A Cultural History of English Language

A Cultural History of the English Language

Gerry Knowles

A member of the Hodder Headline Group
LONDON

First published in Great Britain in 1979 by
Arnold, a member of the Hodder Headline Group.
338 Euston Road, London NW1 3BH
Eighth impression 2004

Distributed in the United States of America by
Oxford University Press Inc.,
198 Madison Avenue, New York, NY 10016

British Library Cataloguing in Publication Data
A catalogue record for this book is available from the British Library

Library of Congress Cataloging-in-Publication Data
A catalog record for this book is available from the Library of Congress

ISBN 0 340 67680 9 (pb)

8 9 10

Typeset by J&L Composition Ltd, Filey, North Yorkshire
Printed and bound in India by Replika Press Pvt. Ltd.

Contents

113072

Preface

The growth of computer-based technology has already fundamentally changed the role of the textbook. In view of the amount of information now available, particularly the kind of detail appearing in the more specialist literature, it is impossible for one short textbook to provide an exhaustive account of the history of English. The analysis of historical corpora is making us reconsider issues which were previously thought to be long since established. Much historical information does not properly belong in a book at all. Sound changes, for example, belong in a relational database, and they are better presented in hypertext with linked sound files than in a conventional book. The aim of this book is therefore to provide a general framework which will be of assistance in the interpretation of historical data.

It is intended as an outline history of the English language for linguists and for students of linguistics and modern English language. In the past, the history of English has typically been studied in the context of English language and literature, and consequently there are large numbers of textbooks which chronicle the changing literary language. There are also many textbooks which are devoted to changes in linguistic form and which trace the history of English phonology, grammar and lexis. However, the scope of linguistics has increasingly extended over recent years to include the social role of language, and this raises such issues as languages in contact, the development of literacy and new text types, and the relationship between standard language and dialects. These things need to be reflected in the historical study of the language. I have sought to take a wider view of the language, and to show how it came to be the way it is. This wider view means that I have not concentrated on the minutiae of linguistic form, and so I have made relatively little use of technical terminology. As a result I hope this book will be more accessible to the general reader.

A consequence of taking a wider view is that one has to reinterpret much of the history of English. Inexplicable gaps must be filled. The peasants' revolt of 1381 and the English revolution of the 1640s both had profound consequences for the language, but they are scarcely mentioned in conventional histories. Secondly, one has to confront the popular myths – many of them of considerable interest and antiquity in their own right – which lie behind the received interpretations. I have attempted to find a deeper explanation than is conventionally given for beliefs about English. Why should English people believe their own language to be inadequate? Why was the English translation of the Bible politically contentious? Why were prescriptive attitudes to English prevalent in the eighteenth century? Why should ideas of 'language deficit' be taken seriously in the twentieth century? In dealing with myths, I have tried to identify the different interests that people have sought to represent and defend. The attitude of the medieval church towards English, for example, may come across as utterly bizarre until one takes into account the economic, intellectual and political power which churchmen of the time were defending. It is more difficult to deal with myths when the political issues are still alive. I find it difficult, for instance, to say anything positive about the intolerant attitudes to language which developed after 1660, and which have profoundly influenced the form which the language takes today.

In preparing this book I have been deeply indebted to many friends, students and colleagues who have provided encouragement and commented on earlier drafts. In particular I would like to thank friends and colleagues at the universities of Lancaster and Helsinki, and a number of individuals including Josef Schmied and Chris Jeffery.

Lancaster, April 1997

1

Introduction

The purpose of this introductory chapter is to raise some of the main issues that are involved in the study of the history of the English language. The first section provides a brief outline history for the reader with no previous historical background, and presents some of the basic historical material which (allowing for some necessary simplification) would be generally accepted by language historians. The remaining sections deal with some general points which are developed further in later chapters. I have used cross-references to make explicit the connections between this chapter and more particular instances in the later chapters.

1.1 *An outline history*

A language related to Modern English has been spoken in Britain since the early fifth century. Before the Roman legions left Britain, the east coast of England was already being subjected to raids from Saxon invaders from beyond the North Sea. In the course of the next century, the newcomers began to settle permanently. According to Bede, a monk from Jarrow writing in the late eighth century, they belonged to three tribes, Angles, Saxons and Jutes. The people are now generally referred to as *Anglo-Saxons*, but their language has always been called *English*. Eventually they conquered the whole of what is now England, and English replaced the Celtic language, which was until then spoken by the mass of the population.

The English speakers were themselves subjected to further raids from across the North Sea, this time from Danes. The first raids date from 797, and eventually the Danes conquered a large part of England north and east of a line stretching from Chester to the Thames. At the time of King Alfred, only the land south and west of this line remained in Anglo-Saxon hands. The Danish invasion and subsequent settlement had a considerable influence on the English language, and many words were borrowed into English, especially into the dialects of the north.

After the Norman conquest in 1066, French became the spoken language of the aristocracy in England, while Latin was adopted as the main written language. English was still spoken by the lower orders of society, but the old written tradition eventually collapsed, and few English written records survive for 200 years after about 1150. French remained in use for some 300 years, until it was gradually replaced by English after the middle of the fourteenth century. The kind of English that emerged, however, was strongly influenced by French, and contained a large number of French words and expressions. The French influence can be seen in the language of Chaucer, who died in 1400.

Caxton introduced printing into England in the 1470s, and written texts became much more widely available than before. Printing was the catalyst for the major upheavals of the sixteenth century which were linked in various ways to the Renaissance and the Reformation. It is from about this time that scholars began to write in English instead of Latin, and as a result many Latin words were borrowed into English. English literature flourished at the end of the sixteenth century, the time of Shakespeare (1564–1616). The Authorized Version of the English Bible was published in 1611.

Modern Standard English can be traced to about the time of Chaucer, but was for a long time variable in spelling, in the use of words, and in the details of English grammar. After the Restoration of Charles II in 1660, there was considerable interest in fixing the language, and in 1712 Jonathan Swift proposed the setting up of an Academy to do this. By default, however, it was left to scholars to decide on what should be included in Standard English. Johnson's dictionary of 1755 did much to standardize spellings and fix the meanings of words. Several grammars were produced, among the more influential being Lowth's grammar of 1762. From the 1760s there was increasing interest in fixing a standard of English pronunciation, which resulted in a tradition of pronouncing dictionaries, of which the most influential was Walker's dictionary of 1791. It was not until the present century that a standard pronunciation was described in detail. This is Daniel Jones's *Received pronunciation*, which was adopted by the BBC in the 1920s as a standard for broadcasting.

1.2 *Language and social change*

Even from this broadly sketched outline it is immediately clear that the history of the language has been determined in various ways by social change. For most of the 1500 years of its history English has been subjected to a pattern of continuous small-scale change interrupted by major events which have brought about dramatic and sudden change. It is these major discontinuities that enable us to divide the history of the language into convenient 'periods'. The first of these continued until shortly after the Norman conquest and is known as *Old English*. The period of French domination is the *Middle English* period, and finally, from about the time of the introduction of printing, when the language becomes recognizably similar to the modern language, it is possible to talk of *Modern English*. In order to understand the details of language change, it is important to investigate the kind of social changes that are involved and how they can bring about changes in the language.

Language contact

The English language has not existed in isolation and has always been in close contact with other European languages. The effect of contact may be to determine which of several languages is used in particular social situations. Conquest by foreign invaders is inevitably followed by the introduction of the languages of the invaders, and this can take several forms. The new language may take hold permanently, as in the case of Anglo-Saxon (see section 2.3), or the invaders may eventually give up their language, as in the case of the Danes (see section 3.4) and the Normans (see section 4.3). Where several languages are in use simultaneously, they may have different functions: for example, after the Norman conquest English and French were used as vernaculars, and Latin was used as the language of record (see section 4.2).

When a language is given up, its users may transfer some of its patterns into the new language. In this way foreign influence has peaked when Danes adopted Anglo-Saxon (see section 3.4), when bureaucrats began to use English rather than French (see section 4.4), and when scholars began to write in English rather than Latin (see section 5.3). The process of adopting features of another language is known as *borrowing*, and the most readily borrowed items are words. English has thousands of words borrowed from Danish, French and Latin. In more recent centuries words have been borrowed from all over the globe as a result of mercantile contact and imperial expansion.

Contact must be taken into account when we consider the origin of the English language. It is self-evident that it is not a single object with a single origin. English vocabulary, expressions and idioms come from a wide range of sources, mainly Latin, French and Germanic, but also Hindi, Hungarian and native American and Australian languages. English pronunciation is largely Anglo-Saxon, but also in part Danish and French. English grammar is basically Germanic, but it has been modified by French and Latin.

Language and power

Language is an important factor in the maintenance of power, and an understanding of power relations is important in tracing the history of a language. In the medieval period, the relevant power was possessed by the church. The important language was Latin, and written English was moulded according to the language practices of the church. Most of our modern literacy practices were closely modelled on those originally developed for Latin. When the power of the church was challenged by the growing power of the state, the prestige of Latin was recreated in English, and the new language of power was a Latinate form of English.

For much of the modern period, English was the language of the English national state, as it grew from a small kingdom to a major empire. The growth of the nation state, the cult of nationalism at the court of Elizabeth, the seventeenth-century revolutions, and worldwide expansion are all reflected in the history of the language. When English was an unimportant vernacular, it was associated with the common people, but after the Glorious Revolution of 1688 it was the language of the 'politest part of the nation'. Soon there was a widespread belief that the common people did not speak proper English at all. Since the middle of the present century power has shifted away from Britain to the United States, and new technologies are creating new relationships which will affect the language in the next millennium in ways we cannot even guess.

A shift of power does not of itself bring about language change, and is mediated by intellectual change, in that shifts of power can affect the basic assumptions people make about their language. Some of the major changes in English in the sixteenth century resulted from the belief of scholars that it was desirable to use English in place of Latin, and from their deliberate efforts to bring change about. The shift of power from the aristocracy to the middle class is reflected in the eighteenth-century concept of politeness (chapter 9), which in turn led to the 'fixing' of standard written English (see section 9.5). The increasing economic power of the working class led to the concept of the Queen's English (see section 10.5) and a narrowed definition of acceptable pronunciation (see section 10.4). In the late twentieth century the assertion and recognition of the rights of women have led to a marked change in the use of the pronouns *he, she* and *they*, and of nouns referring to human beings, such as *poetess* and *chairman*.

Language and fashion

In addition to changes which have an identifiable social origin, there is a large mass of changes which have been the result of prestige and fashion. Although we can never find out how or why some particular innovations occur in the first place, we can nevertheless trace their spread over several

generations. For example, much of the current variation in English pronunciation follows the loss of the [r][1] sound after a vowel in words such as
sure, *square* or *cart*. This can be traced back in some detail to the fourteenth century (Wyld, 1920). The nature of the evidence is such that we can
infer that a new form has emerged, but we are given no idea who started the
new fashion or why. For example, when the captain in Thackeray's *Vanity
fair* says *I'm shaw*, we can infer that he uses the new form of *sure* rhyming
with *law* rather than the old form rhyming with *blüer*, but we do not know
how this new form arose in the first place.

Innovations spread along lines of prestige. The capital imitates the
fashions of the court, and the provincial towns imitate the capital. The
farmer going to market comes into contact with the more prestigious
speech of the town. Of course not all innovations begin at court, and the
farmer will come across more local and regional changes. But these are
unlikely to spread against the tide of prestige, and will remain local dialect
forms (see section 9.2 under *Provincial English*). Innovations eventually
spread to the limits of the sphere of influence of the place in which they
arise, and bring about within that area a greater degree of linguistic
conformity.

In addition to these geographical changes, we have to take into account
age differences and the effects of education. Young people adopt new
styles of speech for the same reasons as they adopt new styles of dress
and other social habits. Traditionally young people adopted the new forms
as they came into fashion in their locality, but this pattern began to change
with the introduction of mass education. Teachers have sought to teach
children what they regarded as the 'correct' forms of English, with the
result that most people are aware of a clash between the English that comes
naturally and the English they have been taught formally. The pattern is
now changing again as the 'younger generation' is constructed by the mass
media as an identifiable group. The long-term effects of this are still
impossible to predict, but already there has emerged a kind of speech
which is neither localized nor based on school norms, and called *Estuary
English* (see section 11.2 under *Estuary English*). The domain within which
patterns of prestige occur has become global.

Because language plays an important role in English society, there have
always been significant differences between the language habits of people
with power and prestige and the mass of the population. Habits of language
– such as dress, diet and gesture – have themselves been categorized as
prestigious or non-prestigious, and the prestigious habits of one generation
have become the arbitrary conventions of the next.

---

1. The square brackets are used to enclose pronunciations.

Language and technology

Language change is facilitated by the development of new technology, in particular technology that leads to improved communications. The effect of technology on language and society depends on who has the power to control the direction of change. In this respect it is two-edged: in the short term it reinforces existing authority, but in the longer term it can alter the distribution of power.

The introduction of printing made possible the development of a written language which became the national standard for England, and later the basis for the modern worldwide Standard English. At first publishers worked for their ecclesiastical and aristocratic masters (see section 4.5), but within 50 years it was clear that the press had generated a new international form of power beyond the control of church and state. Censorship in England at the time of Henry VIII offered a business opportunity to foreign publishers (see section 5.4 under *Bible translations*).

Spoken language was deeply affected by the industrial revolution of the eighteenth and nineteenth centuries. The turnpikes, canals and railways constructed for the transport of freight also brought people into contact, and brought them to the industrial towns. The speech of most people in England is now related to the dialect of one of the major conurbations rather than the local village in which they live (see section 10.3 under *Urban dialects*) and the urban dialects of England are much more homogeneous than the older rural dialects.

Broadcasting and other forms of mass communications developed in the early twentieth century had an initial effect analogous to that of printing, particularly in the spread of Received Pronunciation in Britain (see section 11.2). This has brought about increasing uniformity in speech in England during the present century (see section 10.4), but already the power to control pronunciation has passed from Britain to the United States (see section 11.1). It is too early to predict the longer-term effects of computer-based speech technology and the use of English on the Internet (see section 11.4).

1.3   *Language, evolution and progress*

The major upheavals that punctuate the history of the language were brought about by social events which were not themselves intrinsically involved with language. Social unrest associated with the poll tax in the late fourteenth century eventually brought about the prohibition of the use of English in the area of religion (see section 5.1). Caxton set up his printing press to make money (see section 4.5), not to contribute to the English language. The growth of urban dialects (see section 10.3 under

Urban dialects) was a by-product of the industrial revolution. It would be naïve to imagine these events as the unfolding of a master plan with the English society of the 1990s, or perhaps the 1890s, as its ultimate goal. It would be naïve *a fortiori* to imagine a long-term plan guiding change in the language.

Nevertheless, the notion that sets of changes are connected is widespread, and underlies many beliefs about change in language. It is often claimed, for instance, that the language has in some way improved or deteriorated. This idea can be traced to the sixteenth century (see section 6.5), the fourteenth century (see section 4.3) and indeed to the ancient world. Linguists today still talk about the 'development' of the phonological system or the verbal system, as though sounds and verbs had a sense of historical direction. This has a very real effect on the way they interpret language change, such as sound changes (Milroy, 1994: 25).

Improvement and decay

It is important to realize that, before the middle of the nineteenth century, assumptions about language change followed logically from conventional religious and intellectual beliefs. As it was then understood, a major event in the history of the world was the confusion of languages which followed the building of the tower of Babel by the sons of Noah, calculated to have been in about 2218 BC (Genesis 11: 1–9). This gave a scale of roughly 4000 years for the whole history of human language. The ancient world of Greece and Rome, and for that matter the Old Testament, stretched at least half of the way back. It is thus possible to understand why scholars had such respect for the classical languages, and interpreted change as decay and corruption. There was also a belief that Noah's third son, Japheth, was not involved in Babel, and so his language, and the languages of his descendants, remained pure and uncorrupted. Some linguists went on the trail of Japhetic, as it was called. Van Gorp claimed in 1555 that German was spoken in the Garden of Eden before the fall (see section 6.1 under *Saxon and classical*). Parson's *Remains of Japhet* appeared as late as 1767. The default view that change is inherently bad (see, for example, sections 8.2–8.3) is sometimes given an apparently rational explanation, for example that people borrow too many French or Latin words (see section 7.1).

The Babel story does not of course explain the opposite belief, namely that the language has improved, which typically coincides with social events considered to be evidence of progress, such as the introduction of printing, the Protestant Reformation, or the Restoration of the monarchy. Commentators tend to look back, not to the immediately preceding years, but to the last generation but one. Caxton, in his late middle age, comments on the problems caused by change and looks back to the English 'whiche was vsed and spoken when I was borne', and claims that the English he adopts for his publication is 'lyghter to be vnderstonde than the olde and aucyent englysshe'. Dryden looks back with satisfaction on the improvement in the language since the time of Shakespeare. Swift, by contrast, is dismayed by the deterioration in the language since the 'Great Rebellion of forty-two'. In the 1990s it is sometimes alleged that the language has decayed with respect to some time early in the century, as though language decline had somehow followed the decline of the British empire.

The golden age

A variant of the view of improvement or corruption of languages is that languages rise to a peak and then decay. The classical example is set by Latin, the Golden Latin of Cicero and the Augustan Age being followed by Silver Latin, and eventually the Romance vernaculars. There is still a widespread feeling that English peaked at the end of Queen Elizabeth's reign (see section 6.5), the outstanding linguistic monuments of this golden age being of course the Bible and Shakespeare. Writers in the reign of Queen Anne believed that they themselves were using English at its peak, and sometimes this claim has rather uncritically been taken at face value. Even language historians have used in all seriousness terms such as 'the Augustan Age' (McKnight, 1928: chapter XIII) and 'the century of prose 1660–1760' (Gordon, 1966: chapter 13).

Closely associated with the concept of the golden age is the notion that the language must be defended against the barbarian. It is always worth asking who are the barbarians, and what is the nature of their barbarism. For Sprat (see section 8.1 under *The language of science*) and Dryden (see section 8.2) the barbarians were Puritans. For Defoe (see section 8.3) barbarism was swearing, while for Addison it was the omission of relative pronouns. Swift (1712) warns against the barbarians, but is not clear who exactly they were. Judging by Oldmixon's reply (1712) they were probably Whigs. Present-day complaints that standards of English have declined adduce evidence which makes it clear that the barbarians are the working class (see section 10.3), and by implication look back to the golden age before mass education. King Alfred, in the preface to his translation of *Cura pastoralis*, looks back to a golden age of English literacy, before it was destroyed by barbarians from across the North Sea.

Language evolution

The theory of evolution has exerted a profound influence on the thinking of language scholars. If evolution is linked to a belief in human progress, it is easy to interpret change as progress towards a goal. Natural evolution can be seen as a progress towards *homo sapiens*. In much the same way, language evolution can be seen as a progress towards Standard English.

Natural evolution has its culs-de-sac, species which evolve and die out. Language evolution creates non-standard dialects. Looking back through the natural record, we can trace the main highway that leads from protozoa to *homo sapiens*. Looking back through the linguistic record, we can trace the main highway that leads from early Anglo-Saxon to standard Modern English. Henry Alford actually used the highway metaphor in *The Queen's English* (1864). The story of human evolution has a missing link, and the evolution of written English has a missing link, between the twelfth and fourteenth centuries. Palaeo-anthropologists interpolate change across the gap, and language scholars assert the continuity of English prose (Chambers, 1931), even when it was not actually being written. The evolutionary interpretation of the history of Standard English is reflected in book titles such as *Modern English in the making* (McKnight, 1928) and *The triumph of the English language* (Jones, 1953). Such books give a clear impression that the language is constantly progressing towards a higher goal.

1.4 *Language and myth*

In view of the close connection between language and power, it is impossible to treat the history of the language without reference to politics. That is not to say that these things are party-political issues. When political parties emerged in England after the Restoration, they shared fundamental beliefs about language (see section 8.3), and this has remained the case in Britain ever since. Since language issues are not debated openly, views about language have been passed on by default and unchallenged from one generation to the next. When language has been used for the purposes of propaganda, the propaganda too has been passed on. As a result, the historical facts about the language have come down to us shrouded in myth.

. When people (including linguists) make statements about language in areas which lie beyond their immediate expertise, they are likely to fall back on the common-sense ideas of the society to which they belong. This means giving voice to prevailing myths. In the longer term it creates a problem in interpreting statements about language made in previous centuries. If we are not aware of the myths, we will probably take the statements at face value, and obtain a distorted (if conventional) interpretation of historical events. In studying the history of the English language it is important to strip away the layers of myth, and examine the issues which lie beneath them.

A good sign of myth is when intelligent people put forward in all seriousness linguistic ideas that are inherently absurd. These ideas are taken very seriously while the political issues are still alive, and only afterwards are they subject to ridicule. For example, there must be few people who now believe that Adam and Eve spoke German, and this is now a ridiculous idea. On the other hand, there are many people who seriously believe that the working classes do not speak a proper form of English.

In dealing with myths, it is important to recognize them for what they are in linguistic terms. In some cases the very articulation of the ideas being expressed will reveal their absurdity. It is difficult to take seriously the claim that English was not a fit language for Scripture (see section 5.1), that Charles I was a Norman (see section 7.1), that Shakespeare had an imperfect command of English (see section 8.2) or that English was declining because people used too many monosyllables (see section 8.3). But it is not enough to tackle the problem at the logical level, and in order to understand the controversies we have to dig deeper and find out what the real underlying issues were. In most cases these have nothing to do with language at all. Language is used as an argument in more general social debates and struggles, and we have to understand these more general issues in order to make sense of what people say about language.

Language and race

In tracing the history of a language, it is important to distinguish the history of the language itself from the history of the people who happen to speak it. After a conquest, or under some other kind of social domination, a population may be induced to give up its own language and adopt the language of the dominant group. They do not at that point change their genetic make-up and become ethnic members of the dominant group. They may eventually be accepted as members of it, and be granted full citizenship, but that is a different matter. Acceptance depends on social perception, and citizenship is a political classification. Genetic make-up is changed not by language learning, acceptance or citizenship, but by procreation. The inevitable result of intermarriage between new and old populations is racial mixture.

It is quite common, particularly in dealing with early migratory societies, for groups of related tribes to be identified collectively by the name of a dominant tribe. This usage survives in the use of the word *Angleterre* by the French to refer to the United Kingdom, or the corresponding use of *England* by the Germans. In interpreting these names, we have to consider both race and language. If we refer to the native population of Britain at the time of the Roman occupation as the *British*, that does not mean that the different tribes were — or perceived themselves to be — members of the same race. We certainly cannot assume that they all spoke the same language.

These may be obvious points, but they need making and emphasizing. In the first place, political propaganda sometimes makes implicit or explicit appeal to myths and assumptions about language and race. Expressions such as *Europeans*, *the British* or *the American people* are perfectly good labels for political groupings. On the other hand, it does not make sense to talk about the Scottish race, or to generalize about the racial characteristics of the English.

People who read and write about the English language are just as likely as anyone else to accept racial myths, and to treat them as common sense. It may seem self-evident, for instance, that the Anglo-Saxons were the ancestors of the English, and that the Danes were foreign invaders. The reality is that — leaving aside the British — both Danes and Anglo-Saxons were among the ancestors of the population of the north of England. People who think of themselves as English may support the Anglo-Saxons first against the native British, then against the Danes, and finally against the Normans. But this is the intellectual equivalent of supporting a football team.

Language families

The modern concept of a language family derives from the work of the botanist August Schleicher, who applied the concept of an evolutionary tree to language. Using this model, not only were linguists able to trace the languages of the ancient and modern worlds to their origins, but they also went further back and reconstructed prehistoric proto-languages. Ever since, it has been standard practice to group languages into families, and to position ancient and modern languages on a genealogical tree.

According to the 'family-tree' model, the parent Germanic language gradually evolved into three daughter languages, known as North, East and West Germanic. English, Dutch and German are, in turn, regarded as daughter languages of West Germanic. In some versions, English and Frisian are derived from a separate Anglo-Frisian branch of West Germanic. Scholars worked backwards through the family tree describing languages at earlier stages of development. This was done by making logical inferences from cases of divergence within and among languages. For example, if English has *water* where German has *Wasser*, one or both of them must have changed the consonant in the middle, and in this case Germanic is reconstructed with [t]. Precisely because the method concentrated on divergence, it inevitably followed that, as languages were taken back in time, they appeared to be increasingly homogeneous. As a result, reconstructed Primitive Germanic is much more like classical Greek and Latin — both in form and in its homogeneous nature — than the dialects of the earliest Germanic records.

When this model was first put forward, it was a brilliant hypothesis to account for the relationships among the varieties of Germanic. It works well if we think of an ancient Germanic race whose scions colonize new lands and father new races. It makes much less sense in the conditions of the migratory society of the Iron Age. This is because, as soon became clear from dialect study, the modern languages have resulted not only by divergence from a common source, but also by the convergence of older dialects as a result of language contact. Cultural and political groupings bring dialects together, and as a result differences between them can be obliterated. This is particularly important in the formation of standard languages. Contact is not taken into account in the method of reconstruction, and since the effect of convergence is to obliterate the evidence of earlier differences, these earlier differences can never be reconstructed. Homogeneous dead languages are an artifact of the method of reconstruction.

To take an example, the traditional dialects of Yorkshire have a number of characteristics which they share with Danish (see section 3.4) but not with the dialects of Hampshire. These similarities were brought about by continued contact with the homeland and later between the English and the Danes in the Danelaw. It does not make sense, therefore, to derive Yorkshire and Hampshire English from a common origin in some kind of standard Old English. Nor does it make sense to derive Yorkshire English exclusively from a standard West Germanic. Modern Standard English does not derive from any one dialect of Old English, and in fact it derives in the first instance from the dialects of the East Midlands with a rich admixture of northern forms, western forms and Kentish forms. Its shape was determined in detail within a literacy culture dominated by Latin and French.

Pure Saxon

The first Germanic invaders brought with them a range of different dialects to England, and these gradually converged to form the dialects of the early kingdoms (see section 2.3 under *Early English dialects*). Later immigrants brought different dialects to add to the mix. The migration of Danes and Norwegians to England continued the long-established (and possibly unbroken) pattern. After the partition of England (see section 3.4), the English of the Danelaw began to diverge from the English of the south and west, but inside the Danelaw English and Danish began to converge. Following the reunification of England, northern and southern English presumably began to converge again.

Note that the popular concept of a language does not fit into this dialect pattern. When people talk about Modern English or Danish, they generally take for granted some standardized form of the language, and also assume that one language is clearly different from another. When we refer to the Anglo-Saxon and Danish of the Danelaw, on the other hand, we refer to much more vaguely defined and overlapping groups of dialects. It must be emphasized that there was no such thing as a standard spoken language anywhere in Europe at this time. Latin was the standard written language, and there were moves towards establishing written forms of the vernacular languages, but that is a separate matter.

The concept of pure Saxon English first appears at the time of the Protestant Reformation, and is associated with radical opponents of the medieval church such as Sir John Cheke. The Society of Antiquaries later had political reasons for taking a particular interest in the Saxon past (see section 6.1), and in the seventeenth century Saxon history was used in radical propaganda (see section 7.1). The (Anglo-)Saxon language has since become an important stage in the received account of the origin of English. According to this account Celts took no part whatsoever in the formation of the language, apart from providing some river names such as *Avon* and *Severn*, some topographical terms such as *down* ('hill') and *combe* ('valley'), and the word *brock* ('badger'). The influence of the Vikings and the Normans is likewise minimized.

But this Saxon language was a fiction. 'Saxon' English has remained as a romantic aspiration and has enjoyed apparent prestige. Charles Dickens wrote about it in *Household words* (1858), and the Fowler brothers (1919) set it up as an ideal. It has never in practice seriously challenged Latinate English as the language of real power.

Language as a discrete object

A widespread view of English is that it is a single object which can be examined and described by grammarians and that it remains the same in all circumstances. Such a view is presupposed in the reconstruction of language families. The obvious fact, however, is that like any real language it varies in a number of different ways. In addition to variation of dialect, texts in the language vary according to *register*, or the use to which they are put. Different kinds of English are used in church, in courts of law, in the classroom and by teenagers chatting on a street corner. Writers vary their usage according to whether they are writing a personal letter, a shopping list, a newspaper article or an academic assignment. A skilled writer has a wide choice in the design of a text, including deciding what vocabulary to use, and the complexity of sentence structure.

Register variation is traditionally recognized in the distinction of 'high', 'middle' and 'low' styles, but such a scale is far too crude to be of any practical use. Register is not only multi–dimensional, but the conventions which surround it can vary in the course of time. That is, what is considered appropriate for a particular type of text can be changed. For example, written texts vary in their relationship to conventions of the spoken language.

A widespread but naïve view of writing is that it is speech written down. This has never actually been true of written English. To begin with, the composition of the text is in principle quite separate from the preparation of the physical script. These activities are separated when one person dictates a text for somebody else to write down, something which has always been a normal thing to do. Bede, on his deathbed, dictated the last of his translation of St John's gospel, and the blind Milton dictated the text of *Paradise lost*. Managers still dictate letters to secretaries. By the time a text has been edited and copied by a third person, it is not the creation of any one individual. In any case, the text need not be modelled on conversational speech. The writers of the first English texts were primarily literate in Latin, and they transferred their literacy practices from Latin to English. It is difficult to assess the degree to which this influenced the way they wrote English, especially as many early English texts were translations from Latin.

The relationship between speech and writing is complex and variable. Texts far removed from conversation have been produced since the beginning of writing, and in medieval England this style was used for parish records and business accounts (see section 4.3). On the other hand, some older and more conservative texts are structurally closer to conversation than their modern counterparts. Smith (1568), for example, composed his text as a dialogue between the author and an imaginary companion. Other texts have special phatic sections at the beginning and end which are concerned with the relationship between writer and reader rather than the main business. This remains true of some spoken texts, and, for example, a telephone conversation, whatever its purpose, typically begins and ends with remarks of a personal nature. It is also true of a letter, and even a formal business letter is likely to begin *Dear Sir/Madam* and end *Yours faithfully* before the signature and name of the writer. Phatic elements can be quite startling when they are encountered in situations where they are no longer used: for example, *goodbye!* at the end of a will or charter (Clanchy, 1979: 202–3). It would now be considered rather odd to address the reader from within a book: for example, *Now, o reader, let us consider the remaining case.* This was more familiar in the seventeenth century (see section 7.5).

Some language uses have restricted access. Vernacular uses, such as making a telephone call or reading a popular newspaper, are open to all. People will differ in their individual skills, but there is no organized restriction on access. It is very different in the case of registers dealing with specialized knowledge or the exercise of power. For most of the history of English this variation has involved not registers of English, but actually different languages. In the medieval period, access was tightly controlled by using French or Latin (see sections 4.2 and 5.2), and even when English came to be adopted, new registers were quickly developed which were far removed from the language of ordinary people (see sections 4.3 under *Chancery English*, 4.5 under *Published standard written English*, 5.2 and 5.5). That is not to say that the rich and powerful have deliberately conspired together to rob the people of England of their linguistic birthright, but nevertheless people in positions of power (see section 5.3) or influence (see section 10.5) have acted in accordance with the common sense of the society in which they lived, and thereby created restricted access.

1.5   *Language superiority*

The previous sections have drawn attention to some of the social factors that inevitably affect language change. Ordinary people are influenced by those in positions of power. Myths and propaganda are created to attack or defend positions of power, and these make it more difficult to obtain a clear idea of events. Access to some prestigious uses of language is denied to the unprivileged. Whether the distribution of power is reasonable and equitable is an interesting political question, but it is beyond the scope of this book.

To this mix we have to add the notion of intolerance. The tolerant view accepts the variability and diversity of language on the grounds that that is how language is, and that is where we have to start if we want to understand it. According to the intolerant view, there is something inherently wrong with the language practices of the unprivileged. This intolerant view has been dominant in English society at least since the 1380s, but it leads to beliefs about the language which are demonstrably false. The target of intolerance has changed over time. Before 1660, arguments concerned the adequacy of the English language as a whole. Later the argument was about which individuals and different groups in society were in possession of the correct forms of the language.

Adequate language

The claim that English was not a suitable language for Scripture was repeatedly made over a period of some 200 years. It was originally the outcome of the Oxford conference of 1401, which ironically was a response to the successful translation of the Bible by the Lollards (see section 5.1). In fact the problems of Bible translation had been solved before the conquest, and the real problem was that the Lollard translation was too successful for the liking of the church authorities. The doctrine of the superiority of Latin and the inferiority of English was an effective piece of propaganda to support the suppression of Lollard radicalism. Nevertheless, many Englishmen believed it, and went to great lengths to make their language more adequate (see section 5.3). It is no coincidence that when English scholars ceased to accept church propaganda after the Protestant Reformation, they discovered that English could be used for any purpose whatsoever (chapter 6).

The ideological debate concealed two real practical linguistic problems. The first concerned the exact transference of meaning in translation, and this problem was well understood and discussed by translators from the 1390s to 1611 (see section 5.4 under *Bible translations*). The second concerns the creation of new registers. The problem was tackled in the mid fifteenth century by Bishop Pecock, opinion was divided on how to do it in the sixteenth century, and the same problem confronted scientists in the seventeenth century. Milton's attempt in *Paradise lost* to create an English epic to out-do Homer belongs to the same tradition, but by 1667 it had ceased to be a political issue.

The forms of Modern English have been influenced in many different ways by the belief that English is inferior to Latin. Echoes of this view are heard in the education system down to the present time.

Correct language

In the aftermath of the revolution of the 1640s, there could be no pretending that the English were a united people. Society was divided, and religion was divided. After 1660 insiders who supported the monarchy and the Church of England enjoyed privileges denied to outsiders. During the next 50 years there grows up the belief that the insiders happen also to be in possession of the English language in its pure form. Among the people who allegedly do not have correct English are provincials, Scots, nearly all Irishmen and colonials. This leaves the 'correct' forms as the exclusive property of a small élite group (see sections 8.2–8.5). The criteria for membership of this élite are progressively tightened, especially after the introduction of mass education in the nineteenth century. By the early twentieth century it is impossible to join the group at all unless one happens to have acquired a particular kind of English as a child. Fowler and Fowler (1919: 133), for instance, assert that the correct use of *shall* and *will* 'comes by nature to Southern Englishmen' but that it is 'so complicated that those who are not to the manner born can hardly acquire it' (see section 10.5 under *The King's English*). Several phoneticians in the early twentieth century asserted (see section 10.4) that standard pronunciation – and by implication correct pronunciation – was the property of English public schoolboys. The inference is often stated or implied that people who use the 'correct' forms are thereby enabled to express their meaning effectively, and those who do not use them generate confusion and obscurity.

During periods in which the nature of the correct forms is still a matter of debate, the arbitrary nature of arguments is readily apparent. In the clearest cases, writers simply assert that they belong to (or have close contact with) the élite group who by chance are in possession of the correct forms. Sheridan's claim to possess correct pronunciation, for example, was based on his father's acquaintance with Jonathan Swift. In other cases, writers appeal to logic or grammar to justify what are rather obviously their own prejudices on matters of usage. The situation changes when prescriptive assertions become widely accepted. After generations of repetition, especially when repeated by teachers training children to write, prescriptive rules are inevitably incorporated in educated writing. Irrespective of the original reasons for the condemnation of the forms *you was*, *ain't* or *worser*, it is now an observable fact that such forms are not used by educated writers. What this demonstrates is not that prescriptive writers were right, but that they have been successful.

Standard language

In the last two centuries or so, many standards have been introduced into our culture: standard time, measurements, paper sizes and currency, and even standard screws, jumper chisels and floppy disks. There is an obvious advantage in having a standard at all, and it is often immaterial which of the available options is chosen, even if it is totally arbitrary. In practice the standard is determined by a successful enterprise, and in order to be successful in the first place, it must have answered a social need.

We can think of Standard English in this way. Modern English was standardized from the fourteenth century on by people who had the power to impose their own kind of English, and the process was completed by a wide range of people including schoolmasters, Anglicans, scholars, pedants and gentlemen. Whatever the rights and wrongs of the process by which it came about, the practical result is that, for the first time in history, millions of people literally all over the world have an effective means of communicating with each other.

Unlike standard screws and paper sizes, Standard English is surrounded by all manner of irrational beliefs. Standard forms are believed to be inherently superior, more logical and even more beautiful than others. The effective use of language is confused with the use of standard forms. People's intelligence, personality and employability are often assessed by their linguistic conformity. This creates a standard in the other sense, according to which Standard English represents a standard of achievement which most people never attain.

2

The origins of the English language

In popular discussion, modern European languages are often treated as entirely separate entities, so that English is quite separate from French, German or Italian. As we go back in time, we have to take account of the relationships among languages, and these relationships are broadly of two kinds. First, we find that some groups of languages were formerly much more like each other than they are today, to the extent that they could at one time be regarded as varieties of the same language. Second, languages which are culturally in contact are likely to have an influence on each other. Migrations in the early period brought about many different kinds of contacts between the languages of Europe, and the Roman empire and the Christian religion have between them ensured that contact among languages has continued.

2.1   *The linguistic geography of Europe*

Before examining the language situation in Britain itself, it is as well to consider the wider European context in which the English language first came into being. At the beginning of the Christian era, western Europe was broadly speaking divided into a Celtic-speaking south and a Germanic-speaking north. This pattern was overlaid by the spread of Latin out of the Italian peninsula over much of the Celtic-speaking territory. The picture is further complicated by patterns of migration, particularly by Germanic speakers moving across the frontier into Roman territory.

Language groups

The Celtic languages spread over much of southern and western Europe, including modern France, northern Italy and Spain, in the first millennium BC. The names of some Celtic tribes survive in modern names: for example, the name of the *Belgi* survives in the name of Belgium. The name *Gaul* survives in the adjective *Gallic* used of the French. The Cimbri are first found on the continent, and their name possibly survives in *Cymru*, Welsh for 'Wales', and thence also in *Cambrian*, *Cumberland* and *Cumbria*. Britain and Ireland were invaded and colonized by different groups of Celtic speakers, with the result that there were significant differences between the kind of Celtic spoken in Britain and Ireland in the following centuries. Irish Celtic is referred to as *Gaelic*, while British Celtic was spoken in Britain.

Latin was originally the language of Latium, but came to be the dialect of Rome. The use of Latin spread with the growth of the Roman empire, which included modern Italy, Spain and Portugal, most of Britain, France, and Germany south of the Rhine and the Danube. Beyond Europe it included North Africa and Palestine. Following the decline of the empire from about the fifth century, Latin eventually disappeared as a spoken language on the periphery of the empire, including Africa, south Germany and Britain. It survived in the central areas of continental Europe, where it gradually changed into different varieties which in turn became the modern Romance languages.

Even where Latin did not survive as a spoken language, it remained as the international language of scholarship. This is a role it was to retain throughout Europe for well over a thousand years. As a result, all the major languages of Europe have been profoundly influenced by Latin, not only in their vocabulary, but also in their grammar. When considering the role of Latin in Europe, we have to make a clear distinction between the spoken Latin of the empire, and the later written language which influenced the standard languages of Europe over a thousand years later (see section 5.3).

At the beginning of the Christian era, the Germanic peoples lived in northern Europe. The modern Germanic languages derive from the dialects of the different tribal groups (Frings, 1950). German is a mixture of the dialects spoken south of Denmark. Dutch and Flemish derive from the dialects spoken on the North Sea coast and further inland in the area of the Weser and the Rhine, although the Frisian dialects come more exclusively from the coastal dialects. English derives mainly from the coastal dialects, but with a substantial contribution from the dialects of Denmark and Norway, and perhaps some influence from the Weser–Rhine dialects.

Language contact in Europe

It would be naïve to imagine that in first-century Europe Germanic was spoken by ethnic Germans, Celtic by Celts, and Latin by Romans. Tribes were already genetically mixed, and the language spoken by a particular tribe could change as the result of contact and conquest. When the native populations of Europe adopted Celtic, they did not become ethnic Celts, but Celtic-speaking members of the tribes to which they already belonged. In the conquered territories that became the Roman empire, many people became Roman citizens and spoke Latin. It is easy to assume that they were all Romans, but again this is to confuse language and race. Writers of popular books sometimes imagine that the Roman soldiers stationed in the wind and rain on Hadrian's Wall must have longed for the cloudless skies of Italy. However, the soldiers who fought with the Roman army no more came from the streets of Rome than the Canadians and Gurkhas who fought with the British army came from the streets of London.

The identity of the Germanic peoples remains an enigma. Our use of the words *German*, *Germanic* and *Teutonic* assumes that all the people the Romans called *Germani* and *Teutones* spoke Germanic languages. However, it is unlikely that the Romans considered it necessary to make a clear distinction between the different kinds of barbarian that crossed their frontier from across the Rhine. According to Powell (1980), they may actually have been Celtic speakers. For that matter, we have no reason whatsover to assume that these or any other tribes spoke only one language.

What we do know is that contact between tribal groups led to mutual influence in their languages. Early contact between the Germanic peoples and the Roman world involved trade, and this is illustrated by tracing the Latin word *caupo*, which originally meant 'innkeeper', but came to refer more generally to a trader. From *caupo* derives the German *kaufen* ('buy'), Norwegian *kjøpe* ('buy'), English *cheap*, and the placename *Copenhagen* 'merchants' harbour'. The Germanic peoples learned about new forms of food and drink, and the Germanic words *wine*, *beer* and *cheese* are all of Latin origin.

Apart from trade there were military contacts. Germanic mercenaries, including Alemanns and Saxons, were recruited into the Roman army, and these must have provided useful intelligence about life in the empire for the economic migrants who in the succeeding centuries crossed the frontier of the empire known as *limes* and settled. Most of these eventually gave up their own language and adopted Latin. This has the interesting consequence that the linguistic frontier between Germanic and Latin has hardly moved in nearly 2000 years (Lodge, 1993: 60).

The Germanic tribes are often referred to according to the name of a leading tribe which came into contact with the Roman world. The people identified by the Romans as *Germani* were probably a tribe who came to their attention in central Europe. In contemporary usage the word *Germanic* refers to all tribal groups collectively, whereas *German* refers specifically to the people of modern Germany. The Franks spread up the Rhine and across the border into the empire, where they eventually gave their name to *France*. The Burgundians crossed into Gaul and eventually established the duchy of Burgundy. The Alemanns migrated through what is now eastern France, and the French still call the Germans *Allemands*.

Other waves of migration crossed the North Sea. Saxon pirates settled on the *litus Saxonicum*, 'the Saxon shore', in Roman times, and their name came to be used generically by the Romans for Germanic pirates attacking Britain. The name was adopted into Celtic, where it was narrowed down to refer to the English. The Welsh word for an Englishman is still *Saeson*, and the English language is *Saesneg*; the Scottish word for the English, *Sassenach*, has the same origin. In a later period the Angles became the dominant group, and the various peoples who settled in England from the fifth century called themselves *Engle* ('Angles') and their language *englisc* ('Angle-ish'). The term *Anglo-Saxon* conveniently links the names of the Angles and the Saxons, and is also used to distinguish the kind of Germanic spoken in England from Old Saxon, the language of those who remained on the other side of the North Sea. The modern descendants of Old Saxon are the dialects of the north German plain known as *Plattdeutsch* or 'Low German'.

The northern group took two main routes. One group crossed the Sound to Denmark, and from there in the Viking age went on the eastern coast of England, and to the mouth of the Seine. In England they founded the kingdom of York, and in France the duchy of Normandy. The other group went from Norway round the north of Scotland to Iceland and the Faeroe Islands, and south to the Irish Sea, where they settled on the coast of Ireland, and founded the city of Dublin. They dominated the Irish Sea, and settled on the Isle of Man, and on the western coasts of northern England and southern Scotland. By the early eleventh century England was part of a Danish kingdom that stretched to Skåne in southern Sweden.

2.2 *Language in Britain*

The last section dealt with Europe as a whole. This section will deal specifically with Britain. We know nothing of the language of the aboriginal population of Britain. The earliest fragment of information is the name *Albion*, which is the name by which Britain was known to the Greeks of the colony of Massilia (Marseilles) from the sixth century BC (Powell, 1980: 22). The name was used in Ireland, and could conceivably preserve a pre-Celtic form.

The earliest languages spoken in Britain of which we have any knowledge are the Celtic languages which survive in modern Welsh, Irish and Scots Gaelic. A number of names survive from the early Celtic period. From the fourth century BC Britain and Ireland together were known as the *Pretanic* Islands, and this name survives in the Welsh form *Prydain*. It was adopted by the Romans in the Latin name *Britannia*, and from this in turn we derive the English name *Britain*. It is likely that the name *British* originally belonged to a dominant Celtic-speaking tribe, and that it was later used generically. Other tribes included the Iceni of the south east, the

Brigantes of what is now northern England, and the Picts and Caledonians of the far north. A tribe with a particularly interesting name is the Scots, who originally settled in Northern Ireland but who later migrated to northern Britain.

The Roman army occupied the southern two-thirds of Britain in the years following the visit of Julius Caesar in 55 BC. Latin was introduced as the language of the occupying forces, and it would have been used by people dependent on them, and in the towns which grew up round the Roman forts. Roman soldiers came from all parts of the empire and beyond it. One of the legions stationed on Hadrian's Wall came from Romania, and Lancaster was occupied by a legion from Gaul. We cannot assume that all Roman soldiers were fluent speakers of Latin. A wide range of languages must have been spoken in Britain at this time.

In Britain, Celtic had never been completely replaced by Latin, and its use continued after the withdrawal of the Roman forces in the early fifth century. Leith (1983) speculates that Latin may have survived in the towns of the south east, but this was not in any case to have a permanent effect on language in Britain. (For a detailed discussion of the evidence, see Jackson, 1953: 246–61.) Although Latin has had a considerable influence on English, this is not in any sense a continuation of the Roman occupation. The influence of Latin on English was largely the result of the work of English scholars in the sixteenth century (see section 5.4).

From the early fifth century, some tens of thousands of Germanic migrants crossed the North Sea and settled on the east and south coasts of Britain. These are the people now known as the Anglo-Saxons, and their language is the earliest form of what we now call English. They came from many different places, from modern Denmark, Schleswig-Holstein, the north coast of the Netherlands, and possibly from further inland. They spoke many different dialects, much as 1200 years later the settlers in America took different varieties of English with them. These dialects eventually came to form a recognizable geographical pattern. In order to understand how this happened, we need to trace both the growth of Anglo-Saxon settlements and the effect of political and administrative institutions on the speech of the immigrant population.

The early settlements eventually grew into petty kingdoms. By the end of the sixth century, these lay predominantly to the east of a line from Edinburgh down to the south coast. The names of some of the southern kingdoms – Essex, Middlesex, Surrey, Sussex – survived as county names. By the early ninth century, the petty kingdoms had merged into four major ones. Northumbria extended from Edinburgh to the Humber, and across to the west coast. Mercia was bounded to the west by Offa's dyke, and to the east by the old kingdom of East Anglia, although for some of the time Mercia actually included East Anglia within its borders. To the north it was bounded by a line from the Mersey to the Humber, and to the south by a line from the Severn to the Thames. The old boundary of Mercia and

Northumbria is still reflected in the name of the *Mersey* ('boundary river'). In the south, Wessex stretched from the Tamar in the west to the boundaries of Kent in the east.

2.3 *Early English*

Any detailed knowledge we have of early English necessarily comes from the first written records. In other words we have to make inferences about the spoken language from the written language. This is made difficult by the different patterns of contact. Whereas spoken English was interacting with Celtic in the context of the emerging kingdoms, written English was interacting with Latin as the international language of Christendom.

Early English dialects

There was no such thing at this time as a Standard English language in our modern sense. Not only did the original settlers come from many different tribes, they also arrived over a long period of time, so that there must have been considerable dialect variety in the early kingdoms. As groups achieved some local dominance, their speech was accorded prestige, and the prestigious forms spread over the territory that they dominated. In some cases the immigrants took control of existing Celtic kingdoms, for example Northumbria subsumed the old kingdoms of Bernicia and Deira (Higham, 1986). Here there would already be a communications infrastructure which would enable the prestigious forms to spread. Within their borders, there would thus be a general tendency towards homogeneity in speech. The evidence of the earliest written records suggests a rough correlation between dialects and kingdoms, and the dialects of Anglo-Saxon are conventionally classified by kingdom: Northumbrian, Mercian, West Saxon and Kentish (see map 1). The northern dialects, Northumbrian and Mercian, are usually grouped together under the name *Anglian*. The pattern of change which was established at this period survived until the introduction of mass education in the nineteenth century.

Subsequent development of English dialects can in some cases be traced to shifts in political boundaries. The new Scottish border (see section 3.1), for example, cut the people of the Lowlands off from the rest of Northumbria, with the result that the dialects on either side of the border began to change in different directions. The political boundary between Mercia and Northumbria, for instance, disappeared over 1000 years ago, and yet there are still marked differences in speech north and south of the Mersey. In south-east Lancashire, a consonantal [r] can still be heard in local speech in words such as *learn*, *square*, but this is not heard a few miles away in Cheshire.

Map 1 Old English dialects.

Traces of the old dialect of Kent survive in modern Standard English. There are indications that Kent was settled by some homogeneous tribal group, possibly Jutes or Frisians, and so Kentish may have had marked differences from the earliest times. A distinctive feature of Kentish concerned the pronunciation of the vowel sound written <y>[1] in early English spelling, which elsewhere must have been similar to the French vowel of *tu* [ty] ('you'), or German *kühl* [ky:l] ('cool'). In Kent the corresponding vowel was often written <e>. For example, a word meaning 'give' was *syllan* in Wessex and *sellan* in Kent; it is of course from the Kentish form that we get the modern form *sell*. After the Norman conquest the [y] sound was spelt <u>, and this is retained in the modern spelling of the word *bury*; the pronunciation of this word, however, has the vowel sound [e], and was originally a Kentish form.

When England finally became a single kingdom, innovations would spread across the whole of the country, and begin to cross old borders. Eventually this created a situation in which some features of language are general and others localized. The general features are interesting because they form the nucleus of the later standard language. This point is worth emphasizing, because there is a common misconception that dialects arise as a result of the corruption or fragmentation of an earlier standard language. Such a standard language had never existed. The standard language arose out of the dialects of the old kingdoms.

The beginnings of written English

From about the second century the Germanic tribes had made use of an alphabet of characters called *runes*, which were mainly designed in straight lines and were thus suitable for incising with a chisel. Runes were used for short inscriptions on jewellery and other valuable artifacts, commemorative texts on wood, rocks and stones, and for magical purposes. As Christianity was introduced to the Anglo-Saxon kingdoms, a new literacy culture was introduced with it. The new culture made use of connected texts, and its language was Latin. There are some interesting overlaps between the two cultures, for example the Ruthwell Cross is a late runic monument from the middle of the eighth century, and is incised with runes representing extracts from the Christian poem *The dream of the rood*. One runic panel even represents a phrase of Latin (Sweet, 1978: 103).

The earliest use of English in manuscripts as opposed to inscriptions is found in glosses, which provided an English equivalent for some of the words of the Latin text. To make the earliest glosses, the writer had to find a way of using Latin letters to represent the sounds of English. Some letters, including <c, d, m, p>, had identifiable English counterparts, and

---

1. The angle brackets are used to enclose spellings.

so the use of these letters was straightforward. English also had vowel and consonant sounds which did not exist in Latin, and a means had to be found to represent them. For the sounds now spelt <th>, the runic character <þ> was used interchangeably with a new character <ð>, and another rune *wynn* was used to represent the sound [w]. Another solution for non-Latin sounds was the use of digraphs. Vowel letters were combined in different ways to represent the complex vowel sounds of English, for example the digraph <æ> ('ash') was used for the English vowel intermediate between Latin <a> and <e>. In <ecg> ('edge') the digraph <cg> was used for the consonant [dʒ]. (The pronunciation of this word has not changed: the convention <cg> was later replaced by <dge>.)

The same spellings would be used time and time again, and eventually a convention would develop. The existence of a convention tends to conservatism in spelling, for old conventions can be retained even when pronunciation has changed, or they can be used for another dialect for which they do not quite fit. For example, the English words <fisc> and <scip> originally had phonetic spellings and were pronounced [fisk] and [skip] respectively. The sequence [sk] was replaced in pronunciation by the single sound [ʃ], so that the words were later pronounced [fiʃ, ʃip]. In this way the spelling <sc> became an arbitrary spelling convention. Spelling conventions can thus reflect archaic pronunciations, and any close connection between spoken and written is quickly lost. We still write *knee* with an initial <k> not because we pronounce [k] ourselves, but because it was pronounced in that way when the modern conventions were established many generations ago in the fifteenth century.

There has always been variation in the pronunciation of English words, and so the question must be raised as to whose pronunciation was represented by the spelling. In the first instance, it was more likely that of the person in charge of a scriptorium than of the individual who prepared the manuscript. When new spellings were adopted, they would represent the pronunciation of powerful people: for example, new spellings in the eighth century presumably represented the English spoken at the Mercian court. It follows that although we can usually guess what kind of pronunciation is represented by English spellings, it is far from clear whose pronunciation this is, and it may not be the pronunciation of any individual person. Second, while it is possible by examining orthographic variants to work out roughly where a text comes from, it does not follow that these variants represent the contemporary speech of the local community. Official languages, in particular spellings, are not necessarily close to any spoken form, and are relatively unaffected by subsequent change in the spoken language. The language of early texts was already far removed from the speech of the ordinary people of Tamworth or Winchester, much as it is today.

There is a similar problem with respect to grammar. Some later glosses, for example the Lindisfarne gospels of the mid to late tenth century, take the form of an interlinear translation of groups of words or a whole text.

These raise interesting questions about the relationship between the translation and the original. They were designed to help the reader who was not sufficiently familiar with Latin, and they would not be polished literary translations but more like the kind of translation made today by foreign-language learners to demonstrate their understanding of the foreign text. We cannot infer that the constructions used in these glosses were normal in English at that time. Indeed we sometimes know that they were not. English versions of the Paternoster begin *father our*: but words such as *my* and *our* have always come before the noun in English. The tenth-century Rushworth gospel (Sweet, 1978: 145) continues *beo gehalgad þin noma* for 'sanctificetur nomen tuum'. We cannot conclude from this one example that English could at that time put the subject after the verb. Nor can we tell without further evidence whether *be hallowed* was a normal use of the passive at that time, or whether it was a clumsy attempt to represent the meaning of the Latin word. At the very least, we cannot easily draw conclusions about the forms of early spoken English from a study of written records.

The most typical kind of reading in our modern culture is that undertaken by individuals reading silently to themselves. In medieval times, reading more typically meant reading aloud. St Augustine, in his *Confessions*, comments that St Ambrose read silently, implying that this was unusual (Aston, 1977: 348). We now think of letters representing sounds (which implies that sounds are logically prior to letters), but the medieval term for the sound of a letter was its 'voice' (which implies that letters are prior to sounds). John of Salisbury in *Metalogicon* in the mid twelfth century indicates that silent reading was known but not the normal case: 'Littere autem, id est figure, primo vocum indices sunt; deinde rerum, quas anime per oculorum fenestras opponunt, et frequenter absentium dicta sine voce loquuntur'[2] (quoted by Clanchy, 1979: 202).

This view is consistent with the notion that letters are the smallest units of both written and spoken texts. According to Aelfric's grammar:

> Littera is stæf on englisc and is se læsta dæl on bocum and untodaeledlic. We todælað þa boc to cwydum and syððan ða cwydas to daelum eft ða dælas to stæfgefegum and syððan þa stæfgefegu to stafum.[3] (quoted by Gordon, 1966: 38).

This has been the standard view in grammars and dictionaries up to the nineteenth century.

Second, we normally expect a text to be read aloud in the language in which it is written. There are some exceptions to this. For example, we

2. 'Letters, however, that is characters, are in the first place the indicators of voices, and then of things, which they present to the mind through the windows of the eyes, and frequently speak without a voice the words of people who are absent.'

3. '*Littera* is "letter" in English, and is the smallest part of books ("texts") and indivisible. We divide books into utterances, and then the utterances into parts ("words"), and then the parts into syllables and then the syllables into letters.' (The concept of *syllable* here refers to a group of letters rather than a group of sounds.)

would expect a text in Egyptian hieroglyphics to be simultaneously translated into English rather than read out in ancient Egyptian. The circumstances in which Latin was read out meant that simultaneous translation was a frequent requirement, and a Latin text could be read out in English, or indeed in Welsh. The language in which the text was written was thus independent of the language in which it was read aloud. By the same token, there is no reason to assume that an English text would be read out in the dialect represented by the spellings.

A third important aspect of Latin literacy is that it was controlled by the church. As a powerful international organization, the church had a complex relationship with political states, working through the existing framework but retaining some independence. From the beginning, written English reflects the power of the church. Missionaries from Rome were first sent to Kent in 597, and in 634 Pope Gregory established two archepiscopal sees at London and York. After some initial rivalry with Irish Christianity, the Roman model survived, although in the event the southern see was set up not in London, but in Canterbury, the Kentish capital. As early as 667, the kings of Northumbria and Kent collaborated over the appointment of the archbishop of Canterbury (Whitelock, 1952: 162). Bede's concept of the *gens Anglorum* ('the English people'), or its equivalent *angelcynn* ('Angle-kin'), represents a church view much broader than that of any of the political institutions of the time.

Tension between the wider church view and the narrower political view provides the context in which written English first developed. To begin with, the concept of an English language – as opposed to Kentish or Northumbrian – could at that time only be a church concept. Political states, naturally enough, put their own stamp on the written form. The first English texts were produced in Northumbria, but the earliest surviving texts date from the eighth century, when literacy was already established, and when political leadership had passed from Northumbria to Mercia. The church provided the literacy infrastructure, but in so far as changes in the written form reflected any particular variety of English, it was Mercian. Mercian forms would be used not only in Mercia, but throughout the territory over which it had influence, and, for example, some Mercian spellings were adopted in areas under Mercian control, as far away as Kent (Toon, 1983). The dominant power in the ninth century was Wessex, and the dialect of Wessex, West Saxon, was adopted as an official written language within and beyond the borders of Wessex. After 954 southerners were appointed to the see of York (Whitelock, 1952: 183), and it is unlikely that they would use any variety of English other than West Saxon.

2.4 *The survival of Celtic*

As the Anglo-Saxons settled in eastern England, and took control, there was some movement of population. It is known, for example, that in the fifth century a large number of Britons moved to Armorica, and this movement is reflected in the name *Brittany*. The size of the native population has been estimated at about a million (Hodges, 1984: 42), and the emigrants can have formed only a small proportion of the total. The bulk of the population must have remained where they were. People in positions of power would speak English, and there would be strong incentives for Celtic speakers to learn the new language. Centres of population would go over to English, and from there it would spread to more outlying districts. In the course of time the whole local population would have adopted English, and would have absorbed the newcomers.

English speakers would be in contact with the native population, and the result of this contact is that the native population learned English. This pattern would be repeated continuously as the Anglo-Saxons expanded to the west.

The settlers called the native population of Britain *wealas* ('foreigners') and their language *wælisc* ('foreigner-ish'), or Welsh. The old language continued to be spoken to the north and the west of the Anglo-Saxon settlements, in the Highlands of Scotland, in south-west Scotland and the Lake District, Wales and Cornwall. To the north, the narrow strip of boggy land between the Clyde and Firth of Forth provided a natural barrier between the Celtic and English-speaking populations. The Picts were overrun by a Gaelic-speaking tribe from Ireland called the Scots, so that the Celtic spoken in this part of Britain was different from that spoken further south. Gaelic remained the dominant language of the Highlands until the destruction of the clans in the eighteenth century. The pattern of English-speaking Lowlands and Gaelic-speaking Highlands (see section 3.1) survived for nearly a thousand years, although with a continuous English advance.

South of the Clyde, the old language remained in the west. In the south west, the borders of Wessex were extended to the Severn after the battle of Deorham in 577, and as a result Cornwall was cut off from the Celtic-speaking communities further north. The Celtic-speaking area was restricted further when Wessex reached the Tamar, and Cornish continued in relative isolation until it died out in the eighteenth century. In the north west, when the borders of Northumbria reached the Mersey following the battle of Chester in about 617, the northern Celtic areas were cut off from the west (by land, at any rate), and the Celtic language developed separately in the two areas. At some point the western border of the English-speaking area was formed by *Westmorland*, and Celtic was still spoken in

Cumberland ('the land of the Cymru'). From this time, the main Celtic-speaking area in southern Britain was west of Offa's dyke.

As English political borders moved to the west, the adoption of English was a gradual process, taking several generations. Eventually there would be isolated pockets of Welsh in predominantly English-speaking areas. Such pockets are reflected in placenames beginning with the prefix 'Welsh'. There are, for example, two places called Walworth in Co. Durham, and a place called Walton near Brampton (Higham, 1986: 273). Such a prefix would not be meaningful in border areas where Welsh speech was still common. But as the border moved west, new isolated pockets would be formed. In the Wirral, for instance, just a few miles from the modern Welsh border, there remain isolated Welsh placenames such as Landican, and Welsh must have survived for a time at Wallasey ('island of the Welsh').

As the native people of Northumbria, Mercia and Wessex gave up Celtic and adopted English, they came to regard themselves as English people. The situation was slightly different west of Offa's dyke. The spread of English did not stop at the Mercian border and continued on to the west. However, the place is still called Wales and the people are called the Welsh, long after the majority of them have adopted English. When the word *Welsh* is used for the language, on the other hand, it refers specifically to the modern descendant of the old Celtic language.

The spread of English into Wales has continued until modern times. The ring of castles built in North Wales from the time of Edward I introduced English (and French) speakers into influential positions in the Welsh towns. After the revolt of Owen Glyndwr in the early fifteenth century, the English language was associated with English political and economic control. Welsh speakers were not allowed to acquire land within boroughs or hold municipal office (Williams, 1950: 16). Wales was finally incorporated within the political borders of England by the Act of Union of 1536.

The Acts of 1536 and 1543 set out to establish equality between the English and the Welsh, but using the English language. The 1563 Act for the translation of the Bible and Prayer Book into Welsh was intended to destroy the Welsh language. English and Welsh translations were to be available together in churches so that 'by conferring both tongues together the sooner to attain to the knowledge of the English tongue' (Williams, 1950: 67). In practice, William Morgan's translation, which finally appeared in 1588, was to be an important factor in the preservation of the language.

As in England, the courts used English, and the use of English was a condition of holding office (Williams, 1950: 33, 38). Welsh speakers were excluded from positions of influence, and the process of exclusion reached down the social scale from town corporations to street traders. The guilds in Welsh towns controlled the right to carry on a trade by largely restricting membership to English speakers, and excluding the Welsh, who were even referred to as 'foreigners'. This situation remained until it was overridden by the new social divisions of the seventeenth century.

The decline of Welsh was accelerated by economic factors and the industrial revolution. The growing English conurbations led to the economic decline of Welsh towns, and the emigration of Welsh speakers to England, while in the other direction labour was attracted to the valleys of the south not only from other parts of Wales but also from England. The English attitude towards the Welsh language could be openly hostile. Thomas (1994: 105) quotes *The Times* of 1866: 'the Welsh language . . . is the curse of Wales . . . its prevalence and ignorance of the English language have excluded the Welsh people from the civilisation of their English neighbours.'

2.5 *The British people*

There is an abiding myth that the British population was driven out *en masse* to the fastnesses of Wales and Cornwall by the advancing Anglo-Saxons. The point of the story is clear enough, for it supports the belief that the English race is pure and unmixed with Celtic blood. The question is: who drove them? Certainly there would have been refugees, many of whom would have gone to the west. We also know that refugees from Britain settled in Brittany. But to drive a population out requires a level of technology which was not available in the Iron Age. It needs a highly coordinated army to drive people from their villages and flush them out of the surrounding forests and wastelands. To make the refugees move in the same general direction requires a transport system with a network of roads and railways. Such things can be organized by the German army in the 1940s or the Serbian army in the 1990s, but not by the Anglo-Saxon settlers of post-Roman Britain. Second, if all the British were driven out, who tilled the fields, milked the cows and bore the children? It would indeed be a heroic achievement if the small bands of settlers managed to bring all their population with them and achieve everything out of their own resources.

A much more plausible explanation is that as the Anglo-Saxons took over control in the old Celtic kingdoms, and extended their power by military conquest, they made use of the existing infrastructure. The local population eventually gave up their own language, and began to speak English. This process has continued to the present day, as the English language has followed the spread of English power, to the extent that Welsh survives as a main language only in certain parts of Wales.

There are people today who take for granted that the Welsh and the Irish, in contrast to the English, are Celts. While it may be true that the Welsh and Irish languages are Celtic (and that there are clear political advantages in a romantic appeal to a 'Celtic' past), it cannot be true of the population as a whole. Celtic speech, too, must have followed Celtic power, and must have been adopted by the population already in Britain at the time.

Since the Anglo-Saxon invasions, there have been many additions to the genetic mix that makes up the British population as other groups have invaded and settled. The language, too, has changed fundamentally in this time. The sounds and grammar have changed, and so has the vocabulary. The society and culture in which the language is used have changed. The rate of change has been such that there is no point in history at which the spoken language can be said to have suddenly changed into a different language. This leads some linguists to insist that despite the changes it nevertheless remains the same language, a view that is reinforced by the use of the term *Old English* for Anglo-Saxon. One might as well argue that a broom with a new head and a new handle nevertheless remains the same broom. The belief that the English language that we speak today was first brought to our shores by the Angles, the Saxons and the Jutes is ultimately not a linguistic concept at all, but a political one.

3

English and Danish

From the end of the eighth century to the eleventh, the people of England were in close contact with invaders and settlers from Denmark and Norway. This contact was to have important consequences for the English language in different ways. The contact was much closer in the north than in the south of England, with the result that the influence is much greater on the modern dialects of the north. The most northerly dialect areas of English were annexed by Scotland, with the result that English developed differently on either side of the border, with the older Scottish tongue spoken in the Lowlands, and separated from the dialects of England further south.

The Danes and Norwegians are referred to collectively by several names, including *Norsemen* or 'Northmen'. The generic term now used for their language is *Old Norse*, although this term can refer specifically to Norwegian. When the events were first recorded, the dominant group with whom the people of England came into contact was the Danes, and as a result Anglo-Saxon writers use the term *Dane* in a generic sense. A more romantic term is the *Vikings*, which conjures up the image of raiders intent on looting, pillage and murder. In view of their geographical origin, they are also called *Scandinavians*, but this term ignores the fact that Finland is also part of Scandinavia even though Finnish is not a Germanic language.

3.1 *Old English and Old Norse*

The contrasting labels *English* and *Norse* can give the impression of completely different languages. In fact they were very similar to each other. They had a large number of words in common, including *hus* ('house') and *land*. Norse had (and still has) some peculiarities which differ from the rest of Germanic; for example, the definite article came after the noun, so that where English had *þæt hus* ('the house'), Norse had *husið* ('house the'). But in general, they had the similarities in grammar, vocabulary and pronunciation, and also the differences, that one would expect in languages which had renewed intense contact after several generations of relative separation.

There is some evidence in English dialects to suggest that contact was maintained with the homeland across the North Sea much as Americans later maintained contact across the Atlantic. New forms could have been brought to England by later Angle settlers (Kortlandt, 1986), or in the course of trade. Danes from Jutland may well already have come into contact with Germanic tribes related to the northern English, and been influenced by their speech. One prehistoric example is the similarity in the infinitive[1] in Northumbrian and Danish. The Germanic infinitive originally ended in [n] as in Modern German *singen* ('sing'), and it occurs in early Northumbrian texts: for example, Cædmon's hymn includes the form *hergan* ('praise'). Later it is dropped, and the Lindisfarne gospels include the form *singa* ('sing'). It was also lost in Norse *syngya*. The verb *are* is found in Anglian texts, replacing the older forms *sint* or *beoþ*. It is also found in Danish.

The alternation between forms such as *hath* and *has*, and *goeth* and *goes*, can be traced to Old Northumbrian. The Lindisfarne gospels use both <ð> forms and <s> forms: for example, *eghwelc forðon se ðe giuæð* vel *biddes onfoeð* ('for everyone who asks receives') (Matthew 7: 8). Here there are two alternative words to translate the Latin *petit* ('asks'): *giuæð* with the ending <ð> and *biddes* with <s>. The <ð> corresponds to German <t>, as in *hat*, *geht*, while <s> (probably pronounced [z]) corresponds to Danish <r> as in *har*, *går*. The <s> forms eventually spread from northern English to southern English, and replaced the <th> forms despite their use in the Authorized Version of the English Bible. In the north, the same alternation is found in the plural: for example, *ðer ðeafas ne ofdelfes ne forstelað* ('where thieves neither breaks in nor steals') (Matthew 6: 20). Again the <s> forms correspond to a Norse <r> (cf. Danish *de går* 'they go'), and forms such as *they goes* were characteristic of northern English until at least the seventeenth century. The Norse sound written <r> was phonetically similar to [z], and so the most likely explanation is that this is an innovation which spread across the North Sea to England. In the light of this evidence, Danish influence in English is not to be interpreted as something new, but the intensification of a long-established process.

3.2   *Norse immigration*

The beginnings of contact with the Norsemen can be dated to the year 787, when according to the Anglo-Saxon Chronicle raiders attacked the coast of

---

1. The form of a verb used as a dictionary headword, and also collocated with *to*, e.g. *(to) sing*.

Dorset. A more important raid took place in 793, when the monastery of Lindisfarne was sacked. Anglo-Saxon writers understandably reported their activities in unfavourable terms, emphasizing their barbarity and ferociousness, and concentrating on the atrocities of leaders such as Eric Bloodaxe and Ivar the Boneless. In reality they must have been very similar to the English raiders who had come to Britain a few generations before.

The early raiders seem to have come from Norway rather than Denmark (Geipel, 1971: 34). The main thrust of Norwegian expansion was to the west (see section 2.1 under *Language contact in Europe*), and they later expanded from their settlements in Ireland to the north west of England and south-west Scotland. Their later language was influenced by Irish, and Irish word order is reflected in some of their placenames, for example, *Aspatria* ('Patrick's ash'). They were even referred to as Irishmen, and the village name of Ireby in the Lune valley, for instance, means 'farm of the Irishmen', i.e. Norwegians from Ireland. In general the Norwegians established a large number of small and isolated settlements.

The Danish settlement of England began in the ninth century and led to several larger and organized invasions from the 860s onwards. Danes settled much of the north and the east, in Northumbria and Mercia. These settlements, together with the military strength of the Norsemen, had major political and linguistic consequences. By the late 870s they controlled England with the exception of Wessex, and following the treaty of Wedmore in 886, England was partitioned, with a new boundary roughly following the course of Watling Street running up through the old kingdom of Mercia from London towards Chester (see map 2). The land to the south and west remained in English control, while territory to the north and east was subject to Danish law, and hence the name *Danelaw*. Danish settlements were widespread within this area, but importantly there were also concentrations of population, including York and the Five Boroughs (Stamford, Lincoln, Derby, Leicester and Nottingham).

What remained of England was ruled from the old kingdom of Wessex. Over the next 80 years, Wessex gradually extended its power into the Danelaw, and finally took control in the 950s. In 954 Eric Bloodaxe was expelled from York, and Eadred of Wessex was effectively king of the whole of England. It is easy to think of this as the liberation of the Danelaw from the hand of the foreign invader: but that is to take a Wessex-centred view of the situation. For the people of York, after three generations of contact with the Danes, King Eadred may well have seemed at least as foreign as King Eric.

The Danish kingdom of York had destroyed the old Anglo-Saxon kingdom of Northumbria. The ensuing struggle between York and Wessex gave the king in Scotland an opportunity to extend his southern border. The Scots under Kenneth MacAlpin captured Edinburgh in 960, and eventually secured English territory down to a line from the Solway to the Tweed (Duncan, 1984: 136–7). The England ruled by Eadred did not extend to the

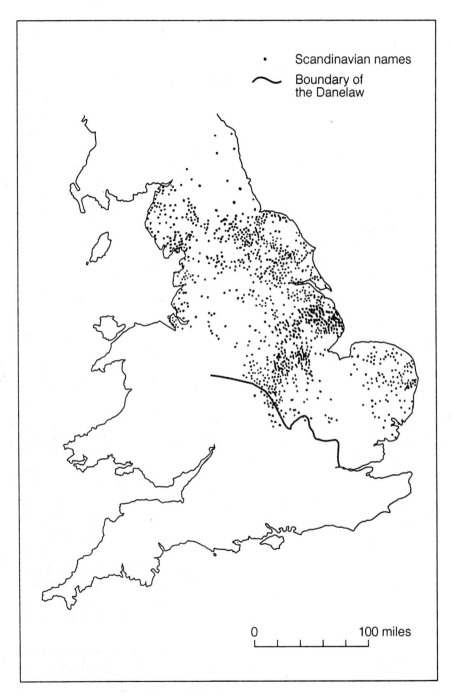

Map 2 The Scandinavian settlements.

former northern parts of Northumbria, and this established a new linguistic geography in the northern half of Britain. Hitherto, Scotland had been a Celtic-speaking area north of the Clyde and the Forth, and English had been the predominant language south of this line. Now the extended Scotland was linguistically divided, with Celtic still spoken in the Highlands, and English in the Lowlands. The name *Scots*, originally the name of Celtic-speaking Highlanders, was eventually transferred to the English speakers of the Lowlands and to their language.

The patterns of Danish migration to eastern England followed major economic changes in Denmark (Randsborg, 1984). Towards the end of the tenth century, England was again invaded and this time conquered by the Danes. Canute and Hardacanute were kings of Denmark and also kings of England, and for a time England was absorbed into the Danish kingdom. Danish power and influence finally declined after the accession in 1042 of Edward the Confessor, who was the son of an English father and a Norman mother. After his death in 1066 he was succeeded after a brief interval by the duke of Normandy, and from this time onward England was oriented not towards the Northmen but towards the Normans.

3.3 *The Anglo-Saxon written tradition*

Much discussion has centred on whether English and Danish were mutually intelligible in the Danelaw. The assumption behind the discussion is that if they were not mutually intelligible, they could be regarded as distinct languages. However, intelligibility is not a good criterion. In the early twentieth century, forestry workers from Gloucestershire and miners from Durham would have had enormous difficulty in understanding each other, but it does not follow that they spoke different languages. Second, intelligibility is not an objectively measurable quantity, and one has to ask *intelligible to whom*? English people would find Danish easier to understand the more they came into contact with it. English and Danish might well have been rather more mutually intelligible for the people of York than for the people of Winchester.

In any case, it is not appropriate to contrast English and Norse as clearly defined and separate languages at this period. Our view of Old English is largely determined by the official language that developed in Wessex after the Norse incursions, and our view of Norse is largely determined by the texts of the sagas written in thirteenth-century Iceland. The comparison of written Late West Saxon and written Old Icelandic does not give us a very clear view of spoken Anglo-Danish contact in the Danelaw in the ninth century. In fact, such a comparison exaggerates the differences.

The Norse raids had destroyed the power of Mercia and with it the Mercian literary tradition. King Alfred, in a famous preface to his translation of *Cura pastoralis*, lamented the decline in learning in England, even north of the Humber. Alfred, of course, was not an objective observer. He was no doubt impressed by the revival of learning at the court of Charlemagne in Aachen, and wished to emulate it, and exaggerated the decline in the Danelaw (Morrish, 1986). Wessex, unlike Northumbria, survived as a kingdom and it was here that English learning eventually revived. By the tenth century the Wessex dialect was the dominant variety of English.

From the 950s the kings of Wessex were powerful enough to claim the title of kings of England. From about this same time England is given its modern name. Hitherto writers had referred to the *angelcynn* ('Angle-kin'); from now on it is *englaland* ('land of the Angles'): an ethnic concept is replaced by a political one. It is important to note that *englaland* is not a descriptive term but a political claim. Edgar, nephew and successor of Eadred, issued coinage bearing the name and title *Adgar rex Anglorum* ('Edgar, king of the English') (Stafford, 1984: 117–19).

A further attribute of the newly united England was a national written language, and the dialect of Wessex became *de facto* a kind of official written standard, now known as *Late West Saxon*. This too is a political concept, and many of the people ruled from Wessex may not have regarded West Saxon as their language at all. Although records survive from before the Norman conquest in different parts of England, the vast majority were written in Wessex in the years after 900, and some of these were copies of documents originally written in other dialects. West Saxon was a language of record, and was used for the histories known as the *Anglo-Saxon chronicle*. It was also a literary language, used for the major Anglo-Saxon poems such as *Beowulf* and *The dream of the rood*. It is for this reason the variety of Old English which is traditionally taught to students to enable them to study the literature of the period.

As an official language, it became to some extent independent of the spoken language, and eventually an archaic language, preserving the features of the language of the time when it became established as a prestige form. Official West Saxon survived the Danish conquest, and for a time the Norman conquest. The English capital moved from Winchester to London, with the result that spoken West Saxon developed not into the standard pronunciation of Modern English, but into the rhotic dialects of the south west. Without power and authority to support it, the speech of the court of King Alfred lost its prestige, and came to be regarded as a rustic dialect.

3.4   *English in the Danelaw*

The survival of Norse varied in different parts of Britain according to different patterns of settlement. The key factors are the status of the settlements, and the distribution of the immigrant population.

In the north west and islands of Scotland, Norse – or *Norn* – was spoken almost until the present century. Orkney and Shetland were Norwegian possessions until they were pledged to Scotland in the 1460s, and the legal right of Norway was still recognized in 1667 (Geipel, 1971: 53–4). The last document written in Norse in Shetland dates from 1607. As recently as 1893–5 Jakob Jakobsen found traces of Norn in Shetland, and spoke to people who remembered the language being spoken (Geipel, 1971: 95–103).

Further south, in south-west Scotland and the Lake District, Norwegian settlements seem to have been scattered and small-scale enterprises, and in many cases made use of land formerly unoccupied. This is reflected in placenames ending in *thwaite* ('clearing'), such as Langthwaite, Stone-thwaite and Rosthwaite ('horse clearing'). Although there were English settlements here, particularly on the Solway plain, it is possible that Welsh also was still spoken. The population is likely to have been so sparse that there was no dominant local language. In addition, the Lake District was remote from centres of power – Northumbria, Scotland, York, Wessex – and none of these powers would have had the means or the motivation to impose its own language. Under these conditions, several languages could survive and co-exist for a long time. Some evidence of the continued use of Norse is provided by a number of runic inscriptions dating from about the year 1100 (Geipel, 1971: 58–60), including a Norse graffito in Carlisle cathedral and a Norse inscription over the church door at Pennington (Cumbria). It must be remembered, of course, that inscriptions tell us how people wrote, but not necessarily how they spoke.

A rather different situation is found in the Wirral peninsula (Mersey-side). The Norse leader Ingemund was expelled from Ireland in 901 and settled in the north of the Wirral. The origin of the settlers is recorded in the village name of Irby ('farm of the Irishmen'). The outline of the settlement is still discernible in local village names. Names ending in *-by* – e.g. *Frankby, Greasby* – may even reflect the names of early land-owners, although Thorsteinn may have taken over an existing English farm at Thursaston ('Thorsteinn's enclosure'). The council or *thing* was held at Thingwall ('thing-field'). Part of the original boundary with English set-tlements can still be traced in the name of Raby ('boundary farm'). Here there was a local concentration of Norwegians in a predominantly Anglo-Saxon area. It must have been in the immigrants' interests to learn English, and eventually Norse died out, leaving no traces in local speech. In the same way, the immigrants in the many smaller settlements throughout the Danelaw must have quickly given up Norse in favour of English.

The kingdom of York, by contrast, was a centre of communication. It was established in the southern part of Northumbria, and the new rulers would have been able to make use of the existing network of communica-tion on land. By sea it was connected to the international trade routes operated by the Danes. Third, it was an ecclesiastical centre, with its own archbishop. A centre of this kind has an influence on the speech of the area which it controls, including perhaps in this case the Five Boroughs south of the Humber. Linguistic forms used in York would be copied by people from outlying districts coming into contact with York speech. To the extent that different areas copied the same forms, the speech of the Danelaw must have become more uniform. At the same time it is likely that changes in the language taking place in the south of England were prevented from crossing the border into York.

In these circumstances it is crucial to know what language was spoken in York, but we can only guess. It is most likely that some kind of English replaced Danish after the fall of York in 954. After this date the kings of Wessex had the power to appoint the archbishops of York, and southwestern English spread to York in the English of the church. Inscriptions from different parts of Yorkshire and the north east which survive from about 1100 (Geipel, 1971: 59–61) contain some Danish personal names and a few other borrowed words, but indicate that English was then in widespread use.

3.5   *Norse influence on English*

Norse influenced English in many different ways in vocabulary, grammar, pronunciation and everyday expressions. The Norse area included the east midlands, which was later to be of importance in the development of Standard English, and in this way a number of modern standard forms derive from the usage of the Danelaw rather than England under the control of Wessex. There are even indications of a southward movement of linguistic influence, presumably from York.

Vocabulary

Some 400 Norwegian and Danish words survive in colloquial and in standard written English (Geipel, 1971: 69–70). Apart from the number, it is important that many of these are also frequent words. There are many more in the dialects of the north, some of them used in colloquial speech in preference to the standard forms.

The earliest loans referred specifically to objects and concepts related to Danish culture, including words for boats (*cnearr, barða*), for currency (*oran, marc*), and for warriors (*dreng*). Some early borrowings are general words such as *law, husband, fellow, husting, call*; by the early twelfth century *die, take, skin* and *knife* had replaced the existing English words (Geipel, 1971: 62–4). After the Norman conquest large numbers of loans appear in English texts, for example in the *Ormulum* and the *Lay of*

Havelock the Dane, which were written in north Lincolnshire towards the beginning and end of the thirteenth century respectively.

Perhaps the most interesting loans are everyday words such as *law* and *sky*, for which perfectly good English words already existed, but which were nevertheless borrowed from Danish. These indicate a close connection between the speakers of English and Danish. Some words such as *bloom, bread, dream, dwell* and *gift* were given new meanings to conform to the Danish meaning; these had formerly meant 'mass of metal', 'fragment', 'joy', 'to make a mistake' and 'dowry'. A *plough* was formerly a measure of land (Jespersen, 1905: 64–5). Other words like *egg* were made to conform to the Danish pronunciation.

Pronunciation

There is a common sound change according to which the consonants [k, g] are modified when they are followed by the vowel sounds [i] or [e]. In popular usage, the original sounds are described as 'hard' and the new modified sounds as 'soft'. Modern German retains the hard [k, g] in words such as *Kinn* ('chin'), *geben* ('give') and *gelb* ('yellow'). These sounds were softened in most other Germanic dialects, including southern English and some varieties of Norse. In English the soft sounds are represented by the spellings <ch, y> in *chin* and *yellow*. On the other hand the hard sounds remained in words such as *kirk* and *give* in an area which included Denmark and the Danelaw. Modern Standard English is mixed, having adopted the southern *church* rather than *kirk*, but it does include the northern *give*. In some English dialects, the [g] of *give* was first softened and the hard sound was restored under Danish influence; but it is possible that in some parts of the Danelaw it was never softened in the first place.

Another north/south difference is found in the pronunciation of words such as *road, whole* and *stone*. The modern spellings represent the southern pronunciation. The northern forms are represented by *raid* and *hale* (now independent words) and the non-standard spelling *stane*. The pronunciation suggested by <stane> is remarkably similar to that suggested by the Old Norse *steinn*. The Yorkshire pronunciation of *nay* is still much closer to the Danish *nej* than to the southern English *no*. In the case of *weak* and *swain* it is only the northern forms that have survived into Modern English.

Danish influence may have brought about the loss of the sound written <gh> in words such as *night, daughter*. This was a velar fricative and it is still found in the German *Nacht, Tochter*, but it is absent from Danish *nat, datter*. Spelling such as <dowter> from the late fourteenth century indicates its loss in areas of Danish settlement (Geipel, 1971: 21).

Danish may also have influenced the pronunciation of an initial <s> or <f> in words such as *fox* and *sing*. In the Danelaw, as in North Germanic, these remain unchanged [s, f], but there is widespread evidence of the pronunciation [z, v] in the area controlled by Wessex (Poussa, 1995). This distribution is confirmed by placename evidence (Fisiak, 1994). Similar forms are found on the European mainland: for example, the <s> of German *singen* is pronounced [z], and the <v> of Dutch *vijf* ('five') is more like an English [v] than [f]. Some [v]-forms have become part of Standard English: for example, *vat* (cf. German *Faß*), and *vixen* alongside *fox*, but otherwise the [s, f] forms have become general, and [z, v] survive only in isolated pockets.

Much of the above analysis remains speculative in view of our lack of knowledge of the detail of the dialects of Scandinavia and the Danelaw. Many of the features regarded as typically English, for example the soft [k, g] in *bench* and *ridge,* are actually found somewhere in the Norse area (Geipel, 1971). Norse typically drops the initial [w] from *worm* and *Wednesday,* but *worm* and *Wonsda* have also been attested. The loss of [l] in *folk* and *half* is typically English, but it has also been found in Scandinavia. Some of the forms believed to be typically English could also be Norse.

Grammar

A particularly interesting effect of Danish pronunciation has been on English word endings. In many Germanic dialects, the sound [z] changed in certain cases to a kind of [r] sound. In *was* the [z]-sound has survived, but it has changed to [r] in the older pronunciation of *were.*[2] The change was more widespread in Norse with the result that modern Danish often has [r] where English has [z]. For example, where English has *is, was,* Danish has *er, var;* and where English forms the plural of nouns with [z] in *stones* [stəunz], Danish has [r] in *stener.*

A remarkable feature of the <s> endings is that they are among the very few that have survived at all into Modern English. Early Old English had a number of morphological endings for nouns, verbs, adjectives and articles, like Latin or modern German. By the twelfth century, most of these had disappeared. Looking at the problem from an English point of view, the usual explanation is that they were dropped in the Danelaw in cases where English and Danish were significantly different. In other words, the English and the Danes communicated in a kind of pidgin Germanic and ignored the endings of words. This does not explain why Danish itself lost most of these endings too. Nor does it explain why nouns, adjectives and articles lost their endings in the Latin of different parts of the Roman empire after the Germanic invasions. This is a widespread phenomenon to be examined on a European scale, and not a local problem of the north of England.

---

2. If you say the word *miserable* [mizrəbl] slowly to yourself, you may be able to feel that these sounds are made in a similar way in Modern English.

In the pronoun system, *they, their* and *them* are of Danish origin. The corresponding English words were *hi, heora* and *hem*, which are confusingly similar to *he, her* and *him*.[3] The old form *hem* survives in the weak form *'em*. The early Old English preposition *with* meant 'against' (cf. German *wider* 'against') and the word meaning 'with' was *mid* (cf. German *mit*). The word *with* has taken on the meaning of the Danish *við*, and this has created an interesting ambiguity in a sentence like *the English fought with the Danes* in that it is not clear whether they are on the same side or opposite sides. Besides this, as in Danish, prepositions can be used in final position: for example, *the Danes that the English fought with.*

Norse in English dialects

The examples given in the last two sections were borrowed in the Danelaw but eventually spread to other varieties of English and were later included as the standard forms. There are other words, such as *leik* ('play'), *skrike* ('cry'), *bairn* ('child'), which survive in local dialects. There must have been many thousands more which have died out over the last few centuries. Some of these old words were recorded by Ray in 1691, and later in the nineteenth century by Joseph Wright in his *English dialect dictionary*. An interesting subset of these words is nowadays associated specifically with the Lake District. People who normally talk about hills, streams and ponds will nevertheless refer to fells, becks and tarns in the Lake District.

The Yorkshire use of *us* in the sense of 'our' (e.g. *When can we have us dinner?*) may be another case of English <s> matching Danish <r>, but this time not in the standard language. A similar usage can be found in the Lindisfarne gospel: *suæ ue forgefon scyldgum usum* ('as we forgive us debtors'). Further south, the expected form for 'our' would be *urum*. Among the grammatical details which were to be condemned by prescriptive grammarians of the eighteenth century (see section 8.5) were a number of Danish borrowings: expressions such as *it's me; the best of two;* or *this here book.* Both languages have also confused the uses of the relative pronouns *who* and *whom*, although in different ways, and both languages can omit the relative particle as in *the man I saw.* In these cases English shares grammatical details with Danish. Both languages are different in these respects from German, and the Danish types survive as informal or non-standard forms.

Many of the Norse features have been lost as a result of later influences on the language. Some of its earlier influence can be discerned if we look at

---

3. Another pronoun *heo* was also similar to *he* and *hi*. This was replaced with the new pronoun *she*, which is not Danish but derives from the feminine definite article. This solution has caused problems for non-sexist language in the late twentieth century, whenever a sex-neutral pronoun is required.

texts not in standard written English, but in spoken northern English. One of William Wordsworth's neighbours in Rydal said of the poet in about 1825 that he was 'not a man as folk could crack wi'. *Folk* is both English and Norse, but it has survived as a normal word more in the north than the south. The use of *as* as a relative pronoun is found in dialects of the north rather than the south, and corresponds to the Norse use of *som* ('as'). The sense of the preposition *with* is Norse, and the use of the preposition in final position is itself characteristic of Norse grammar.

The influence of Norse adds a complication to the linguistic map which makes it difficult to generalize about the kind of English spoken in the last decades before the Norman conquest. This has important consequences for our understanding of the *dialects* of this period, and also for the concept of a spoken Anglo-Saxon *language*. The pattern formed by the dialects of the old kingdoms (see section 2.3) was overlaid by the influence of Danish and Norwegian in the Danelaw. Here there must have been a very complex socio-linguistic situation, with differing degrees of influence. At one extreme, and at certain times, new immigrants from Denmark would speak Danish, while immigrants from Dublin would speak Norwegian influenced by Irish. There must have been surviving pockets of Anglo-Saxon in Danish areas – giving rise to placenames such as Ingleby ('farm of the Angles') – much as Celtic pockets had survived the Anglo-Saxon settlements some centuries before. The bulk of the population of the Danelaw must have spoken mixed Anglo-Norse dialects, ranging from anglicized Norse to English influenced by Danish. Judging by later events, it is this last type which eventually emerged as the dominant one. Meanwhile, in the south and west, the Anglo-Saxon dialects continued with relatively little Norse influence.

This situation did not remain stable, but changed with social and military events. As political power passed to Wessex, south-western English features would spread north and east, and into the old Danelaw. Words and other features of speech which had already been replaced by Danish would change back to English, but to the new southern English rather than the original northern English. Now when we examine the later records, it is the Danish words and expressions that manage to survive that are the natural object of interest. The occurrence of English words in later texts from the Danelaw does not excite comment. It is impossible to distinguish cases in which English words replaced earlier Danish ones, and cases of purely English development. It follows that the impression given by the later evidence can be only an underestimate of the general level of Danish influence.

After the Norman conquest, the main linguistic divisions in England remained between the north and east on the one hand and the south and west on the other. This can be seen quite clearly in the maps of the late Middle English dialect survey (McIntosh *et al.*, 1986). The royal capital was later moved from Winchester to London, which was in the overlap area. An important consequence of this is that a number of Danelaw features – usually rather misleadingly referred to as 'northern' – became part of London English. At this time London English was beginning to assume its dominant role in determining the standard form of English, and northern English began to be the object of ridicule and attack (Bailey, 1991: 24–6). Even so, York English was still sufficiently important in the fourteenth century to merit a vitriolic attack from Ranulph Higden from Chester, and his translator John of Trevisa from Cornwall: 'Al þe longage of þe Norþhumbres, and specialych at ʒork, ys so scharp, slytting, and frotyng, and vnshape, þat we Souþeron men may þat longage vnneþe vnderstonde.'[4]

Looking back from the twentieth century, we know the eventual outcome of Anglo-Norse contact, and it might seem that this outcome was inevitable. In reality, the Standard English with which we are familiar is the chance product of social and military events that had nothing at all to do with language. If York had defeated Wessex, it is quite possible that Anglo-Saxon would have died out, and that Modern English would have been been a northern-based Anglo-Norse dominated by York. At the time of Canute, it must have seemed quite likely that England would be merged into the Danish empire; if this had happened, Anglo-Saxon might have been replaced by Danish. It was not until after 1042, when the son of the Norman Queen Emma came to the English throne, that the actual outcome would have appeared even as a remote possibility.

---

4. 'All the language north of the Humber, and specially at York, is so sharp, piercing, and grating, and mis-shapen, that we Southerners can scarcely understand that language.'

4

English and French

Following the accession of Edward the Confessor in 1042, England was reoriented towards France and the former Roman empire, and away from Denmark and the north of Europe. Undoubtedly the best-remembered single event was the Norman conquest of England, which followed the battle of Hastings on 14 October 1066. English and French remained in close contact for over 300 years. When English reemerged as the written language of England, and as the spoken language of the upper classes, it was deeply influenced in many different ways by French. These influences were to prove permanent.

4.1 *England and France*

Eleventh-century French was not a language like modern French. At the time of Hastings there were two main dialect groups, or languages, spoken in France and conventionally identified by the word used for *yes*: the language of the north is called *langue d'oïl* – *oïl* being an older form of the modern *oui* – and the language of the south, *langue d'oc*. Modern French is the language of a unified national state, and it is used for a range of purposes both spoken and written.

There was a king in Paris who ruled the area known as the Ile de France and who claimed suzerainty over neighbouring duchies, including Normandy, Burgundy and Brittany. Some of these duchies were sufficiently independent to conduct their own foreign policy, and the dukes could rule territory outside France. After 1066, the duke of Normandy ruled England, and later the duke of Burgundy ruled what is now the Netherlands and Belgium. In such cases the ruling class and the people they ruled would speak completely different languages. In England, as land passed from English to Norman owners, and high offices of church and state were taken over by Normans, French became the spoken language of the ruling class, and English remained as the spoken language of the ruled. The duchies would also have different kinds of French, and the French brought to England from Normandy was markedly different from *francien,* the French of the Ile de France.

Within three generations or so, the expatriate Normans began to regard themselves as Englishmen. According to Richard FitzNeal in 1179, the Normans and the English were no longer distinguishable (Clanchy, 1979: 168). At the same time, there was considerable animosity between them and the Normans of France. According to French invective of the time, Englishmen had tails, they were better at feasting and boozing than at fighting, and were a bit dozy on account of the damp and foggy climate (Crouch, 1994: 64–5). The links which remained among the upper aristocracy were effectively broken when in 1204 the king of France crushed the duchy of Normandy and brought it under central control.

The increased power of the king of France had an effect also on the French language, in that *francien* spread with central control, and eventually became the standard variety for the whole of France. The kind of French spoken in England lost its prestige in France, and within a short time Parisian French was being taught in England as a foreign language. Some time after 1250, Walter of Bibbesworth wrote a treatise to help ladies improve their French (Clanchy, 1979: 151–2). His compilation of a list of French words marks the beginning of French lexicography. John Barton produced a French conversation manual for foreign travellers in about 1400. The French linguistic tradition effectively began in fourteenth-century England (von Wartburg, 1946: 114).

4.2 Literacy in the medieval period

The popular image is of the haughty Norman lord speaking French and the Saxon serf speaking English. In reality there must have been widespread bilingualism. Orderic Vitalis was born near Shrewsbury in 1075, the son of a French father and English mother. He was educated from the age of 5 but heard and knew no French until he went to Normandy at the age of 10. On the other hand he would have been familiar with Latin. Both English and French were regarded in the early medieval period as inferior to Latin.

Latin was the language of record, which means that it was used as a matter of course for any document that was felt to be sufficiently important to be left to posterity. The vernaculars French and English were both used for certain limited purposes. French was the main auxiliary written language until the mid fourteenth century, after which it was gradually replaced by English.

Latin and the vernaculars

A consequence of the Norman use of Latin as the language of record was that the use of English as a written language gradually declined. According to the radical propaganda of the reign of James I (see section 7.1), the Normans set out to destroy the English language, but recent research has shown that, on the contrary, they took written English very seriously. They particularly valued English law as formulated by Alfred and Ine (Richards, 1986) and codified later by the Danish king Canute. The translation of English law into Latin in the twelfth century (Frantzen, 1986: 12) indicates that the old legal system was considered so important that it needed to be preserved for posterity. The Norman use of Latin as the language of record represents not the destruction of the Anglo-Saxon heritage, but the transfer from a national standard to the prevailing European standard.

If the Normans did not value English as a vernacular, this is to be interpreted not as a repressive language policy towards English, but as consistent with the prevailing view of vernaculars. They had themselves a few generations before given up their own Germanic language in favour of Latin and French. English could not survive as a language of record without the active support of the civil power and public authorities, and these the Normans could not be expected to provide.

What is remarkable is that Anglo-Saxon survived as a written language for another hundred years even though there was no authoritative group with a motivation to promote its use. Anglo-Saxon texts, including law texts, continued to be copied long after the conquest, and some texts exist only in twelfth-century copies. There were bilingual English–Latin documents, including a continuation of the *Anglo-Saxon chronicle*, and a trilingual Psalter produced at Canterbury (Clanchy, 1979: 166). The final collapse of the Anglo-Saxon tradition is well described by Clanchy (1979: 167). The version of the *Chronicle* continued at Peterborough was, until 1121, copied from an earlier original. From 1122 the same scribe continued, but his spellings showed the influence of the contemporary spoken language. A different scribe compiled the record for 1132 to 1154, and he used not the archaic forms of Wessex, but new forms based on the contemporary dialect of the east midlands. The Anglo-Saxon written language died out because no-one any longer knew how to write it.

Literacy in French

Norman French was used as the language of courtly literature, and since French was the language of the upper classes, French literacy essentially reflects the aristocratic taste of the time. Wace's *Roman de Brut*, a history of Britain, was based on the work of Geoffrey of Monmouth, and his *Roman de Rou*, a history of Normandy, was commissioned by Henry II.

Richard I wrote poetry in Norman French. There was a demand for romances, and tales of courtly love. A *romance* was originally a story written in the Romance (i.e. in this case French) language, but its modern associations reflect the kind of story originally written in French. An important group of stories in this tradition was those which concerned King Arthur. Originally Arthur was a Celtic hero, but after the Norman conquest the stories were taken over and adapted by the Norman ruling class. Arthur and the Knights of the Round Table became the models of the French concepts of chivalry and courtesy.

From the middle of the thirteenth century, French was beginning to be accepted as an alternative language of record. In courts of law (Clanchy, 1979: 161–3), the previous practice with regard to Latin was transferred to French, and the words of people speaking English were recorded in French. There is thus no means of ascertaining what language was actually spoken in court unless this is itself explicitly recorded.

Literacy in English

The few English texts that survive from the early medieval period fall into several categories. The earliest, i.e. those written within about a hundred years of the conquest, represent the end of the late West Saxon tradition, and English was eventually replaced in these functions by Latin and French. English continued to be used as a spoken language by the ordinary people of England, and also for some public purposes, such as sermons which ordinary people would not understand in French.

Following the fall of Normandy, English versions of French literary texts began to appear. For example, Laȝamon's *Brut*, based on the work of Wace, appeared in the early thirteenth century. At about the same time appeared the *Ormulum*, the work of an Augustinian canon called Orm, consisting of a set of verse sermons for use in church. Orm was particularly concerned with the pronunciation, and devised a regular system of spelling which he used rigorously. All written English texts show strong French influence, and aristocratic literature rather more so than texts intended for popular use.

French influence is most obviously marked in the spelling. The introduction of French spelling conventions gives the superficial impression that English changed very rapidly in the years following the Norman conquest. For example, new conventions were used for the [ʃ] sound, producing spellings such as <fisshe, fishe, fische> and eventually <fish>. In the same way, new conventions were developed for the initial consonants of <thin, chin> and <whin>, and for some vowel sounds. The word *house* at this time had an [u:] sound, like the vowel in the modern pronunciation of *moose*. The Old English spelling was <hus>. However, a similar vowel sound was represented by <ou> in French, and so the spelling was changed to <hous>. The actual pronunciation did not change until much later.

An aspect of Norman spelling which can be confusing for the modern reader is that no distinction was made between the letters <u> and <v>. Both characters were used for the vowel [u] and for the consonant [v]. The angled shape of <v> was sometimes used at the beginning of a word, and the rounded shape of <u> elsewhere. Up to the seventeenth century we consequently find *us* written <vs> and *give* written <giue>.

4.3   *The reemergence of English*

The first hint of the reemergence of English is heard in 1258 at the time of the Barons' revolt. The struggle mainly concerned the arbitrary exercise of royal power, but a particular issue was the appointment of Frenchmen to prominent positions in church and state. Simon de Montfort – who was actually born in France – demanded *inter alia* the restoration of English. Henry III subsequently issued a proclamation in English as well as in French. Such events would be difficult to explain if the English aristocracy were themselves at this time typically monolingual French speakers. It is also from this time that aristocratic literature begins to appear in English. Later in the century Robert of Gloucester complains that only 'Vor bote a man conne Frenss me telþ of him lute'[1] and 'lowe men holdeþ to Engliss' (ll. 7542–3), but he goes on to point out (l. 7546) that 'Ac wel me wot uor to conne boþe wel it is',[2] which suggests that some people were bilingual. Among the 'lowe men', incidentally, were novice monks and undergraduates, for from the late thirteenth century there are several decrees and regulations: for example in Oxford in the 1320s, requiring them to keep to French or Latin.

A significant impetus to change was provided by the outbreak in 1337, in the reign of Edward III, of the extended period of warfare between England and France known as the Hundred Years War. One of the effects was to force Englishmen and Frenchmen to see themselves as belonging to different peoples. The separation of English and French was not confined to language, and covered other areas of culture. Until this time, for example, English architecture had generally followed French architecture; English perpendicular architecture of the fifteenth century is independent of the French flamboyant style.

---

1. 'For unless a man knows French people think little of him.'
2. 'But people know that it is as well to know both [languages].'

Social change

Throughout the course of the war, English progressively took over the various roles previously assigned to French. An indication of the decline of the use of French as a spoken language among the nobility is given by Ranulph Higden's *Polychronicon*, originally written in Latin in about 1352, and translated into English by John of Trevisa in 1387. Higden argued that the original English language had in the past been impaired ('apeyred' in the translation) by contact first with Danes and then with Normans. In his time, French rather than English was used in school and among the nobility:

> Þis apeyryng of þe burþtonge ys bycause of twey þinges. On[e] is chyldern in scole, aȝenes þe vsage and manere of al oþer nacions, buþ compelled for to leue here oune longage, and for to construe here lessons and here þinges a Freynsch, and habbeþ suþthe þe Normans come furst into Engelond. Also gentil men children buþ ytauȝt for to speke Freynsch fram tyme þat a buþ yrokked in here cradel.

Already in the 1350s Higden is implying that French is not really the first language of the upper classes, but one they learn at school. Then as now, it would be dangerous to infer that people who learn French at school habitually use it as the language of everyday conversation. Later in the century, Trevisa comments that Higden was actually describing the situation before the Black Death in 1349, and that since then the situation had changed again. In 1385, 'in al þe gramerscoles of Engelond childern leueþ Frensch, and construeþ and lurneþ an Englysch'.

From 1362 English was used in courts of law, all legal cases being tried in English. However, English was not used consistently in recording the proceedings of courts of law until the eighteenth century (Prins, 1952: 27). English was used in the formal opening of parliament in 1363. The earliest known testament (i.e. a bequest of goods and chattels) in English dates from 1389, although the first will (i.e. a bequest of real property) dates from 1479 (Chambers and Daunt, 1931).

There are reports that by 1350 English was in use in the royal court (McKnight, 1928: 7). Nevertheless, in 1375, a German merchant in London wrote to two Hanse merchants in Bruges advising them to bring a French interpreter with them in order to do business in London, particularly for dealing with the royal court (Viereck, 1993: 73). French remained the first language of the king until the end of the century. Henry IV, who came to the throne in 1399, was the first king of England since the conquest who had English as his mother tongue. But Henry also knew and used French.

Economic change

By the fourteenth century, we have to take account of a new group in society, separate from the nobility, and of rapidly increasing power and importance. This is the growing middle class of manufacturers, traders and merchants. This development has two important aspects. First, it was based on London and the towns rather than the countryside, which was still in the control of feudal landlords. London has had a continuous and increasing influence on English in England and beyond. Second, a number of English merchants had an international outlook. They were beginning at this period to take control of their own international trade, particularly with Bruges and Antwerp. English merchants at first exported raw wool, but in the first half of the fourteenth century they were exporting finished cloth. German merchants of the Hanseatic League from Cologne, Hamburg and Lübeck had in about 1281 (or possibly earlier) established an office in London which came to be known as the Steelyard. By the end of the fourteenth century, English merchants had set up their own rival organization, the Merchant Adventurers. By the time Caxton brought his printing press to England, the book trade was already organized on an international scale. Published English has never been confined to England.

The importance of merchants is primarily economic, but it also has linguistic consequences. Their approach to language seems to have been essentially pragmatic, and for a time they kept records in Latin as a matter of course. But from the 1380s the London guilds began to use English for their records. In 1384 the City of London issued a proclamation in English, the importance in this case being not that it was read aloud in English but that it was actually written in English. In 1422 the London brewers decided that in future their proceedings would be conducted in English, instead of Latin. By the middle of the fifteenth century, London tradesmen formed a significant literate group apart from churchmen and the nobility. They were even classed as *literati* (Clanchy, 1979: 185). The timing of these changes is significant, as they coincide with other events which were to have a profound effect on the language.

In a study of London business accounts, Laura Wright (1994) shows how in the fifteenth century and later English phrases could be incorporated in texts of Latin or French. All three languages could occur together: for example, *13 les bordes voc shelfes quatuor les pryntyng presses* ('13 boards called shelves, 4 printing presses') (p. 451). Latin words were abbreviated, and special characters were used in a written language with no obvious spoken counterpart. For instance, a symbol like '&' is a stylized version of Latin *et*, but it can just as easily be read out as *and*. For that matter *voc* does not need to be expanded into its full Latin form, and can be read out directly as *called*. The words of a phrase such as *attendenc[e] & labore* (p. 450) could eventually be regarded as English. In business texts of this kind it is not quite clear where English ends and Latin and French begin.

Chancery English

In view of the variety of Middle English dialects, one might reasonably expect the shift from French to English to be accompanied by a sudden burgeoning of dialect texts. This appears not to have happened. There is substantial agreement among language historians that already by the end of the fourteenth century there is a recognizable variety of written English which can be traced to the modern standard. As more people became literate in English, they used not their own local dialect but a special written form. The new standard was essentially London English, which was based largely on the dialect of the east midlands, but incorporated a number of northern elements, including the forms *they* and *though* which had spread from the Danelaw. Samuels (1963) identifies four different incipient standard varieties, showing different regional influences, and demonstrates how the dialect of the midlands came to dominate London English. These are the English of Wycliffite writings, early London dialect, later London dialect influenced by immigration from the central midlands, and a Chancery standard which developed in the fifteenth century.

All these incipient standards were written rather than spoken. There is nothing surprising in the fact that people should write a form of English different from the one they spoke. This was true in eighth-century Mercia, and in eleventh-century Wessex, and it is true today. It was also true of people who were literate in French, for the French written in England was not the variety that people spoke. What is not clear is the nature of the agency that could have brought this situation about. Before the conquest, the Mercian and the Wessex standards had resulted from the cooperation of the church and secular powers. This was not the role in the fourteenth century of the church (see section 5.1), nor of a French-speaking court. Nor could it have been the role of creative writers using different regional dialects of English.

It was the economic activity of middle-class merchants and traders that led to the growth of towns, and eventually to the dominant position of London. The growth of towns led in turn to the development of town dialects, including London English. Economic activity organized on a national scale ensured that features of the spoken dialect of London eventually spread more or less to the whole of England. The wool trade alone, for example, established links between London and East Anglia, the Yorkshire dales, Cumbria, the Cotswolds and the South Downs. The influence of the meat trade extended beyond the borders of England, into Wales and Galloway. Such everyday contacts provided the infrastructure which made possible the spread of prestigious forms and the eventual acceptance of national norms.

The dialects of the hilly areas of the north and west, away from the centre of economic activity, became the subject of jokes and adverse comment. Trevisa, in his translation of Higden, ridicules 'oplondysch men' who 'wol lykne hamsylf to gentil men and fondeþ wiþ gret bysynes for to speke Freynsch, for to be more ytold of',[3] and goes on to attack the speech of York (see section 4.5). Nevertheless he is quite aware of the importance of economic factors, since in the south there is 'betre cornlond, more people, more noble cytes, and more profytable hauenes'.

The most likely explanation for the emerging written standard is that it began as the commercial language of London, and spread along existing lines of communication. This commercial language would be the obvious one to use when English began to be used for official purposes from the 1360s on. It was also the obvious variety for a London civil servant like Geoffrey Chaucer. In the north west, however, the author of *Sir Gawayne and the Grene Knight* and *The pearl* was still using local dialect in the third quarter of the century.

For prestige, national coverage and sheer volume, nothing could compete with the royal bureaucracy, which by the 1420s was routinely using English. Fisher (1977) makes a very powerful case for the influence of the Chancery, which until the end of the fifteenth century 'comprised virtually all of the national bureaucracy of England except for the closely allied Exchequer'. Until the fourteenth century it followed the king on his royal progress, but from the time of Edward III it was located at Westminster, where it became a self-perpetuating bureaucracy of about 120 clerks. Richardson (1980) traces Chancery English to the usage of Henry V's Signet Office. Henry clearly used English as a propaganda weapon in his war against France, and began to use English in his correspondence four days after landing in France in August 1417. The variety established during his reign was continued after his death in 1422. It was in this same year that the London brewers adopted English, noting that 'the English tongue hath in modern days begun to be honourably enlarged and adorned'.

The relationship of Chancery English to Wycliffite English and the commercial dialect of London is not yet fully clarified. Nevertheless it was established by about 1440, and in regular use. Chancery clerks would be literate not only in English, but also in French and Latin. From the first, official English was in close contact with the traditional foreign written languages.

---

3. 'want to liken themselves to men of gentle birth, and strive with great effort to speak French, in order to be accounted more highly'.

4.4   *English under French influence*

The length and nature of the contact between English and French resulted in the large-scale borrowing into English of French words and expressions, and even grammar and other features of usage. There are two routes from French to English: through speech and through writing. Early borrowings are consistent with what one might expect from a relatively stable situation in which French is the language of the rulers, and English the language of the ruled. English speakers coming into contact with French-speaking superiors would need to learn some key French expressions. By the fourteenth century, French was the language of the national enemy, and as the upper classes adopted English they retained many of the linguistic habits of French. At about the same time, written English began to assume some of the functions formerly carried out in French, and English-speaking clerks would borrow features of written French into English.

Code switching

During the transition period, many people would know at least two languages. Bilinguals talking and writing to each other would be able to switch from one language to the other in the course of a conversation or written text. The following extracts are taken from a letter from Richard Kyngston, dean of Windsor, to Henry IV on 13 September 1403.

> Please a vostre tresgraciouse Seignourie entendre que a-jourduy apres noone . . . q'ils furent venuz deinz nostre countie pluis de cccc des les rebelz de Owyne, Glyn, Talgard, et pluseours autres rebelz des voz marches de Galys, et ount prisez et robbez deinz vostre countie de Hereford pluseours gentz, et bestaille a graunte nombre.[4]

The first thing to notice is just how many words used in the French have since been borrowed into English: *noon, countie, rebel, march, rob, number*. *Please* is used grammatically as a French word, but it actually has the English spelling. In the middle of his letter, Kyngston switches to English:

> Warfore, for goddesake, thinketh on ȝour beste frende, god, and thanke hym as he hath deserued to ȝowe! And leueth nought that ȝe ne come for no man that may counsaille ȝowe the contrarie; for, by the trouthe that I schal be to ȝowe ȝet, this day the Walshmen supposed and trusten, that ȝe schulle nought come there, and therefore, for goddesloue, make them fals men!

---

4. 'May it please your most gracious Lordship to understand that today after noon . . . that they had come into our county more than 400 of the rebels of Owen, Glyn, Talgard, and several other rebels from your marches of Wales, and have taken and robbed within your county of Hereford several people, and cattle in large number[s].'

Notice the number of French words which have been incorporated into the English text: *deserve, counsel, contrary, suppose, false.* Kyngston switches between languages in the middle of what we would now regard as a grammatical sentence:

> Jeo prie a la benoit trinite que vous ottroie bone vie ove tresentier sauntee a treslonge durre,[5] and sende зowe sone to ows in help and prosperitee.

> Escript a Hereford, en tresgraunte haste, a trois de la clocke apres noone.

The language of the ending is presumably French, but some words including *haste* and *noon* could equally well be English. If it is French, then *clocke* is the only English word to appear in the French text. Code switching of this kind survived in legal usage until the seventeenth century. Chambers (1932: p. lxxxii) quotes an example from 1631: *Il jecte un graund brickbat que narrowly mist.*

A very similar mixing of English and French is found in texts drafted by Chancery clerks. Here for comparison are the openings of two pleas (both quoted by Fisher, 1977). The first is in French and addressed to Henry IV in about 1406:

> Plese a nostre tresexcellent seigneur le Roy grantier a vostre humble servant Jehan Hethe, un des poevres clercs escrivantz en l'office de vostre prive seel . . .

The second is in English and addressed to Henry VI in 1438:

> Please it to the king oure souerain Lord of your benigne grace to graunte to youre humble servant and oratoure Sir William Wakysby, Tresorer with the Quene youre moder : . .

One can almost describe a text like this as written in French but using English words.

English vocabulary

Early French loans reflect the contact between rulers and ruled. The Peterborough *Chronicle* entry for 1137 contains the words *chancellor, prison and justice*, and the proclamation of Henry III (1258) has *sign* and *seal*. From the beginning English and French elements are mixed, the *Chronicle* entry has *sotlice* (French *sot* 'foolish' + English *lice* 'ly'), and the Proclamation has *crowning* (French *crown* + English *ing*). It was John Wallis (1653) who first observed that animals with English names (e.g. *ox, pig, sheep*) took on French names (cf. *beef, pork, mutton*) when served up as meat on the lord's table. Eventually words were borrowed from a wide range of different areas: government, law, hunting, sport, social relation-

---

5. 'I pray to the Blessed Trinity to grant you a good life with perfect health and of long duration.'

ships, etiquette, morals, fashion, cuisine, etc. Examples taken from the London guilds in 1380 (Chambers and Daunt, 1931) include *suggestion, mayor, sergeant, appear, recorder, accused* and *court*. The rate of borrowing peaked in the fourteenth century – i.e. at the time of the shift from French to English – and began to decline in the last quarter of the century (Dekeyser, 1986).

Apart from individual words, a number of collocations and expressions were borrowed from French. The following list of examples is taken more or less at random from Prins (1952): *par cause de* ('because of'); *avant la main* ('beforehand'); *condamner à mort* ('condemn to death'); *Comment le faites-vous?* ('How do you do?'); *faire quelqu'un un bon tour* ('to do someone a good turn'); *tomber malade/amoureux* ('to fall ill/in love'); *faire une requeste* ('to make a request'); *ennemi mortel* ('mortal enemy'); *l'ordre du jour* ('the order of the day'); *mettre à l'épée* ('to put to the sword'); *prendre vengeance* ('to take vengeance'); *le cri et le hu* ('the hue and cry'); *s'il vous plaît* ('if you please'); *prêter l'oreille* ('to lend an ear'); *prendre quelqu'un au mot* ('to take someone at their word'); *prendre quelque chose en bonne part* ('to take something in good part'); *prendre quelque chose en considération/à coeur* ('to take something into consideration/to heart'); *sans faille* ('without fail'). Even as prototypically English an expression as Shakespeare's *lend me your ears* has its origins in French.

English grammar

The borrowing of French words and expressions had a deep impact on English grammar, many parts of which were refashioned on the French model. The use of *who*, for example, was remodelled on French *qui*. Old English used *hwa* ('who') to ask a question such as *who did it?*, and this corresponds to one use of *qui*. But French also used *qui* in a relative clause such as *the man* who *lives next door*, for which Old English used the completely different word *þe*. Under French influence, Middle English began to use *who* as a relative pronoun (Mustanoja, 1960: 187–206). Old English, like modern German, used the verb *weorþan* ('become') to form passive expressions such as *the king was killed*, but this became rare after the eleventh century (Mustanoja, 1960: 438–9). Modern English, like modern French, uses the verb *to be*.

Perhaps the change which is of the greatest historical interest concerns the second person pronouns. Originally English made a distinction between *thou*, used to address one person, and the plural *ye* for more than one person. These were subject forms, e.g. *thou art my friend, ye are my friends,* and contrasted with *thee* and *you* used for the object or after a preposition, cf. *I saw thee/you; I gave it to thee/you.* Two types of change take place in this system. First, the ambiguity of French *vous* is recreated in English, and *you* takes over the functions of *ye,* so that it becomes grammatical to say *you are my friends*. This is perfectly normal in Modern English, but originally must have been as strange as **him is my friend.*[6] We also sometimes find *I gave it to ye*, and this is still common in some varieties of English.

The other change is that *you* takes over the functions of *thou*, so that the distinction between singular and plural is lost. This is usually analysed in terms of power and solidarity (Brown and Gilman, 1960); *thou* is used to intimates and people of lower social status, and *you* to people who are in a more distant or a superior relationship. This is the kind of pattern found at the beginning of the fifteenth century. In the letter to Henry IV above, the king is addressed as *vous* in French, and this is paralleled exactly by the use of the plural *ye* in English. In 1417, Margery Kempe was examined for heresy by the archbishop of York (Sutherland, 1953), and while she used *ye* to him, he used *thou* to her:

York: I her seyn thu art a ryth wikked woman.
Kempe: Ser, so I her seyn that ye arn a wikked man.

The *you* forms were used symmetrically between social equals at this time.

If the predominant message conveyed by the use of the singular form is not 'we are intimates' but 'I am superior', it can easily become a marked form, especially when it is routinely used by an Anglo-French aristocracy when addressing English subordinates. At any rate, the use of *thou* among intimates declined sharply. In a study of 89 conversations containing a total of 377 pronoun forms in Durham court records, Hope (1993) found that, already by the 1570s, *you* had become the normal form of address. In view of the social relationships between men and women, we might expect men to use *thou* to their wives and receive *you* in return; but this is not confirmed. Nor do siblings use *thou* to each other. Members of the lower classes also use *you* by default. *Thou* was by this time used not for intimacy but to insult, particular a person in an inferior position, as in the following examples from Hope:

Roger Donn: For although ye be a gent., and I a poore man, my honestye
                 shalbe as good as yours.
Mr Ratcliff: What saith thou? liknes thou thy honestye to myn?
James Warton: thou drouken horemonger preist
Richard Mylner: I preye yow to leave such talk. . . .
                 (later) I will come to the perchance when thou art in
                 better mynd.

The highly marked nature of *thou* must be borne in mind when interpreting its use by political and religious radicals (see section 7.5).

---

6. Unattested or impossible examples are conventionally marked with an asterisk.

Pronunciation

In view of the transfer of French vocabulary, expressions and grammar into English, one might also expect a significant influence on pronunciation. However, English texts were written by clerks familiar with English and not by aristocratic learners of English. French influence leaves no traces until it affects not only the way native speakers pronounce their words but also the way they spell them. There have been many changes in English pronunciation which have been traced back to the late medieval period (Wyld, 1920) and which could well have begun as features of a prestigious foreign accent: loss of the [r] sound after a vowel, changing [θ] to [f], and simplifying consonant clusters, such as [wr, kn, hw] as in *wrong, knee, what*. While a French origin for these is possible, it cannot be proved. In any case, some of the most profound changes in English pronunciation which also began in the late medieval period – including the so-called 'great vowel shift' – have remarkable parallels in Dutch and German, and cannot be ascribed to French influence.

There are parallels between medieval French and medieval English pronunciation which are unlikely to be due entirely to chance. For example, French confused the sounds represented by <er> and <ar>, so that Latin *perfectum* has become *parfait* ('perfect'), and *sacramentum* is now *serment* ('oath'). In English the word *person* appears also in the form *parson*, and *varmint* and *varsity* appear alongside *vermin* and *university*. We also have words such as *clerk* and *Derby* which are spelt <er> but pronounced in some dialects as though they were spelt <ar>. Another example concerns the quality of vowels according to whether they are final in the syllable or followed by a consonant. A French pair such as the modern *céder* but *cède* has a parallel in an English pair such as *keep(en)* but *kept*. Even here, however, it is difficult to ascertain the exact relationship between the French and English patterns.

Some relatively rare English sounds became more common as a result of French loans. The vowel sound [juː] mostly derives from the English attempt at the French [y] vowel, as in *view* or *music*, but occurs also in the English word *new* (except in dialects where this has been changed to [nuː]). The consonant [dʒ] spelt <j> as in *jury* or <ge> as in *village* preserves the older French pronunciation, but it also occurs in the English *ridge* and *edge*. English had [v] in certain positions, as in *wolves*, but now it could also occur initially, as in *vine*. The diphthong [oi] is typically and possibly exclusively French, and the pronunciation of *joy* has not changed since it was borrowed. Finally, [ʒ] is found in later loans from French, such as *rouge*, but it is also found in the English pronunciation of Latin loan words such as *invasion*.

4.5   *Printing*

The nature and extent of Anglo-French contact explains why so many French forms were transferred into English. What it does not explain is why the influence proved permanent. It would have been quite possible, for example, for the rejection of French to be followed by a rejection of French forms in English. There are two important factors here. First, the introduction of printing in the 1470s ensured the permanence of the emerging official standard. Second, William Caxton's publishing enterprise was designed to appeal to an aristocratic market, and English aristocratic taste in the fifteenth century was heavily dependent on the duchy of Burgundy. War with the king of France did not necessarily involve war with the duke of Burgundy, and Burgundian fashion was an important influence in England. Since Caxton was successful, the language he adopted set the precedent for future publishing. Modern Standard English consequently derives from the French-influenced official London English of the late fifteenth century.

Incunabula[7]

William Caxton was a businessman who operated for a long time from Bruges, in modern Belgium. At that time the Low Countries were ruled by Burgundy, and Caxton's Burgundian contacts put him in a good position to exploit the aristocratic book market. When he transferred his printing press to England, he set it up in Westminster, which was not only close to the Chancery, but also the ideal place for him to contact his aristocratic customers. With the benefit of hindsight we know he was successful. But in the 1470s it must have been far from obvious that publishing in the vernacular was going to succeed at all. Publishing in Latin for an international readership might have looked more promising, but Caxton's competitors in this area failed (Blake, 1969: 211–12). Nor was the aristocratic market promising, for England was at the time embroiled in the internal dynastic struggles known as the Wars of the Roses. The fall of an aristocratic patron could have serious consequences for a businessman who was dependent on him to determine what was fashionable, and thus for the credibility of his literary publications.

Aristocratic taste determined what Caxton decided to publish. He published the works of Chaucer, Gower and Lydgate rather than Langland and the northern poets (Blake, 1969: 70–1). In 1485 he published Malory's *Le morte d'Arthur*. Some 28 of his 106 publications were translations from other languages (Blake, 1969: 150). However, taste determined not only

---

7. Works printed before 1500.

what to publish, but the kind of English used. Caxton praises English influenced by French and denigrates native English. In his preface to the second edition (1484) of *The Canterbury tales* (Blake, 1969: 161) he praises Chaucer, the 'laureate poete' who had 'enbelysshyd, ornated and made faire our Englisshe' which before was 'rude speche and incongrue'.

Since Caxton could not himself be an arbiter of taste in language, it was prudent to apologize in advance for any lapses he might inadvertently make. He included in some of his prefaces a humility formula (Blake, 1969: 17) of a kind that was to be frequently copied in the following century. In the preface to his translation of *Eneydos* (1490) he complains of the difficulties arising from 'dyuersite and chaunge of langage'. He claims that '[I] toke an old boke and redde therin / and certaynly the englysshe was so rude and brood that I coude not wele vnderstande it'. In the same preface he tells the now famous story of the northerner who asked a Kentish woman for 'eggys And the good wyf answerde. that she coude speke no frenshe'. Beneath the apparent humility, Caxton is making quite clear that he is aware of the difference between old-fashioned and fashionable, and between provincial and courtly usage. The translation was intended 'not for a rude and vplondyssh man' but for 'clerkys and very gentylmen that vnderstande gentylnes and scyence' and was dedicated to Arthur, prince of Wales. Caxton's argument is surely a gross and contentious exaggeration, but it makes good advertising copy.

Published standard written English

The printing press was originally intended to improve the production of manuscripts. By the fifteenth century the trade was no longer a church monopoly, and book merchants had developed more efficient methods of production in their writing houses or scriptoria. Before printing, actually writing the words on to the page was still the most labour-intensive part of the process, but now the time invested in preparing the type paid off in print runs of 200 or more copies.

The development of scriptoria meant that the form of the text was left less to the discretion of the scribe, and became a matter for managerial decision. After the introduction of printing, printing houses developed their own house styles, deciding how words should be spelt and texts punctuated (Blake, 1969: 172–5). The preparation of the text became the responsibility of the editor, and the published form of the text became independent of the spoken form used by the original author. In other words, the written language became free to develop its own forms and norms, independently of the spoken language.

It is difficult for a manual copyist to work with total accuracy, and so errors and modifications inevitably creep in, and texts appear in slightly different versions in different manuscripts. The print run, on the other hand, produces a large number of identical copies. Given the technology to control this variation, it makes sense for the first time to raise the question of the correct or canonical form of a text. In other words, the new technology raises the question of standardization.

The size of print runs makes a larger number of texts available. This has the effect of shifting some of the uses of literacy from the public domain to the private. When manuscripts are rare they will be read aloud in public. Texts are read at mealtimes to the monks in the refectory. A teacher reads and interprets a manuscript with students. When books are readily available, they can be read and studied privately by an individual. Hand-written texts are extremely expensive, and only rich institutions and individuals can afford them. Long print runs meant that book prices came down, and eventually ordinary people were able to buy books. The growth of popular literacy, and the reading and private study of books – especially the English Bible – were to have major political consequences (see section 7.2 under *Literacy and radicalism*).

By the time Caxton died in 1491, he had already established a number of precedents for publishing in English. Published English was already removed from the language of ordinary people. It was based on London English, but it was not simply regionally based, since it contained elements from a range of dialects. It showed the influence of the aristocracy and the Civil Service. Above all it was a written form already largely independent of the spoken language. It was not yet standardized in the modern sense, but the technology was in place that would make standardization feasible.

5

English and Latin

The conditions that led to the use of English in the place of French also led
at about the same time to the struggle between English and Latin. Latin in
the medieval period (see section 4.2 under *Latin and the vernaculars*) was
the language of a European culture which embraced religion and scholarship, and which was supported by the powers of church and state. Change
was eventually brought about by a successful challenge to the power of the
medieval church in England. As the culture began to be challenged, so
Latin was challenged with it. In order to understand how English came to
replace Latin in the sixteenth century, it is important to investigate the
earlier events and changes which brought about a new social context in
which English was perceived as the natural language of England.

5.1   *The Lollards*

One of the most remarkable linguistic developments of fourteenth-century
England was the association that was created between the use of English
and opposition to church and state. Opposition to the church is associated
with the Oxford theologian John Wyclif, who in 1356 attacked the church
in his Latin treatise *The last age of the church*. In the 1370s, he turned his
attention to more central matters of doctrine, emphasizing the authority of
the Bible instead of traditional church teachings, thus anticipating the
views of later Protestant reformers. Political opposition was a popular
reaction to government policy. In 1377, in view of the need for revenue
to fight the war with France, the government introduced the poll tax at a flat
rate of fourpence per head of the population, taking no account of the
ability to pay. When it was raised to a shilling (5p) in 1381, the peasants of
the southern counties rose in revolt, and captured London, where they
beheaded the archbishop of Canterbury. By the end of the century, the
religious and social issues had come together in the Lollard movement.

The defiant use of English can be traced to 1382, when John Aston was tried for heresy before the archbishop of Canterbury, and spoke in English in order to be heard by the public, ignoring the court's instruction to speak Latin (Trevelyan, 1899: 304). It was at about this time, towards the end of his life, that Wyclif grasped the full significance of the use of English (Hudson, 1985). The Bible was then available in French, but no English translation had been made since before the Norman conquest. Lollard translators produced an English version of the complete Bible towards the end of the century.

If scholars went to the effort of making this translation, then there must have been a large and potentially powerful group of people who were literate in English and who had the money to buy books and the education and leisure to read them. Among these were merchants (see section 4.3 under *Economic change*), some of whom were involved in the book trade. According to Hudson (1985: 188–9), Lollard texts already indicated meticulous editing practices which anticipated those of early printing houses (see section 4.5 under *Published standard written English*), and there may have been a centre for book production somewhere in the east midlands. Lollard English was one of the strands of the incipient written standard adopted by the national bureaucracy at the time of Henry V (see section 4.3 under *Chancery English*).

Literacy in English was also spreading among the lower orders of society, to the extent that already in 1391 the Commons had petitioned the king – in the event unsuccessfully – to make it illegal for serfs and villeins to learn to read (Lawson and Silver, 1973: 83–4). Businessmen and labourers would in general have had very different interests, just as they do now; but their interests were different from those of the church, and they both had an interest in the use of English.

Fear of the masses, and mass education, led to some remarkable developments at the beginning of the fifteenth century. A debate took place in Oxford in 1401 (Hudson, 1985: 67–84) to discuss the suitability of English as a language for Bible translation. The orthodox scholar Richard Ullerston defended English against the charge that it was a barbarous language with no grammatical structure, and that it lacked a vocabulary suitable for Scripture. The view that prevailed, however, was that English was not a suitable language for Bible translation. Since English had in reality been used for Bible translation for several centuries (see section 2.3 under *The beginnings of written English*), this was clearly not a linguistic judgement, but a political one. The year 1401 was also the one in which parliament passed the Act for the burning of heretics, *de hæretico comburendo*, which linked popular literacy to sedition: heretics were accused of making unlawful conventicles and confederations, setting up schools, writing books and wickedly instructing and informing the people (Aston, 1977: 352).

In 1407, the use of English in any area within the church's domain was prohibited by the ecclesiastical legislation of Thomas Arundel, archbishop of Canterbury. The key passage has been identified by Hudson (1985: 148) in the seventh constitution:

> statuimus igitur et ordinamus, ut nemo deinceps aliquem textum sacrae scrip-turae auctoritate sua in linguam Anglicanam, vel aliam transferat, per viam libri, libelli, aut tractatus, nec legatur aliquis hujusmodi liber, libellus, aut tractatus jam noviter tempore dicti Johannis Wycliff, sive citra, compositus, aut in pos-terum componendus, in parte vel in toto,.publice, vel occulte.[1]

The church's policy towards English proved to be an extremely effec-tive counter-measure, at least in the short term, to a popular threat to its power and authority. The issue was not so much what was being dis-cussed but who was doing the discussing, and it remained legal to discuss heresy or church abuses as long as it was in Latin. The problem for the church was that the English version of the Bible was made available to *þe trewe prechours of þe gospel*, the itinerant poor priests who disseminated Lollard ideas among simple and ordinary people. Despite the ban, under-ground reading parties continued to be discovered by the authorities (Aston, 1977: 353).

Since the church effectively controlled scholarly knowledge, any scho-larly writing in English could be deemed close to heresy. The Lollard tract *Tractatus de regibus* begins 'Sythen . . . trouthe schuld be openly known to alle manere of folke, trowthe moueth mony men to speke sentencis in Yngelysche that thai han gedired in Latyne, and herfore bene men holden heretikis' (quoted by Hudson, 1985: 141). The most surprising works came under suspicion of heresy. *The Canterbury tales* were cited in the 1460s, and by the 1520s even English versions of the Paternoster and the ten commandments were considered dangerous (Aston, 1977: 370). John Colet was suspended in 1513 for translating the Paternoster into English.

Even with a good text, translators have the problem of conveying the exact meaning of the original. Lollards writing in English had to tackle the same problem of expressing in English the kind of ideas which had for-merly been expressed in Latin, and to do this, they used native English words, but also borrowed from French and Latin. In order to attack the Lollards, the bishop of Chichester, Reginald Pecock, in his *The repressor of over much blaming of the clergy* of about 1455, found it necessary to write not in Latin but 'in the comoun peplis langage'. He faced exactly the same linguistic problems as his opponents, and he invented from native materials or borrowed familiar terms from French and Latin. Among the 'English' words he invented are *unstondabilnes* ('instability'), *agenseie*

---

1. 'We therefore state and ordain that no-one shall henceforth translate any text of holy Scripture on his own authority into the English language or any other, by way of book, pamphlet or tract, and that any such book, pamphlet or tract either composed recently in or since the time of the said John Wyclif or to be composed in the future, shall not be read either in part or as a whole, in public or in private.'

('contradict') and *untobethoughtupon* ('inconceivable') (Gordon, 1966: 67–8). Pecock fell in 1457 in the incipient power struggle between Lancaster and York. He was himself charged with heresy, was forced to recant, and died in obscurity in about 1461 (Green, 1945).

5.2   *Classical scholarship*

The consequences of more widespread literacy were not restricted to religion. There was a more general demand for education, and for works of secular scholarship in English. Nevertheless there were powerful interests invested in the use of Latin, and it continued to be used as the language of conservative scholarship.

Medieval education

Typical medieval education was a kind of apprenticeship, whether for the law or the church, or for the skilled trades (Lawson and Silver, 1973: 72–5). The training provided by the church would begin with the first three liberal arts (the *trivium*) – namely, rhetoric, logic and grammar – and go on to the final four (the *quadrivium*), consisting of arithmetic, geometry, astronomy and music. Higher studies included Aristotelian philosophy, civil and canon law, medicine and theology.

In some cases, notably the church and the Inns of Court, the training had a wider appeal which was not restricted to intending entrants to the profession. Literacy skills, in particular, proved to be of wider social relevance, and by the fifteenth century grammar schools were being attended by boys who had no intention of becoming priests. Eventually secular bodies such as the guilds took an interest in education and in some cases took control. St Paul's School was reendowed by John Colet in 1510–12, and transferred from the dean and chapter of St Paul's to the London Company of Mercers. The first headmaster, William Lily, was a layman (McKnight, 1928: 92). In the long term, church training became what we now think of as general education.

The professions

By the early sixteenth century there was a growing body of secular knowledge – including knowledge of the New World – which people needed to know about but which was not catered for in traditional church scholarship. One might therefore have expected the new secular education to bring in a new curriculum. Now that English was established as a written language, a published language and an official language, one might have expected English to be adopted as the language of scholarship.

But the Latin curriculum remained, and grammars were produced to teach it. John Stanbridge's *Accidence* of 1496 contained a number of grammatical aphorisms which must already have been traditional and which remain familiar: for example, 'all maner thyng that a man may see fele. here. or vnderstonde that berith the name of a thyng is a nown'. Thomas Linacre produced a grammar in 1523. The curriculum also survived the Reformation, and by far the most influential work, generally known as 'Lily's grammar', was a compilation of the work of William Lily and John Colet which was published in 1549 and which was made compulsory in grammar schools. In one form or another it remained in use for 300 years. This was accompanied from 1595 by a Greek grammar written by William Camden.

Latin was used not only by the church and in education, but by the other professions. The use of English presented an obvious threat, for example, to doctors of medicine. In his *Castel of helth* of 1541, Sir Thomas Elyot defends writing 'phisike in englyshe' on the grounds that the Greeks and Romans wrote in their native languages. Note that Elyot defends something new not on account of its intrinsic merit but by citing precedents from the ancient past. Thomas Phaer, in his translation of Jehan Goeurot's *Regiment of lyfe* of 1544, is quite explicit in his aim to attack vested interests, and seeks 'to distrybute in Englysshe to them that are vnlearned part of the treasure that is in other languages, to prouoke them that are of better lernyng, to vtter theyr knowledge in such lyke attemptes: finallye to declare that to the vse of many, which ought not to be secrete for Lucre of a fewe' (Jones, 1953: 48–9). To the scholar who had spent years acquiring his scholarship in Latin, the use of English must have seemed an unfair shortcut.

The Greek controversy

The Lollard translators had expounded a sensitive and scholarly theory of translation, emphasizing the importance of having a reliable original text to work from (Hudson, 1986: 91). Higher standards of accuracy in written texts were achieved following the introduction of the new printing technology. In 1512–13, for example, Gavin Douglas criticized Caxton for the textual inaccuracy of his translation of the *Aeneid* (Blake, 1969: 195). Accuracy of text and attention to detail were part of the new standards of scholarship established by Erasmus during his time as professor of Greek at Cambridge from 1509 to 1524. Among his achievements was a Greek New Testament with a Latin version by 1516. Among his followers were the two Englishmen whose reputation extended beyond the Channel, namely Thomas

Linacre and Thomas More. In 1524 Linacre wrote his *De emendata struc-tura latini sermonis,*[2] dealing with style in writing Latin.

Erasmus' attention to the detail of Greek texts extended to the question of how they should be pronounced. According to the pronunciation con-ventionally used at the time, some different Greek vowel letters were pronounced alike. Erasmus inferred that they must formerly have been pronounced differently. He advocated what he regarded as the original pronunciation in his *Dialogus de recta latini graecique sermonis pronun-tiatione*[3] of 1528.

After the Reformation, Roman canon law was abolished as a university subject, and Greek was introduced as an exciting new subject (Lawson and Silver, 1973: 95). An important pioneer was Sir John Cheke (1514–57), who taught Greek at Cambridge and was appointed professor of Greek in 1540. Cheke's efforts to introduce the reformed pronunciation at Cam-bridge were opposed by Stephen Gardiner, the university chancellor, who issued a decree in 1542 forbidding its use. He argued 'none should philo-sophize at all in sounds, but all use the present'. Erasmus' views on pronunciation also encountered opposition in Paris, where they were denounced as 'grammatical heresy'. His writings were later put on the papal index of works which Catholics were forbidden to read.

It is difficult to believe that Gardiner was threatened by sounds and the study of pronunciation. What did present a threat, and a serious one, was the precise study of texts. This point had been understood by the Lollard translators. The Bible was at this time increasingly proclaimed by refor-mers as the ultimate authority, and, the more scholarly and accurate the written text, the more effectively it could be used to challenge the tradi-tional oral authority of the church.

Gardiner was extremely conservative not only in language but also in politics and religion. When, after 1553, Queen Mary sought to return the English church to Rome, Gardiner was her lord chancellor; and in this capacity he played a role in the burning of heretics, and one of his potential victims – had he not recanted – was Sir John Cheke.[4] After Gardiner's death in 1555, Cheke published the correspondence between himself and Gardiner under the title *Disputationes de pronuntiatione graecae linguae.*[5] What is important and perhaps surprising in this story is that the study of pronunciation could be regarded as a political issue.

---

2. 'Concerning the amended structure of Latin discourse'.
3. 'Dialogue concerning the correct pronunciation of Latin and Greek'.
4. The issues were not just about pronunciation. Cheke was a major government figure under Edward VI, and on Edward's death was involved in the plot to put Lady Jane Grey on the throne.
5. 'Disputations concerning the pronunciation of the Greek language'.

5.3 *Scholarly writing in English*

Well over a hundred years after the Oxford conference, there were numerous echoes in print of the rejection of English as a scriptural language. English, it was argued, was a barbarous language, unfit for Scripture or the great works of antiquity; to write in English is to cast pearls before swine. The power of this argument is demonstrated by the fact that even many of the scholars who wrote in English actually agreed that English was a rude, vile, barbarous language (Jones, 1953: 3–31).

By the sixteenth century, there was a growing demand for books in English. If English was an impoverished language, this obviously presented the scholarly writer with a problem. In order to write on topics normally discussed in Latin, the writer had to find words to express concepts which had no conventional English equivalents. The means adopted – borrowing from Latin and French, and inventing new English words – were the same as those used in the fifteenth century by the Lollards and their opponents. But now it was on a bigger scale, in both the number of words, and the range of texts.

Inkhorn terms

The new fashion for taking words wholesale from Latin and using them in English texts is usually associated with Sir Thomas Elyot, who borrowed words 'of the latin tonge for the insufficiencie of our owne langage'. In *The boke named the gouernour*, which appeared in 1531, he set out 'to augment our Englyshe tongue' by new words which were to be 'declared so playnely by one mene or other to a diligent reader that no sentence is therby made derke or harde to vnderstande'. Words brought into use would quickly become familiar like other words. Among the many words that Elyot introduced in this book are *abbreviate, acceleration, accommodate, aristocracy, barbarously, circumscription, democracy, education, encyclopedia, historian, inflection, modesty, society, temperature, tolerate* and *venereal*. These have all survived. *Comprobate* and *vendicate* survived into the seventeenth century, and *obtestation* into the nineteenth. Other words, including *operatrice, rigorosity* and *talliation,* were introduced by Elyot but never used again.

Elyot's views were echoed by Thomas Lupset in 1533 in his *A treatise of charitie*: 'whan we be driuen to speake of thynges that lacke the names in oure tonge, we be also driuen to borowe the wordes, that we haue not, sometyme out of latin, sometyme out of greke . . . And though now at fyrst heryng, this word stondethe straungelye with you, yet by vse it shall waxe familiar' (quoted by Jones, 1953: 75). Technical terms (or 'terms of art') were a special case, as John Dolman points out in his translation (1561) of

Cicero's *Those fyue questions*: 'I haue vsed none but the playne and accustomed termes' except in the case of 'such thinges as the Lodgicians terme names of arte, for the whych, we haue no proper Englyse words'.

Elyot's approach was a compromise between traditional Latin writing, and a kind of writing which sought to be wholly English. It was subject to criticism both from conservatives who thought scholars should not be writing in English at all, and from radicals who thought it was not English enough. Another view was that words could be found in the English of the past. According to Thomas Berthelette (1532, quoted by Jones, 1953: 116), dedicating his edition of Gower's *Confessio amantis* to Henry VIII, there were 'plenty of englysshe wordes and vulgars / . . . whiche old englysshe wordes and vulgars no wise man / bycause of theyr antiquite / wyll throwe asyde'. If a writer needs more words he can 'resorte to this worthy old wryter John Gower / that shall as a lanterne gyue hym lyghte to wryte counnyngly / and to garnysshe his sentences in our vulgar tonge'.

As a result, borrowing as a whole later came under attack, and the foreign borrowings were dubbed 'inkhorn' terms. Ascham in 1545, in his dedication to *Toxophilus*, took the view that 'He that wyll wryte well in any tongue, muste folowe thys councel of Aristotle, to speake as the common people do, to thinke as wise men do'. He objected to the fact that 'Many English writers haue not done so, but vsinge straunge wordes as latin, french, and Italian, do make all thinges darke and harde'. He may have been the first to call borrowed words 'inkhorne termes'. Sir Thomas Chaloner, in his translation of Erasmus' *In praise of folly* in 1549, attacks scholars who 'mingle their writings with words sought out of strange langages, as if it were alonely thyng for theim to poudre their bokes with ynkehorne termes, although perchaunce as unaptly applied as a gold rynge in a sowes nose'.

In the next decade, Sir John Cheke was equally sanguine about the sufficiency of native materials. He wrote to Sir Thomas Hoby on 16 July 1557, commenting on Sir Thomas's translation of Castiglione's *The courtier*: 'I am of the opinion that our own tung shold be written cleane and pure, vnmixt and vnmangled with borowing of other tunges . . . For then doth our tung naturallie and praisablie vtter her meaning, whan she bouroweth no counterfeitness of other tunges to attire her self withall, but vseth plainlie her own.' Cheke put his ideas into practice in his translation of St Matthew's gospel. Among the 'native' words he fashioned were *moond* ('lunatic'), *ground-wrought* ('founded'), *hunderder* ('centurion'), *tollers* ('publicans'), *biwordes* ('parables') and *crossed* ('crucified'). On the surface, the views of Cheke are directly opposed to those of Elyot. But Elyot was trying to get scholarly writing in English accepted, and by the 1550s that battle had long since been won.

The written sentence

In addition to individual words, scholars influenced the way in which words were grouped together to form sentences. In early printed texts, words were grouped according to the way they would be spoken aloud, perhaps by someone dictating to a scribe. Consider this example from Caxton's prologue to his translation of *Eneydos* of 1490:

> After dyverse werkes made / translated and achieued / hauyng noo werke in hande. I sittyng in my studye where as laye many dyuerse paunflettis and bookys. happened that to my hande cam a lytyl booke in frenshe. whiche late was translated oute of latyn by some noble clerke of fraunce whiche booke is named Eneydos / made in latyn by that noble poete & grete clerke vyrgyle / whiche booke I sawe ouer and redde therin. How after the generall destruccyon of the grete Troye. Eneas departed berynge his olde fader anchise vpon his sholdres / his lytyl son yolus on his honde.

If you read this text aloud, pausing at a full stop and at a forward slash ('/', known as a *virgule*), you will have little difficulty in understanding it. You will probably find yourself making additional pauses which are not marked in the written text. From the point of view of meaning, the groups of words marked off with virgules can be regarded as the parts of bigger groups marked off with full stops.

If you try to divide the text into sentences, you will find it impossible. That is because it is not written in sentences. Some scholars (see, for example, Blake, 1969) have concluded that Caxton was not a good writer. But texts constructed in this way are found from Old English times onwards, and are based on the word groupings of the spoken language. By the 1530s we find word groupings remodelled according to the Latin sentence, and from this time texts can be divided into familiar sentences. The Latin sentence, unlike Latin vocabulary, has never been socially contentious, and (leaving aside some twentieth-century writers such as James Joyce) has never been challenged. At most, there have been minor variations making the English sentence more or less close to the original Latin model. Linguists today take it for granted that texts are constructed in sentences.

5.4 *The English Bible*

Vernacular translations of the Bible had long been a matter of controversy. The Synod of Toulouse had in 1229 proscribed vernacular translations of the complete Bible. But in practice the prohibition had been relaxed, and by 1500 printed Bibles were available in Spanish, Italian, French, Dutch, German and Czech. In addition, the Latin Vulgate was available, and the

Hebrew text of the Old Testament was published in 1488. The ban still applied in England on account of the association of the English Bible with the Lollards.

It might superficially appear that the English translation simply reproduces the meaning of the Latin text in English words. In reality, the translator has to make an interpretation of the text in order to find an English equivalent. This point was well understood, and had been argued by Richard Ullerston at the Oxford conference in 1401. The traditional view was that the biblical text could be properly interpreted only by someone who was professionally trained, and this was an argument for retaining the Latin version. Someone reading the English translation was still given an interpretation, but by the translator rather than the priest. A further problem is that the reader could be misled by the meaning of everyday English words, and fail to grasp the exact meaning of the original.

Bible translations

Among the people influenced by Erasmus' work at Cambridge was William Tyndale, who moved from Oxford in about 1510 in order to study Greek. Whereas Erasmus seems to have sought to work within the established order, Tyndale's aims were more radical. With his English translation of the Bible 'he would cause a boy that driveth a plough to know more of the Scriptures than [the pope] did'. He dismissed the arguments against the use of English: 'Thei will saye it can not be translated into our tonge / it is so rude. It is not so rude as thei are false lyers' (*The obedience of a Christen man*, 1528).

From 1515, the lord chancellor of England was a churchman, Cardinal Wolsey, and Henry VIII had himself been given the title *Fidei Defensor* ('Defender of the Faith') by the pope for his attack on heresy. Bible translation was a dangerous activity in England, and Tyndale worked abroad. At Hamburg in 1524 he translated the gospels of Matthew and Mark; and he completed the New Testament at Cologne in 1525, where he was supported by English merchants. (The international nature of the book trade has already been noted above, see section 4.5). In 1529, Wolsey was succeeded as chancellor by Sir Thomas More, who was vehemently opposed to the work of Tyndale (Partridge, 1973: 43–6). Tyndale stayed abroad and in the early 1530s completed the first five books of the Old Testament, and added the Book of Jonah in 1534. He was eventually arrested in 1535 and burnt as a heretic in October 1536.

By this time the situation in England had already changed. Henry VIII had broken away from Rome following the pope's refusal to grant him a divorce. The pope excommunicated Henry, who then had himself declared supreme head of the Church of England by the Act of Supremacy in 1534. More fell in the controversy and was replaced by Thomas Cromwell, who was neither churchman nor scholar. English translations of the Bible, the work of Miles Coverdale, appeared legally in England for the first time in 1535. Tyndale's work, annotated by John Rogers, appeared in 1537 with royal assent under the name of the *Matthew Bible* (Partridge, 1973: 53, 70). By 1540 the Great Bible, a revised translation supervised by Coverdale and with a preface by Archbishop Cranmer, was required by statute to be available in every parish church (Partridge, 1973: 70).

Fear of popular literacy was reasserted in 1543 in an Act for the advancement of religion (Aston, 1977: 368–9). Reading of the English Bible was restricted according to rank. The nobility and gentry were allowed to read it to their households, but their womenfolk – like merchants – were allowed to read it only to themselves. It was once again banned for the lower sort, including common women, artificers, apprentices, journeymen, serving men, husbandmen and labourers.

Twenty years later, England had undergone the Protestant Reformation under Edward VI, the conservative reaction under Mary, and a return to Protestantism under Elizabeth. The Geneva Bible, which first appeared in 1560, was clearly Protestant in orientation, both in the translation and in the marginal notes (Partridge, 1973: 76–86). But already there were divisions in the Church of England between the radicals and those who retained many traditional beliefs. In 1567 Bishop John Jewel expressed the old view on translation: 'The Vnlearned people were keapte from the Readinge of Scriptures by the special prouidence of God, that pretious stoanes should not be throwen before Swine' (quoted by Jones, 1953: 63–4). The Geneva Bible was followed in 1568 by an Anglican version, the Bishops' Bible.

By this time the conservative refusal to countenance a vernacular translation at all had long ceased to have any force, and a Catholic translation of the text of the Vulgate, the Rheims Bible, appeared in 1582. This was based on the kind of precise scholarship and close study of the text which had caused such trouble earlier in the century. Some 'sacred wordes and speaches' were kept in their Latin or Greek forms, given 'how easily the voluntarie Translatour may misse the true sense of the Holy Ghost'. Anthony Marten in 1583 (Jones, 1953: 112) complained of the 'new inkpot termes', including *chalice*, *penance*, *euangelize* and *propiciate*. Finally, a revised Anglican version was completed in 1611 (see section 7.2 under *The King James Bible*).

Contested words

There are a number of key words in the Bible, the interpretation of which has consequences for the interpretation of the biblical message as a whole. The Greek word αγγελος, for example, meant 'messenger', which suggests an ordinary human being. If, instead of being translated as *messenger*, the Greek word is borrowed into English as *angel*, it suggests a supernatural being with wings. In the case of this word, there were no disagreements between radicals and conservatives because they all believed in angels, and so the use of *angel* was uncontroversial. Other key words involved the authority of the medieval church. Radical translators gave an ordinary everyday meaning to Greek words, while conservative translators incorporated traditional church beliefs.

Bishop Gardiner, at the time of the Greek pronunciation controversy, made a list of 99 words which he regarded as sacred, and which should therefore not be translated into English. It would be misleading, for example, to translate *sacramentalem panem* as 'sacramental bread' because Latin *panis* does not mean quite the same thing as English 'bread', and refers to food in general. As part of a general theory of translation, this is a subtle and well-made point, but in this and many similar cases it is a specious argument. It is unlikely that anybody has ever been confused about the meaning of *daily bread* in the English Paternoster. The real issue was the church's belief about the status of the bread used in the celebration of the mass.

The Greek word εκκλησια meant something like 'assembly of people'. The more radical translators were inconsistent, but tended to translate it as *congregation*; while conservatives preferred *church*, which gave apparent biblical support to the medieval church as an institution. For example, in 1 Corinthians 4: 17, the Authorized Version of 1611 has 'as I teach every where in every church', where Tyndale and most of his successors had *congregation*. The Rheims Bible of 1582 used *church*. Similarly, in Philemon 2, the Authorized Version following the Rheims Bible has 'the church in thy house', but Tyndale and Coverdale use *congregation*. Very significantly, Tyndale uses *congregation* in Matthew 16: 18: 'Apon this roocke I wyll bylde my congregacion.'

The word *church* was convenient for conservatives because it included several meanings: the church at Ephesus was a group of early Christians, the Catholic Church is an institution, while the church in the village is a building. The survival of the church as an institution was not an issue for the Lollard translators, and they consistently used *church*. This ambiguity was a problem for later radicals. Some early Protestants refused to use the word *church* for the building and called it a *steeple house* instead, a usage which was associated with Quakers until the eighteenth century.

The word *priest* derives from Greek πρεσβυτερος, which originally meant 'older man', and it was used for the elders of the Jewish Sanhedrin and the Apostolic church. The Vulgate usually translated it as *senior* but in some cases transliterated the Greek word as *presbyter*. Radical translators from the Lollards on regularly used the translation *elder*. The Rheims Bible used *priest* for *presbyter*, and otherwise *auncient* or *senior*. The use of *priest* of course brings with it the assumption that in order to become a presbyter one had first to be ordained by the medieval church.

The Greek word επισκοπος originally meant 'overseer' and is translated *bishop* by the Lollards. They did not object to bishops *per se* and indeed referred to Christ as their bishop: they objected to the wealth of the church and used *prelate* as a term of abuse (Hudson, 1985: 172–3). Protestant translators from Tyndale onwards, however, avoid *bishop* and use *overseer*: for example, in Acts 20: 28 the Authorized Version of 1611 has 'the flock over the which the Holy Ghost hath made you overseers'. The Rheims translators used *bishop*. The validity of the hierarchical structure of the medieval church is assumed by *bishop* and challenged by *overseer*.

In some cases a contentious translation involved secular issues. In translating St Paul's sermon in 1 Corinthians 13, Tyndale used *love* and Rheims translators used *charitie*, and in this they were followed in the Authorized Version. When poverty was regarded as a holy state, almsgiving was a noble act. With Protestantism came a harsher attitude towards poverty, which was later clearly articulated by William Perkins (Hill, 1968: 212–33), and charity was associated with indiscriminate and counter-productive almsgiving.

5.5   *The legacy of Latin*

The medieval belief in the superiority of Latin survived long after the language had ceased to have any practical use for the majority of learners. It was retained as the language of the universities, and it continued to be taught in the grammar schools, reinforced by a powerful vested interest. Its very uselessness was part of the attraction, and for a long time the knowledge of a dead language was considered a suitable qualification for a privileged position, second only to being born into a respectable family. New educational establishments more concerned with real-life problems were developed, such as Gresham College and the dissenting academies, and although these taught the modern knowledge that superseded ancient knowledge, they did not enjoy the same prestige. Latin was to continue as an essential part of the conservative educational curriculum in the universities and the grammar schools until the late twentieth century. Eventually women won the right to learn it.

Latin had been the language of power for over a thousand years, and as it gradually lost ground to English, many of the features and trappings of Latin were recreated in English. Inkhorn terms represented the beginnings of the process of creating Latinate English, the kind of English that was to become the new language of power in England. The attacks on inkhorn terms marked the beginning of another long tradition of opposition to Latin, often associated with 'Saxon' English, which can be traced to the present day. Cherished beliefs about Saxon English have continued to be the stuff of myth and propaganda, and they have made a deep impression on the way that linguists think about language, but they have never seriously challenged the underlying prestige of Latinate English.

The practice of wholesale borrowing from other languages, already familiar in medieval times, and developed by chancery clerks in the fifteenth century, continued despite the objections of the radicals. When people learned new concepts it made no difference in practice whether the labels for these concepts were Latin or English. As a result we now take for granted that we have on the one hand a basic vocabulary of everyday words, such as *mother, road* or *egg*, which everybody knows and which in the main are Germanic in origin, and on the other hand an extensive vocabulary of learned words, such as *contemporary, simultaneous* or *epistemic*, which typically come from Latin and Greek. Inkhorn terms became a permanent feature of the language, and even people who want to complain about them have to draw on a vocabulary of classical origin in order to do so. The problems faced by people without a Latin background were solved by the first dictionaries, which were written to help people who could read English but did not know Latin and Greek (see section 6.4 under *The first dictionaries*). Sir Thomas Elyot was proved right.

The decline of Latin as a practically useful language was accompanied by increased attention to the grammatical detail of the classical language, which in turn led to the concept of correct and incorrect language, and was later reflected in the belief in correct English grammar. The Greek pronunciation controversy led to a belief in correct spelling and pronunciation, and to the beginnings of English phonetics (see section 6.3 under *Spelling reform*). After the Restoration, the former roles of English and Latin were reproduced in the English of a privileged minority, now furnished with established traditions of linguistics and literature, and the vernacular English of ordinary people (see section 8.2).

The connection between Latinate English and power is illustrated by the production of gobbledegook, language which is incomprehensible to the intended recipient. Stephen Gardiner has had many disciples. Gobbledegook is used in the professions, not only by priests and theologians, but also by doctors and lawyers. In our modern society we do not employ priests to interpret biblical texts, but we do employ solicitors and accountants to interpret conveyancing law or income-tax regulations. Academic subjects have drawn on Latin (along with Greek) to develop their own kinds of gobbledegook, and invented classical technical terms until the development of computer technology by unLatined boffins. University students still spend a lot of time learning classical words. Producers of gobbledegook can always claim that their usage is for the sake of precision, while recipients are in no position to judge. It has been a formidable weapon in the hands of the Civil Service (see section 10.5 under *The King's English*).

6

The language of England

At the beginning of the sixteenth century, writers routinely apologized for writing in English. They felt that English was a rude, vile, barbarous language. At the end of the sixteenth century, writers expressed great pride in the English language. In later times writers and romantics were to look back on this period as the golden age of the English language. The Bible and Prayer Book, in particular, are still sometimes said to have captured the rhythms and cadences of a language far superior to our own and much more beautiful than the one we use today.

For William Tyndale, English was the language of the 'boy that driveth the plough'; 50 years later it was the language of Good Queen Bess. Elizabeth came to the throne on the death of her sister Mary in 1558. Under Elizabeth, the Church of England established a successful compromise between Catholicism and Protestantism, and England enjoyed relative peace when much of Europe was at war. Elizabeth's government survived rebellion and conspiracy at home, excommunication by the pope, and the threat of invasion from abroad. After the defeat of the northern rebellion in 1569, England began to celebrate 17 November, the anniversary of Elizabeth's accession. In the 1580s, Drake plundered Spanish shipping, sailed round the world and became a national hero. The failure of the Spanish Armada in 1588 is remembered as a great English naval victory. Overseas, England dominated Ireland and began to experiment with colonies in the New World. In the arts, this was the golden age of English music: Tallis was followed amongst others by Morley, Dowland and Byrd. The Immortal Bard was born at Stratford in 1564. John Aylmer, the Anglican bishop of London, discovered that God was an Englishman.

English was now the national language of England. Like the state itself, the national language was centred on the queen, her court and her capital. Antiquarians begin to provide the language with an illustrious past. At a time when Englishmen were beginning to out-do the men of the ancient world, who knew nothing of gunpowder, the compass, or of America, patriotic Englishmen were beginning to assert that English was the equal of the languages of Greece and Rome. English writers sought to improve upon the writers of the ancient world, and scholars applied their knowledge to English instead of Latin. In the view of Richard Mulcaster (1582: 75), English had reached a state of excellence 'of most and best account, and therefor fittest to be made a pattern for others to follow', comparable to Greek at the time of Demosthenes, and Latin at the time of Tullie. In the same work (1582: 254) he made his famous remark: '*I loue* Rome, *but* London *better*, *I favor* Italie, *but* England *more*, *I honor the* Latin, *but I worship the* English.'

6.1   *Saxon English*

When scholars began writing in English instead of Latin (see section 5.4), the dominant approach was perceived as a compromise by more radical scholars. This more radical group, which included Sir John Cheke and his associates, was more concerned with the development of native English materials. The concerns of this group developed into a new interest in non-classical antiquity and England's Saxon past.

Saxon and classical

The English interest in the Saxons is part of a wider continental interest in the Germanic peoples, which began with the work of the Flemish physician van Gorp (Jones, 1953: 215 ff.) from the middle of the century. According to van Gorp, Germanic was the original language of Paradise, spoken in the Garden of Eden. The Germanic peoples were not involved in the building of the tower of Babel, and so their language remained unconfused. This in his view made it superior to the confused classical languages, Hebrew, Greek and Latin. One of the virtues of Germanic is that it has a large stock of vowels and consonants, which means that they can be combined in different ways to form a large vocabulary of short, monosyllabic words. A large vocabulary has in turn the advantage that a wide range of meanings can be expressed without ambiguity. The development of van Gorp's ideas was to have important consequences on the continent, particularly in nineteenth-century Germany, in comparative philology and the reconstruction of the Germanic family of languages. The assumed superiority of Germanic over Hebrew was to have a dark side when linked to anti-Semitism, but our concern here is with more immediate consequences in England between the Reformation and the English revolution.

Note the importance of van Gorp's claim that Germanic words are unambiguous. The alleged problem with a language like Hebrew, which according to van Gorp had an impoverished vocabulary, was that words were used in many different senses. This meant that texts had to be subjected to a process of commentary and interpretation before they could be understood. The medieval church had long maintained that the biblical text had to be given a professional interpretation. That may be true if the text is written in Latin or Greek, but for the Protestant Englishman reading his Bible in unambiguous Saxon, that was clearly unnecessary.

The influence of van Gorp in England can be traced to the work of members of the Society of Antiquaries, which was founded in about 1580. Among the important members of the society were William Camden and Richard Verstegan (see section 7.1). The latter's original name was actually Rowlands, but he had adopted the German name of his maternal grandfather. He was also rather unusual in that he was a Roman Catholic who held radical views on English. In political terms, the interest in Saxon English was part of a wider political movement which was more radical than the Church of England (see section 5.3). During Elizabeth's reign the movement can be taken to be generally supportive of the authorities of church and state, but this was to change in the new political circumstances after her death.

Native materials

Interest in the use of native materials manifested itself in praise for the Saxon attributes of English, including monosyllables and the use of compounds, and also denigration of the use of foreign words, especially French words (Jones, 1953: 241ff.). Some writers extolled the virtues of northern English on the grounds that it was a conservative form of English, and therefore closer to the Saxon original.

One of the most obvious differences between content words (i.e. words such as nouns, adjectives and verbs) in English and Latin is that English has a large number of monosyllables. Latin words, by contrast, have endings which add at least one syllable to the root. Monosyllables were approved of by patriotic radicals, and opposed by conservatives. For example, George Gasgoigne advised the poet in 1575 to 'thrust as few wordes of many sillables into your verse as may be: and hereunto I might alledge many reasons: first that the most aunciant English wordes are of one sillable, so that the more monasyllables you use, the truer Englishman you shall seeme, and the lesse you shall smell of the Inkehorne' (Jones, 1953: 115).

Opinion was divided on whether monosyllables were an advantage or a disadvantage in verse. Gil (1621) argues in his preface that they are unsuitable for metre in that they clog up the verse movement. (Note, incidentally, the use of the verb *clog*: it is repeatedly used in the next 100 years with respect to monosyllables.) On the other hand, Chapman, in his translation of Homer, thought that they lent themselves to rhyme:

> Our Monosyllables, so kindly fall
> And meete, opposed in rime, as they did kisse.

Monosyllables were to prove controversial after 1660 (see sections 8.2–8.3).

The formation of compound words out of words which already existed in the language was one way of avoiding borrowing from other languages. Arthur Golding in *A woorke concerning the trewnesse of the Christian religion* (1587) used a number of compounds, including *tragediewryter*, *leachcraft*, *fleshstrings* ('muscles'), *bacemynded* and *grossewitted*. But by this time compounds were already linked to monosyllables. The link had been recognized by Ralph Lever in 1573: 'the moste parte of Englyshe wordes are shorte, and stande on one sillable a peece. So that two or three of them are ofte times fitly ioyned in one' (Jones, 1953: 126). Lever's title *The arte of reason, rightly termed, witcraft* illustrates the point. He uses *witcraft* ('logic' or 'reason'), *saywhat* ('definition') and *endsay* ('conclusion'). Although his preface is called the *forespeache*, he changes style in order to seek the patronage of the earl of Essex and writes an *epistle dedicatory*.

The antiquarian interest in older English found literary expression in the work of Edmund Spenser, who was probably influenced during his time at Merchant Taylors' School by the headmaster Richard Mulcaster. The writer of the preface to *The shepheardes calender* (1579), known by the initials E. K., commented: 'he hath laboured to restore, as to theyr rightfull heritage such good and naturall English words, as haue ben long time out of vse'. Spenser had taken old words from Chaucer, 'the Loadestarre of our Language', whose work is 'the well of English undefyled'. Among these words are *eke* ('also'), *quoth* ('said'), *whilom* ('formerly'), *ycleped* ('called'). The use of archaic words was to be copied by the young Milton, under whose influence they were to survive for a long time in so-called 'poetic diction'. Spenser's *The faerie queene* was dedicated to Queen Elizabeth in 1596. When he died three years later, Elizabeth honoured him by ordering a monument for his tomb in Westminster Abbey. She forgot to pay for it.

6.2   *The language arts*

The first three liberal arts in medieval education were grammar, rhetoric and logic, and dealt with language, albeit in a rather confused way. The art of rhetoric was originally concerned with the effective use of language, in particular the use of language to impress or persuade in courts of law. By the Renaissance period it was more or less fossilized into a set of rules for constructing and embellishing a text. Grammar was defined as the art of speaking well – *grammatica ars est bene loquendi* – but actually dealt with the forms of the written language. The study of language forms was itself sometimes confused with logic.

These subjects were confused partly because they were based on precedent and authority. To understand prevailing sixteenth-century views about English, one also has to start with contemporary perceptions of Latin. For example, given that Latin was the language of ancient texts, one can understand the assumption that language is manifest primarily in written texts, and that speech is consequently writing read aloud. These are not the conclusions that can be drawn from the observation of the language behaviour of ordinary people in the sixteenth century or at any other time.

As English began to take over the functions of Latin, scholars began to transfer the language arts to English. Since English literacy was based on Latin in the first place, this was generally a reasonable thing to do. The first of the arts to be transferred was rhetoric, and this gives us an insight into what was highly valued at the time. Among the most important rhetorics was Thomas Wilson's *The arte of rhetorique*, which appeared first in 1553 and again in 1567. Wilson defines what is required of an orator as 'to teach, to delight, And to perswade' (p. 2). Although oratory strictly involves speaking in public, Wilson is actually talking about written texts. He deals with the composition of a text (p. 6), which amounts to finding something to say, putting it together and delivering it effectively. The parts of an oration (p. 7) include the beginning or *Enterance*, in which 'the will of the standersby, or of the Iudge is sought for, and required to heere the matter', the middle, and the end, 'a clarkly gathering of the matter spoken before'.

Although the book is overtly concerned with the structuring of texts, Wilson stresses the importance of using native English materials: 'Among all the other lessons this should first be learned, that wee neuer affect any straunge ynkehorne termes, but to speake as is commonly receiued' (p. 162). He attacks the fashion for using words and phrases of French and Italian, which is 'counterfeiting the Kings English'. He even denies the need for foreign words for rhetorical purposes: 'I know them that thinke *Rhetorique* to stande wholie vpon darke wordes, and hee that can catche an ynke horne terme by the taile, him they coumpt to be a fine Englisheman, and a good *Rhetorician*' (p. 162). On the other hand, he has no objection to received words of whatever origin, including *letters patent, communion* and *prerogative* (p. 165).

George Puttenham (1589) in *The arte of English poesie* (Book 3 'Of ornament', chapter 4 'Of Language', pp. 120–1) linked rhetoric to the court. He recommends as a model 'the vsual speach of the Court, and that of London and the shires lying about London with(in) lx myles, and not much aboue', the English of 'gentlemen and others that speake but specially write as good Southerne as we of Middlesex or Surrey do, but not the common people of euery shire'. He specifically excludes 'terms of Northern-men, such as they vse in dayly talke', the speech of 'marches and frontiers, or in port townes, wher straungers haunt for traffike sake' or 'any vplandish village . . . where is no resort but of poore rusticall or vnciuall people', or 'speech of a craftes man or carter, or other of the inferiour sort . . . for such persons doe abuse good speaches by strange accents or ill shapen soundes, and false ortographie'. In view of the use of Latin terms, he excludes the usage of universities 'where Schollars vse much peeuish affectation of words out of the primitiue languages'. Puttenham has often been misinterpreted as though he were suggesting that everybody should use courtly language. His model is recommended for the writing of courtly poetry.

A characteristic of some of the rhetorical writing that was highly prized at the time is artifice. The aim, far from conveying meaning effectively, is to create a text that is regarded as aesthetically pleasing. John Lily, grandson of the grammarian William Lily, created a style that has come to be known as euphuism. Here is an extract from *Euphues: the anatomy of wit* (1579):

> Ah wretched wench Lucilla how art thou perplexed? what a doubtful fight dost thou feel betwixt faith and fancy? hope & fear? conscience and concupiscence? O my Euphues, little dost thou know the sudden sorrow that I sustain for thy sweet sake. Whose wit hath betwitched me, whose rare qualities have deprived me of mine old quality, whose courteous behaviour without curiosity, whose comely feature without fault, whose filed speech without fraud, hath wrapped me in this misfortune.

This is essentially an exercise in formal decoration, including alliteration (*feel . . . faith . . . fancy; sudden sorrow . . . sweet sake*), assonance (*wretched wench . . . perplexed*) and syntactic parallelism (*whose* [adjective] [noun] *without* [noun]). To understand what it means it helps to know that Lucilla had begun 'to fry in the flames of love' for Euphues and that she is talking to herself; but ultimately a text of this kind exists for its own sake, not to convey a practical meaning.

Rhetoric was associated not only with courtly language but also with the universities. Well into the seventeenth century, scholars would be trained to follow the rules of Latin rhetoric. Among the surviving papers of John Milton are some undergraduate assignments which he undertook at Cambridge. These are oratorical exercises, usually called *prolusions* according to the Latin name. Prolusion 1, *Utrum Dies an Nox præstantior sit?* ('Whether Day is more excellent than Night'), examines the question from two opposing points of view. The outstanding characteristic of this and similar exercises is the utter pointlessness of the content of the text. The exercises deal with the form of the text, but they are not clearly spoken orations or written texts. What mattered was what writers had done in the past, not the practical needs of contemporary orators and writers. In defence of Milton's tutor, however, it should be pointed out that in the event this exercise resulted in the composition of the two companion poems *L'allegro* and *Il penseroso*.

Manuals for teaching Latin were slightly modified to produce the first grammars of English. William Bullockar expressed the need in his *Pamphlet for grammar* in 1586. Paul Greaves's *Grammatica anglicana* appeared in 1594 but it was written in Latin and made English look like Latin. It contained a Latin–English glossary or *dictionariolum*, and – oddly enough, but in the spirit of the time (see section 6.1 under *Native materials*) – a list of Chaucerian words, in which, for example, *yore* is glossed as 'long agoe'. In the next century, the English grammatical tradition was to develop under the shadow of Lily, and the word *grammarian* became almost a term of abuse. There were great classical scholars such as Cheke and Mulcaster, who were also champions of English, who must have had a sufficient awareness of grammar to understand the problems of tackling the structure of a language so different from Latin and Greek. But these are not the people who determined the course of events.

6.3   *English spelling and pronunciation*

The medieval concept of spelling (see section 2.3 under *The beginnings of written English*) presupposed a kind of *phonetic spelling*, in which there is a close match between the way words are spelt and the way they are pronounced. Erasmus assumed phonetic spelling in his work on Greek pronunciation (see section 5.2 under *The Greek controversy*). English has never had phonetic spelling, and the relationship between letters and sounds has always been a complex one. By the sixteenth century, English spelling was already extremely archaic. Scholars who attempted to apply Erasmus' thinking to English consequently found their task a difficult one, and called for spelling reform.

Archaic spelling

Pronunciation has constantly changed, and changes in spelling have lagged behind, with the result that spelling has always represented the pronunciation of several generations or even centuries before. Pronunciation increasingly diverged from spelling in the medieval period, and many late medieval spellings were permanently fossilized following the introduction of printing. Modern spelling still largely represents medieval pronunciation, and the discrepancies between sounds and spellings were already marked in the sixteenth century.

Over the last 500 years or so the relationship between sound and spelling has been further obscured in all varieties of English by changes in the long vowels which have come to be known as the *Great Vowel Shift* (Knowles, 1987). The <i> of *time*, formerly pronounced as in *machine*, moved to its modern value [ai], and <ou> of *house*, formerly pronounced as in French *vous*, became [au]. The double vowel letters of *green* and *moon*, which formerly represented long [e] and [o] respectively, were now used for vowels similar to the old values of long <i> and <ou>. The spellings <ea, oa> of *meat* and *road* were used for long vowels intermediate in value between [e] and [a], and [o] and. [a] respectively; these now took up the former values of <ee> and <oo>. Later on, vowels spelt with <ea> in most cases merged with <ee> so that *meat* is now pronounced exactly like *meet*. The vowel of *make* and *day* also shifted, to take up the former value of <ea>. Even with a knowledge of phonetics and phonology it is difficult to keep track of these changes. Scholars of the sixteenth century who sought to understand English spelling had only their understanding of the Latin alphabet to guide them.

These vowel changes affected not only the pronunciation of English, but also the English pronunciation of Latin, and English Latin became markedly different from continental Latin. This led to the first of several reforms in the pronunciation of English Latin, and also to scholarly interest in English pronunciation.

Spelling reform

There was considerable interest in the second half of the century in the spelling and pronunciation of English. Erasmus' work on Greek pronunciation (see section 5.2 under *The professions*) stimulated interest in spelling in France, and in England Sir John Cheke extended his interest in Greek pronunciation to English. An account of his views is given by John Strype (1705), *The life of the learned Sir John Cheke*. He sought to make minor changes to bring spelling closer to pronunciation, e.g. *gud* ('good'), *britil* ('brittle'). He advocated the removal of silent letters, e.g. *faut* ('fault'), *dout* ('doubt'), including silent final -*e* in *giv* and *prais*. The letter <y> was to be replaced with <i> in *mi, sai* and by <ee> as a suffix in *necessitee* or *adversitee*; long vowels were to be represented by double letters, *maad* ('made'), *weer* ('where'), *liif* ('life'), *thoos* ('those'). An exception was that the long -u of *presume* was to be marked with a macron.

The first major work on spelling, however, was produced by Cheke's associate Sir Thomas Smith, whose *De recta and emendata linguæ anglicæ scriptione, dialogus*[1] appeared in 1568. Smith started with two assumptions, namely that spelling should be a 'picture' of speech – 'Est autem scriptura, imitatio sermonis, vt pictura corporis'[2] – and that each letter had associated with it a natural sound. It followed that in a written text there should be a one-to-one correspondence between the letters and the sounds of the language. He observed that English did not have enough letters for

---

1. 'Dialogue concerning the correct and amended writing of the English language'.
2. 'For writing is a representation of discourse as a painting is of the body.'

all the different sounds, and objected to the use of one letter for different sounds, which he considered an abuse of letters. He invented some special letters for sounds which could not be represented conventionally, and saw no use for <c> and <q>, which always overlapped with other letters. He also held the interesting view that English orthography had been satisfactory in Anglo-Saxon times, but that it had been confused after the Norman conquest (cf. section 7.1).

The kind of representation described by Smith is very familiar to linguists today, but it is regarded not as spelling but as phonemic transcription (see Knowles, 1987). First, he reverses the traditional view of speech as writing read aloud, and sees writing as speech written down. Whereas Erasmus saw the need to reform the pronunciation to match the spelling, Smith sees the need to modify the representation to match the pronunciation. Second, instead of treating words as part of the text, he examines them as isolated objects: the pronunciations he assumes are not the forms of words in context, but words as individual dictionary entries. For example, a word like *and* when it occurs in a text can be pronounced in many different ways – [ænd, ənd, ən, əm] etc. – but spelling reformers from Smith onwards have taken for granted that the spelling should represent the dictionary form, so that <and> counts as a phonetic spelling.

Similar ideas were expressed by John Hart, whose *An orthographie* appeared in 1569. He had already been interested in the topic for twenty years, and in 1551 he had written *The opening of the unreasonable writing of our Inglish tongue*, which remained in manuscript. Hart sought 'to vse as many letters in our writing, as we doe voyces or breathes in speaking, and no more; and neuer to abuse one for another, and to write as we speake: which we must needes doe if we will euer haue our writing perfite'. He consequently objected to capital letters, on the grounds that these constitute a second set of symbols related to sounds. Hart's approach assumes that there is only one pronunciation to be represented, and this was taken for granted as the pronunciation of the court, 'for that vnto these two places, do dayly resort from all townes and Countries, of the best of all professions, aswel as of the own landsmen, as of aliens and straungers, and therefore they haue the best meanes to take the best and leaue the worst' (Hart, 1570).

Hart still looked forward to a perfect language. Within a few years some scholars were beginning to assume that the language had already reached a peak. An early example is found in John Baret's three-language dictionary of 1573, entitled *An alvearie or triple dictionarie, in Englishe, Latin and French*. Baret repeats the ideas of Smith and Hart, and argues that orthography of the language needs to be diligently worked at, or else, if we 'suffer it to fall into decay, as not being able to kepe it now in reparation, we shal be all worthy of perpetuall shame'. Baret also hints at the need for a government agency to control the language. In this he was followed by William Bullockar (1580), who believed that, with a dictionary to preserve the reformed orthography and a grammar to stabilize the language, the vernacular could become 'a perfect ruled tongue'.

Mulcaster was also interested in spelling reform, but he strongly attacked the view that spelling should be based on sound alone, and insists on the role of reason and custom (1582: 67 ff.). He thought there were too many letters in *putt, grubb, ledd* and too few in *fech, scrach, herafter, singlie* (p. 105). (He wanted a <t> in *fetch* and *scratch*, and a third syllable in *singlelie*.) He also saw a problem in the case of homographs, i.e. words such as *use* (noun) and *use* (verb) which are pronounced differently but are spelt the same. However, he saw clearly the problem of variability in sound, and the difficulty of overcoming established custom and practice.

Mulcaster saw the need for a dictionary and argued that it would be praiseworthy to 'gather all the words which we vse in our English tung, whether naturall or incorporate, out of all professions, as well learned as not, into one dictionarie, and besides the right writing, which is incident to the Alphabete, wold open vnto vs therein, both their naturall force, and their proper vse' (1582: 166).

6.4   *The study of words*

Spelling reformers took the important step of abstracting words from their occurrence in texts and assessing them as objects of the language in their own right. If we examine a word as an object, we need to be able to refer to it: this is straightforward if we have a standard spelling, but problematical if the word can be spelt in different ways. We also need to be able to generalize about its meaning in different contexts. And at a time when the use of words is politically contentious, it is important to know something of a word's etymology, and if it is borrowed, to be able to say which language it comes from. Early works concentrate on such things as the origin of words, on their spelling and their meaning. All these factors are prerequisites to the development of English dictionaries.

Etymology

Etymology is for most people nowadays an arcane branch of knowledge to be found in etymological dictionaries. It was different for sixteenth-century scholars. English was not widely known outside England, and English scholars needed to know other languages, including Latin, as a matter of course.

There was already a tradition of linguistic scholarship in England, and there were books designed to teach foreign languages. French linguistic scholarship began in England in the fourteenth century (see section 4.1), and the tradition was continued. Pierre Valence's *Introductions in frensshe or Introdvctions en francois* appeared in 1528, probably printed by Wynkyn de Worde. This was followed by the anonymous *A very necessary boke* in 1550 and *A plaine pathway to the French tongue* in 1575 by de la Pichonnaye (1575), and by Bellot's *Englishe scholemaister* in 1580. Italian grammars appeared, reflecting the growing interest in Italian literature, including Thomas (1550) and Grantham (1575). The first Spanish grammar, Antonie del Corro's *The Spanish grammer*, appeared in 1590, two years after the Spanish Armada. A Welsh grammar by John Davies appeared in 1621.

In these circumstances the origin of words was all but self-evident to polyglot scholars. John Hart, in his *Method* of 1570, made a long list of words of French origin used in English: 'we doe vse Biscuyte, which signifieth twise baekt: and for Ouenheader, furner, deriued from *Four* an Ouen: *Barbier* of *Barbe*, we say Barber . . . : the like for *Rasoer*, a shaver, or euen maker'. Other French loans included:

> a garde, or warde, a keepe or defence: a Gardebras, or wardebras, an arme keeper: a Portier or gate wayter, or gater: a Porteur, a bearer, or burdener: a Pantier or Pantler, a Breadseruer: a Bottelier, a Bottleseruer: a Cordoanier, a Shoonmaker: a Marenier, a Seaman, or sayler: a Scribe, or Scriuener, a Plumber, of Plumb, for lead: a Tailour, a cutter, or shaper, as we say for a woman Shapester: a Marchaunt, a Monger, a Lauadier and Lauandiere, a washer, and many others.

Hart's work has two interesting features. First, instead of just objecting to curious words, he is able to characterize the words he is talking about quite specifically. Second, he is aware of the requirements of different styles, and different users. With respect to borrowing, he says:

> Howbeit, I must confesse it beautifieth an Orators tale, which knoweth what he speaketh, and to whom: but it hindreth the vnlearned from vnderstanding of the matter, and causeth many of the Countrie men to speake chalke for cheese, and so nickname such straunge termes as it pleaseth many well to heare them: as to say for temperate, temporall: for surrender, sullender: for stature, statute, for abiect, obiect: for heare, heier: certisfied, for both certified, and satisfied: dispence, for suspence: defende, for offende: surgiant, for surgian: which the French term *chirurgian*, which is flesh clenser.

The first dictionaries

The need for a dictionary was perceived by Mulcaster and others from the 1580s. Edmund Coote's *English schoole-maister* (1596) was concerned with reading and writing, and spelling and word division. It included a list of about 1500 'hard english words for vnskilfull persons' to help them read the Scriptures and sermons. A particularly interesting aspect of this work is that it is intended for a new kind of literate public, for 'people without Latin . . . and such men and women of trades (as Taylors, Weavers, Shop-keepers, Seamsters, and such other) as haue vndertaken the charge of teaching others'.

The book usually recognized as the first English dictionary was produced by Robert Cawdrey, schoolmaster at the 'Grammer schoole at Okeham in the County of Rutland':

> A Table Alphabeticall, conteyning and teaching the true writing, and vnderstanding of hard vsuall English wordes, borrowed from the Hebrew, Greeke, Latine, or French. &c. With the interpretation thereof by *plaine English words, gathered for the benefit and helpe of Ladies, Gentlewomen, or any other vnskilfull persons.* Whereby they may the more easilie and better vnderstand many harde English wordes, which they shall heare or read in Scriptures, Sermons, or elsewhere, and also be made able to vse the same aptly themselves . . . At London, . . . 1604.

This is clearly a response to the need for help with new words, particularly Latin words, which had come into English, and which literate people unfamiliar with Latin would not understand. Note that Cawdrey takes for granted that he has a female readership: literate women would not learn Latin at this time. The dictionary contained about 3000 words, and for each headword gives a brief account of the meaning:

> *Aggravate,* make more grievous, and more heavie.

> *Circumspect,* heedie, quick of sight, wise, and dooing matters advisedly.

> *Hecticke,* inflaming the heart and soundest part of the bodie.

> *Hipocrite,* such a one as in his outward apparell, countenance and behaviour, pretendeth to be another man, then he is indeede, or a deceiver.

> *Incorporate,* to graft one thing into the bodie of another, to make one bodie or substance.

> *Maladie,* disease.

Cawdrey was followed in 1616 by John Bullockar's *An English expositor: teaching the interpretation of the hardest words vsed in our language*, and by Henry Cockeram (1623) whose *The English dictionarie* contained 'some thousands of words'. Cockeram is interesting because he addresses a new readership, and his dictionary is subtitled:

> or, an interpreter of hard English words. Enabling as well Ladies and Gentlewomen, young Schollers, Clarkes, Merchants, as also Strangers of every Nation, to the vnderstanding of the more difficult Authors already printed in our Language.

Whatever scholars might have said about Saxon English, the evidence from early dictionaries shows that Sir Thomas Elyot's view (see section 5.4 under *Bible translations*) was proved right in practice.

6.5 *Elizabethan English*

So the English language arrived at its golden age in the reign of Elizabeth. But whose language was it? It was the language of bishops and courtiers, and the traditional nobility, and the language described and codified in scholarly books. In order to assess Elizabethan English it is essential to realize that we are dealing not just with claimed linguistic facts but with highly successful propaganda. The English language was used to glorify the English national state and the queen as its embodiment. The language historian who looks for some substance behind the myth faces a problem, for it is difficult to point to any permanent feature of the language that was demonstrably brought about by the cult of English nationalism at the court of Good Queen Bess.

The standard language has retained the prestige given to it in Elizabeth's time. It is still true today that by default the term *the English language* refers to the official written language, and if we wish to refer to spoken language or the language of ordinary people we have to make this explicit, as though such kinds of English were in some way deviant or abnormal. The dominant position of London in determining the direction of change in the language increased and continued until the middle of the twentieth century. The social status of the kind of people believed to be in possession of the best English gradually changed: now it was courtiers, but after 1688 it was to be supporters of the monarchy and the state church (see section 8.5). The Church of England was to have a role in perpetuating conservative views of language.

English words are still combined to form compounds, and Germanic monosyllables are still among the commonest words in English texts. But compounding was not developed to the same extent as other Germanic languages, and the bulk of new words continued to be borrowed or formed on classical models. When words are listed in dictionaries (ignoring their frequency in texts), classical words appear to dominate the English vocabulary, and give it a richness with which other languages cannot compete. The myth is Saxon, but the reality is Latin.

The ideas of Sir Thomas Smith have been repeated many times by would-be spelling reformers, but they have had no effect whatsoever, partly because they were already irrelevant and out of date when they were first put forward. A reform of the spelling to match the pronunciation of the court would have made little practical difference to someone reading to an audience in York or Bristol. Smith published in 1568, when spelling and pronunciation were no longer political issues. The fact that he published in Paris a book written in Latin suggests that he was writing essentially for the international scholarly readership and that his aim was of a theoretical and linguistic nature. If he had really wanted to influence spelling practice he would surely have written in English. Mulcaster wrote in English, and Mulcaster's view of spelling has prevailed. From this period the alphabets of many European languages were augmented with accents and other diacritics. Apart from the emergence of <j, v> as separate letters independent of <i, u>, the English alphabet has remained unchanged.

Scholarly influence on spelling has if anything taken it further from phonetic spelling, and led to the introduction of etymological letters and errors. *Debt* and *doubt* now contain a <b> to reflect their origin in Latin *debitum* and *dubitum*; these words come from French *dette* and *doute*, and the <b> has never been pronounced in English. *Island* has been given an <s> to bring it into line with *isle*, a word with which it has no historical connection; and similarly *delight* has been given <gh> to make it more like the totally unconnected word *light*.

The scholars who celebrated the greatness of the English language used at the court of Queen Elizabeth had nothing to say about the businessmen who were printing and selling their books, or about the practical needs of readers. In the long run, the practice of printers was to have a much greater effect on the way English texts were produced than the theoretical writings of scholars. What has always mattered to skilled readers, processing the text for meaning rather than form, is efficient word recognition. Fast reading requires rapid recognition of word shapes as a whole, and there is no time to map individual letters on to the sounds of speech. Publishers speeded up the process by the introduction of new fonts with more easily recognizable letter shapes. Exact letter–sound correspondences and indications of the origins of words are not actually very important. English spelling has continued to be heavily influenced by the gradually changing house styles of different publishers.

We cannot leave the myth of Elizabethan English without referring to the Bible and Shakespeare. The Church of England had a Bible and a Prayer Book in English, and English was used in church services. But the important translation of this period is the Geneva Bible, not the official Anglican one (see section 5.3), and the so-called Authorized Version belongs to the next reign (see section 7.2 under *The King James Bible*). Anglican propaganda, directed against Papists on the one hand and against Puritans on the other, has a distant echo in the quaint belief that Anglican texts of this period (particularly those written by Cranmer) were in some indefinable way especially beautiful.

If Shakespeare is by common consent acclaimed the greatest of English writers, this says something about English literature, and not the language of his time. If he used the language in a particularly brilliant way, the credit for that must go to Shakespeare and not to the language, and certainly not to the authorities of church and state. Later creative writers used the works of Shakespeare as an unattributed source, much as they used the classical writers of Greece and Rome, and radical writers used the Bible (see section 7.3). But this says something about how later writers thought that texts should be produced (see section 7.5), and has to be seen in the context of the new scientific writing against which it is a conservative reaction (see section 8.1). There is no linguistic reason to believe that the language had any special features to justify the romantic claim that it was at its peak at this time.

7

The language of revolution

When Queen Elizabeth died in 1603, the linguistic battles of the preceding century had long since been won. English had replaced Latin as the language of the Church of England, it was a successful literary language, and it was becoming increasingly established in other fields. The new king faced new problems, and these were to have linguistic consequences of a new kind. The political struggle was to become internal, between the established authorities of church and state and their opponents. Radicals challenged the traditional authority of the king and the nobility, and of the Church of England. By the middle of the century, the linguistic repercussions of the debate are to be traced in secular linguistic theories and opinions, in the use made of the English Bible, and in the way texts came to be written.

The Civil War that broke out in 1642 was followed by the republican government of the 1650s, and then the restored monarchy in 1660. After 1660, texts quite suddenly begin to look remarkably modern. In fact language historians sometimes identify the period from Caxton to the death of Shakespeare in 1616 as a separate period, *early Modern English*. Texts written in this earlier period have for the modern reader a certain strangeness and unfamiliarity about them. It is not so much in the words themselves – although these will have unfamiliar spellings and will be used in unfamiliar senses – nor is it in the grammar. It is in the way people express themselves, and how they take for granted that texts should be constructed. After 1660, words are still used in unfamiliar senses and still have unfamiliar spellings, but the texts as a whole are much more straightforward for the modern reader and easier to understand. It can be concluded that the revolutionary decades were an important period of linguistic transition.

7.1   *The Norman yoke*

The Society of Antiquaries (see section 6.1) developed the view that the English language had a purely Saxon origin. The Saxons had, according to

Camden (1605), made 'a full conquest, viz. the alteration of lawes, language and attire', which meant that their Saxon English remained unaffected by native Celtic. It was subsequently influenced but not fundamentally changed by the Danes and the Normans, who had tried and failed to destroy the English language. According to Camden, 'the Normans . . . as a monument of their Conquest, would have yoaked the English vnder their tongue, as they did vnder their command'. Richard Verstegan likewise argued (1605: 222) that the Normans 'could not conquer the English language as they did the land' (quoted by Hill, 1968: 79). The important point that these writers sought to establish was that the English language as a whole was independent of Norman French.

The significance of this is that early in James I's reign the relationship between Saxons and Normans became an issue in different interpretations of the king's right to rule. According to a contemporary interpretation of the Norman conquest (discussed at length by Hill, 1968: 58–125), the free Saxon people of England had been subjected to the 'Norman yoke' by the usurper William the Bastard, and had ever since remained in captivity. The ruling class – including the monarchy – could trace its ancestry to Norman conquerors. It was clearly not English at all, but French.

Camden was developing an alternative interpretation of English history to challenge the dominant political views of his day, some of which were based on the stories of King Arthur, the British hero who stood against the Saxons. The Tudor dynasty claimed Welsh descent from Arthur, and Henry VII called his first son Arthur.[1] James I claimed descent from King Arthur through the Scottish line as well as the Tudors (Hill, 1968: 68). The new interpretation of history was not one to appeal to the monarchy or the ruling class, and the Society of Antiquaries ceased to meet following the disapproval of James I. Nevertheless, interest in its ideas continued to develop. A lectureship in Anglo-Saxon was founded at Cambridge in about 1623 by Sir Henry Spelman, a former member of the society.

Although the arguments were superficially about the origin of the English language (Jones, 1953: 222–36), at a deeper level they concerned the validity of English law (Hill, 1968: 58–125). The assertion was that the Normans acted in total disregard of the law, treated with contempt the traditional laws of the free Anglo-Saxon people, and attempted to destroy the English language (cf. section 4.2 under *Latin and the vernaculars*). In the revolutionary years, the Norman yoke and Saxon English had an obvious appeal to radicals who wished to right the wrong, and echoes are heard in the writings of not only scholars such as John Hare (1647) and Meric Casaubon (1650) but also Levellers and Diggers. The Digger Gerrard Winstanley, for example, wrote to Fairfax and the Council of War in 1649: 'the common people of England, by joynt consent of person and purse, have caste out Charles, our Norman oppressour' (quoted by Tawney,

---

1. In the event Arthur died before he could succeed to the throne.

1926). Hare's book, the title of which, *St Edwards ghost*, looks back to the time of Edward the Confessor, also has the subtitle *or Anti-Normanisme*. His proposals make for the modern reader a rather odd list: for William to be deprived of his title of Conqueror, for King Charles to abandon his claim by conquest, for the nobility to repudiate their Norman names and titles, and for Norman laws to be abolished and the laws of Edward the Confessor to be restored and written in English. The final demand was to purify the language of French words.

The period of Hare's 'Anti-Normanisme' coincides with the growth of popular literacy on the one hand, and on the other with the new scientific outlook usually associated with Francis Bacon. These three movements are based on quite different ideologies, but what they share is a desire for plainness and simplicity in the use of the English language, a goal that was to be realized after the Restoration. The ideas of Camden and Verstegan were reinforced by nineteenth-century philologists and still survive as the received view of the origin of English (see section 1.5 under *Correct language*).

7.2   *The Bible and literacy*

Among the linguistically important events of the early decades of the century was the new translation of the Bible, increasing access to the biblical text, and the use of the text in political polemic.

The King James Bible

The new translation of the Bible was an outcome of the Hampton Court conference chaired by King James in 1604, close to the beginning of his reign. In the seventeenth century, a hierarchically ordered church could be seen as the counterpart of a hierarchically ordered society, and the conference had the political aim of supporting the hierarchy of the Church of England against the Presbyterians. This was the occasion of James's famous outburst 'No bishop, no king, no nobility!' The new translation was intended as a revision of the Bishops' Bible, and to counter the influence of the Geneva Bible (see section 5.4 under *Bible translations*). It left out the Geneva notes, which the king regarded as 'very partial, untrue, seditious and savouring too much of dangerous and traitorous conceits'. Contested translations (see section 5.4 under *Contested words*) were settled in favour of an Anglican interpretation. The word *bishop* crept back, and indeed it was used four times, although *overseers* remained in Acts 20: 28. A key verse is 1 Peter 2: 13, in which the king is referred to in the Geneva version as the 'superior' and the new translation uses the term 'supreme'.

The political stance was made quite clear in the dedication to King James, in which the adulation of the king is complemented by rude comments on 'Popish persons' on the one hand, and 'selfconceited Brethren' on the other.

The new translation, which came to be known as the 'Authorized' Version, was extremely successful, and became the dominant translation in regular use in Britain, at least until the appearance of the New English Bible in the 1960s. After 1616 the Geneva Bible remained in widespread use among the radicals, but it had to be imported illegally from the Netherlands, and it ceased to be printed after 1644 (Hill 1993: 58, 66). By this time its notes had already succeeded in providing ordinary people with the means of interpreting the Bible for themselves. These popular interpretations were to have an important impact on radical writing in the revolutionary decades.

Literacy and radicalism

Following the breakdown of censorship in the revolutionary period, the publication of books and pamphlets on a wide range of topics proliferated. Hill comments (1993: 198) that 'anyone could get into print who could persuade a printer that there was money in his or her idea'. In 1640, 22 pamphlets were published in England; in 1642 the figure was 1966 (Hill, 1980b: 49). In 1645, some 700 newspaper titles appeared (Stone, 1969: 99). The number of pamphlets and newspapers which appeared between 1640 and 1660 has been estimated at 22 000.

Publication on this scale presupposes the existence of a reading public who can make use of it. Literacy had by this time long since ceased to be the preserve of the church and the aristocracy, and we can take for granted widespread literacy among merchants of the growing capitalist class. Schoolbooks were beginning to cater for the practical needs of a much wider readership. One of the first English spelling books to appear was Francis Clement's *The petie schole*, which appeared in 1587. It was designed for children 'taught by men or women altogeather rude, and vtterly ignoraunt of the due composing and iust spelling of wordes'. John Evans's *Palace of profitable pleasure* of 1621 was dedicated to James I. It was designed to assist with Bible reading, and to assist those that 'were not brought up in the facultie of reading, themselues depriued of manuy vnspeakable comforts, proceeding from serious meditation in the law of God'. Literacy was reaching the lower orders of society, and when a pamphlet was read aloud in alehouses, its message reached many more who could not read for themselves.

In the absence of public libraries, or even of appropriate secular literature, the reading of many of the newly literate was largely confined to the Bible and what we would now class as religion. Already in 1604, Cawdrey's dictionary was intended to help ordinary people read sermons and the Bible (see section 6.3). Indeed, Bible reading would be a strong motivation for learning to read in the first place, since it enabled the reader to form opinions independently of the traditional authorities of church and state (Hill, 1993). This is why the Geneva Bible with its marginal notes was so important, and why the state needed a new official translation to counteract its influence.

Ordinary people reading the Bible would approach the text with their assumptions about contemporary events and problems: the treatment of the poor, the enclosure of common land, or even the divine right of kings. A superficial similarity would be sufficient for them to conclude that the Bible was actually referring to contemporary events. Some of the radicals, such as Arise Evans, would explicitly assume that the biblical text referred to revolutionary England, while others would use the Bible to illustrate their arguments (Hill, 1975: 93–4). This use of an exotic text to interpret everyday events is an aspect of popular literacy that survives in the way people interpret their horoscopes in newspapers and magazines. People who took for granted that the Bible was the word of God would also be able to draw from the text inferences about the actions God required them to take. Widespread discussion of the Bible by people who shared similar assumptions would lead to what is in modern terms a political programme. For example, the belief that the events of the Book of Revelation were due to take place in the 1650s gave a particular urgency to social reform. We would now distinguish Biblical scholarship from sociology, social administration and political theory: but these academic subjects belong to a later world.

The need to reach the new reading public affected the way texts were written. The kind of Latinate prose written by Milton might impress scholars, and even members of parliament, but its erudition would be lost on an alehouse audience. Public opinion was being formed by writers who did not conform to the old conventions, and who used a kind of language more generally understood. The more radical writers – Levellers and Diggers, Ranters and Quakers – used a new language to spread a social message. The biblical text provided a store of knowledge shared by writers and their readers, and effective writers made full use of it.

An important effect of the spread of popular literacy was that it became normal for ordinary people to hold independent opinions on a wide range of topics. In a previous generation they would have been burnt for religious heresy. Heresy was no longer regarded as a capital offence in England, and *de haeretico comburendo*, the 1401 Act for the burning of heretics, was eventually repealed in 1677, long after it has ceased to be effective anyway. However, there was a changing official attitude towards popular literacy itself, and it was regarded as a threat to the institutions of the state, and therefore something to be controlled. It is perhaps no coincidence that the return of censorship was soon accompanied by attempts to restrict the kind of English regarded as polite and acceptable (see section 8.2).

7.3 *Language, ideology and the Bible*

An important characteristic of the language of seventeenth-century radicals is the use of the Bible and religious concepts to convey a political and social message. In order to make sense of a radical text, one has to imagine oneself in their literacy culture, and play the role of someone whose political views derive from the Bible. Take, for example, this extract from Milton's *The tenure of kings and magistrates* of 1649:

> Surely it is not for nothing that tyrants, by a kind of natural instinct, both hate and fear none more than the true church and saints of God, as the most dangerous enemies and subverters of monarchy, though indeed of tyranny; hath not this been the perpetual cry of courtiers and court-prelates?

There are plenty of biblical references which can be used to give apparent justification to the belief that the authorities of church and state are fundamentally corrupt and ill-intentioned, and that monarchy is to be equated with tyranny. By a similar process 'the true church and the saints of God' can be equated with the radicals. In other words, the text is saying that the bishops and the court support the king against the radicals. True enough. But the point of the text is not to make a logical claim but to harness the feelings already channelled by the study of the Bible.

It must be emphasized that the interpretation is not there 'in the text', but depends on the assumptions the reader is willing to make. The reader who assumes that kings rule by divine right may simply dismiss a writer who accuses the king of tyranny. Some readers may not accept that biblical references are relevant to contemporary events. The modern reader may not see any connection at all between the passage and the Bible, and conclude that it is merely incoherent and bizarre.

At the crudest level, biblical language was used for invective. This was not a new invention, and belonged to a long-established tradition. In the 1390s, Walter Brute, writing in his own defence on a charge of heresy, denounced Rome as the 'daughter of Babylon', 'the great whore sitting upon many waters with whom the kings of the earth have committed fornication', and identified the pope with the Beast of the Book of Revelation (Trevelyan, 1899: 325). Tyndale took for granted that the pope was a usurper. Edward VI wrote in his notebook that the pope was the minister of Lucifer (Chapman, 1961: 171), and James I agreed with the radicals that the pope was the Antichrist. What was new was the manner in which biblical references could as a matter of course be incorporated into texts, and used effectively as political propaganda for a wide range of the population. Writers could be confident that their readers – and their hearers – would not only recognize the references, but draw the intended inferences from them. The biblical language in which their views were expressed can give the modern reader the impression that Puritans were obsessed with the

Old Testament and the Book of Revelation. But this is to impose modern conventions on to seventeenth-century texts. If we examine them through their own conventions, we obtain a much clearer view of the issues they were attempting to tackle.

Bible-based metaphor

Many people are familiar with the words of Handel's *Messiah*: *Every valley shall be exalted, and every mountain and hill made low . . . Thou shalt break [the kings of the earth] with a rod of iron; Thou shalt dash them to pieces like a potter's vessel.* Following royal precedent, we stand at the beginning of the Hallelujah chorus. The *Messiah* is an established part of the English Christmas. A radical of the 1640s would have seen a very different connection with the Establishment, for mountains and valleys were likened to the high and the low of English society, and Charles Stuart was a king of the earth. These metaphors could be taken to provide biblical justification for revolution and eventual regicide.

Biblical metaphors were used in just this way during the English revolution (Hill, 1993: 109 ff.). William Greenhill in a sermon to the House of Commons in 1643 used several references to the cutting-down of trees, and the cutting-off of kings by the root. In this case the metaphor is explicitly explained by the Geneva Bible, in which, according to a marginal note to Isaiah 2: 14, 'by high trees and mountains are meant them that are proud and lofty, and think themselves most strong in this world' (Hill, 1993). Gerrard Winstanley in a Digger pamphlet first uses and then explains the metaphor with a mixture of metaphors: 'a monarchical army lifts up mountains and makes valleys, viz. advances tyrants and treads the oppressed in the barren lanes of poverty' (Hill, 1993: 121). Thomas Goodwin when addressing the House of Commons in 1642 explained that 'A mountain is a similitude frequent in Scripture, to note out high and potent opposition lying in the way of God's proceedings' (Hill, 1993: 117).

These metaphors are different in kind from everyday metaphors such as *John is a fox* or literary metaphors such as *all the world's a stage*, because common-sense beliefs, assumptions and associations are insinuated along with the overt comparison. Winstanley not only equated monarchy and tyranny, but also took for granted that it was wrong to widen the gulf between rich and poor. Goodwin took for granted that the actions of the proud and lofty were contrary to the will of God. The reader who shares these assumptions may be led to the inference that the righteous have a duty to implement God's will, and bring down God's enemies, including the rulers of the English church and state.

Biblical precedent

There are other ways in addition to metaphor in which the language of radical writing was influenced by the Bible. There were many events and stories which could be taken as precedents to contemporary events, and used as a guide to action. There were several Old Testament kings – Pharoah, Nimrod, Ahab, Jereboam – whose wicked actions could be compared with those of Charles I. The names of places which in the Bible have negative connotations – Babylon, Egypt, Sodom – could be used to refer to places or institutions of which the writer disapproved. The contrasting term is Israel; England could be referred to as Israel or even as the Promised Land. People could be dubbed Lucifer or the Antichrist, or hailed as Moses. Oliver Cromwell was a second Moses who had brought his people out of Egypt (Hill, 1993: 113–14), but if he had taken the crown that would have effectively taken them back to Egypt.

Precedents, like metaphors, were interpreted according to a whole set of assumptions and a complex network of beliefs. An example of this is found in Numbers 35: 33: 'Blood defileth the land, and the land cannot be cleansed but by the death of him that caused it to be shed' (discussed by Hill, 1993: 324–31). Given the assumption that the biblical text refers to England in the 1640s, that England needed cleansing, and that Charles was responsible for the shedding of blood in the years of the Civil Wars, it followed that this verse was referring to Charles, and that the people of England were under a moral responsibility to put Charles to death. Such a responsibility is indicated quite clearly by George Cockayn in a fast sermon (a sermon given on a fast day) to the House of Commons on 29 November 1648:

> Honourable and worthy, if God do not lead you to do Justice upon those that have been the great Actors in shedding innocent Blood, never think to gain their love by sparing of them (Jeffs, 1970: vol. 32, p. 42).

The phrase *the man of blood* was used of King Charles by his opponents, and the scriptural verse was quoted at Charles's trial.

In view of the detailed and widespread knowledge of the Bible, metaphors and precedents need not be used self-consciously as such, but could be used in a routine fashion like ordinary words. When Matthew Newcomen addressed parliament in 1642 (Hill, 1993: 92), his message was no doubt clearer to his audience than to his modern readers when he complained that:

> the church of God hath had . . . sad experience of this . . . consequence of marrying with idolators and those that are enemies to the church [in the case of] Christian kings and princes . . . when they have matched . . . with such as professed the Christian religion, only not in purity.

The key word here is *idolators*, which refers in the first place to the second commandment, which at this time was given a very wide interpretation, and included Catholic rituals. The *church* is the assembly of true believers rather than the Church of England. Newcomen was indirectly and retrospectively alluding to the marriage of King Charles and the French Catholic Queen Henrietta Maria in 1625. Biblical images were also like ordinary words in that they could be freely combined, as in this extract from Cornelius Burges's fast sermon to parliament on 17 November 1640:

> *Babylon* began to besiege *Hierusalem*, and *Antichrist* began to pull of his vizzard . . . *Pictures* and *Images* began first to be set up in *churches*, for . . . *adoration* and worship (Jeffs, 1970: vol. 1, p. 38).

As the thinking of the extreme radicals such as Ranters and Diggers began to break out of the traditional Christian mould, the links between biblical references and their use became increasingly tenuous, as in this passage from Gerrard Winstanley:

> He that works for another, either for wages or to pay him rent, works unrighteously . . . but they that are resolved to work and eat together, making the earth a common treasury, doth join hands with Christ to lift up the nation from bondage, and restores all things from the curse (quoted by Hill, 1975: 129).

This smacks more of communism than of Christianity. The nation in bondage is not the chosen people in Egypt, but the English lower classes who exist only to be ruled. (After 1660 the word *nation* is often used to exclude the lower classes, and this usage probably goes unnoticed as it is so familiar.) The curse that followed the fall of Adam is not work or sin but private property. This Christ is a radical, not the respectable Christ of Presbyterians and Anglicans.

Similar examples can be found in scholarly writing. In his attack on the proposed Restoration (*The ready and easy way to establish a free commonwealth*, 1660), Milton condemns 'this noxious humour of returning to bondage, instilled of late by some deceivers'. The inferences are routine: the Chosen People of England are once again to be subjected, this time to the Pharoah Charles II. In *Samson Agonistes* (1671) Samson labours not under the Norman yoke but under the Philistine yoke:

> Promise was that I
> Should Israel from Philistian yoke deliver;
> Ask for this great Deliverer now, and find him
> Eyeless in Gaza at the mill with slaves,
> Himself in bonds under Philistian yoke (ll. 38–42).

After several decades of use, these metaphors and precedents must have become increasingly tired and hackneyed.

7.4 *The intellectual revolution*

Inseparable from the political revolution there was an intellectual revolution taking place. The traditional view of scholarship regarded it as an authoritative body of inherited knowledge. The sources of religious knowledge were the Bible and the writings of the Fathers of the church, and the sources of such secular knowledge as existed were the classical writings of Greece and Rome. In this tradition, scholars could do little more than preserve and expound received views and interpretations. As late as 1636, anatomy lecturers at Oxford had to expound Hippocrates and Galen and accept the authority of Aristotle (Hill, 1972: 54–5).

The authority of the ancients on a range of matters which we now regard as the province of science was challenged in the late sixteenth century by a number of writers whose ideas came together in the work of Francis Bacon. In the first book of axioms of *Novum organum* (1620), Bacon argues that there are two ways to knowledge, the conventional path by deduction, and the true path by induction from observation (Axiom XIX). Bacon separated natural science from theology, and later political science and economics emerged as autonomous fields of inquiry (Hill 1980b: 65). The full significance of Bacon's ideas, particularly the notion of empirical knowledge based on observation, was not fully appreciated until the revolutionary years of the 1640s. After the Restoration, Bacon's ideas were to have full expression in the work of the Royal Society (see section 8.1).

The importance of this for the history of the language is a negative one, in that the study of language remained authoritarian and relatively unaffected by scientific thinking. By this time, Latin had largely ceased to have any practical function, except for scholars writing for an international readership. Nevertheless, Lily's grammar of 1549 (see section 5.2 under *The professions*) maintained its dominant position, and a number of Latin manuals appeared at this time to accompany or supersede it, and in either case leave the priviledged position of Latin unchallenged. The Catholic Joseph Webbe attacked grammarians (1622: 6) and sought to develop new methods of teaching which almost anticipate the direct method and the communicative approach (1622: 10–27), but he appears not to have questioned the purpose of teaching Latin in the first place. His Puritan contemporary, John Brinsley, sought to use Latin for the teaching of English, which had the effect of transferring old attitudes from Latin to English. Brinsley's *The posing of the past* (1612b) was 'for the perpetual benefit of church and Common-wealth' and dedicated to Prince Charles.[2] Brinsley was followed by Hewes (1633), Danes (1637) and Farnaby (1641), this last being commissioned by Charles I. Edmundson's (1655) attempted alternative to Lily was, interestingly enough, designed to help students with

---

2. This did not protect Brinsley from being suspended from his teaching post in 1620.

their English vocabulary. Other books did the reverse, and used English as a guide to Latin, such as Hewes (1624) and Poole (1646). English grammars of the seventeenth century continued the tradition begun in the 1580s (see section 6.2) of confusing the grammar of English with the grammar of Latin. Latin was used as a guide to English, and English grammars continued to be written in Latin. Gil (1621) dealt with grammar, spelling and pronunciation. Ben Jonson's grammar, published posthumously in 1640, was based on the Latin grammar of Ramus[3] (1585), and like Shirley (1651) made English look like Latin.

Erasmus' work on Greek (see section 5.2 under *The Greek controversy*) had ironically created the belief that there was a correct pronunciation of texts. A consequence of the transfer of authoritarian attitudes to English was that grammarians began to assert that there was a correct form of English, including pronunciation. In 1640 Simon Daines's *Orthoepia anglicana* 'the Art of right speaking and pronouncing English' asserted what he claimed to be the correct pronunciation, but he gave no criteria for his judgements. John Wallis, whose *Grammatica linguæ anglicanæ* of 1653 is sometimes credited with being based on observation, referred (p. 73) to 'puram et genuinam linguae Anglicanae pronunciationem' as opposed to 'singulas vero locorum dialectos' (quoted by Lass, 1994: 83). Wallis's grammar also included an explanation (pp. 86, 88) of the word *thou*, a word which had largely disappeared from speech, but which was to survive for a long time in grammar books.

By 1660 the teaching of English had developed on the model of traditional Latin teaching, and the dominant approach to English, reinforced in schools, transferred authoritarian views about Latin to English, and treated English as though it were a dead language. This whole way of thinking drew on the authoritarian view of knowledge and was fundamentally incompatible with the new scientific approach. Despite some early attempts to study language scientifically (see section 8.1), language was effectively excluded from the domain of science.

7.5   *The linguistic outcome of the English revolution*

The influence of the revolution is to be found not in the forms of English – in such things as spellings[4] and pronunciation, grammar, or the meanings of words – but in the way the language was used. The construction of written texts at any period is governed partly by the need to convey the writer's

---

3. The Latin name of Pierre de la Ramée.
4. Since this was written, it has become clear from a study of texts from the Lampeter corpus that spelling was already close to standardization in the early 1640s, and even more so 20 years later.

meaning, and partly by general beliefs about the way in which texts should be produced. Sixteenth-century texts were influenced by Renaissance rhetoric, and beliefs about style and vocabulary. After the revolution, a more utilitarian approach was taken, and the meaning was conveyed in simpler language. At the same time we can trace the beginnings of a new intolerant approach to language, in particular other people's use of language.

As an example of a text written according to principles which are no longer used, consider the opening sentence of Milton's pamphlet on divorce (1644), which was addressed to parliament:

> If it were seriously asked, (and it would be no untimely question,) renowned parliament, select assembly! who of all teachers and masters, that have ever taught, hath drawn the most disciples after him, both in religion and in manners, it might not untruly be answered, custom.

This extract has some features which in modern times would be regarded as appropriate in speech but not in writing. For instance, Milton identifies his intended readers explicitly and addresses them directly from within the text. The text begins with a long preamble of the kind we might now expect in an after-dinner speech but not a formal written text. To discuss divorce in writing in this way now appears old-fashioned. Just a few years later, Lord Brouncker was writing on the recoil of guns (included in Sprat, 1667: 233 ff.). His preamble is limited to a brief reference to the society's command 'to make some Experiments of the Recoiling of Guns'. He then describes his experiments directly and clearly, and to clarify his argument further he includes tables of figures and mathematical proofs. There is no trace of the speaker here, and some parts of the essay are difficult to read out at all, as for example when he refers to points in a diagram on the previous page. This is a modern written text.

There were also differences in the way information was conveyed. The use of the Bible as an authoritative source of information, complemented by the similar use of ancient classical writings, belonged to an intellectual world in which there was a fixed body of knowledge held in common by scholars. The reader of this kind of text is required to refer to the same sources in order to make sense of it, and this in practice restricts the number of people who can gain access to it. Classical allusions convey nothing to the pamphleteer's alehouse audience or the unLatined modern reader. Biblical references were extremely effective in decades when people spent their time studying the Bible, but convey nothing to people who have never heard of Leviticus. Consider, for example, Milton's first comment on divorce in the monograph referred to above:

> [a] most injured statute of Moses: not repealed ever by him who only had the authority, but thrown aside with much inconsiderate neglect, under the rubbish of canonical ignorance; as once the whole law was by some such like conveyance in Josiah's time.

To understand this, you need to know that the laws of Moses included divorce, and that in Milton's time it was a matter of debate whether or not it had been superseded. 'Canonical ignorance' is an interestingly ambiguous reference to the Church of Rome or the Church of England. You also have to know who Josiah was. I assumed when I first read the passage that he was a wicked Old Testament king who kindled the wrath of God; actually he was a good king (Kings 22) who rent his clothes when he realized that the law had not been observed. But this was written by a mature scholar, and might be regarded as an extreme case. In fact, the modern reader is likely to have much the same difficulty with a poem such as 'On the morning of Christ's nativity', which Milton wrote at the age of 10.

Radical writers who used the Bible as their authority (and biblical sources as a new kind of rhetoric) used an ancient manner of expression for a modern way of thinking. By drawing their ideas by a process of deduction from biblical precedent they ironically accepted 'ancient' assumptions about the nature of knowledge. However, the manner in which they attempted to fit biblical texts to contemporary situations reveals deeper assumptions about such things as the distribution of wealth and the way society should be organized. Already William Perkins, who died in 1602, had argued that Scripture 'comprehendeth many holy sciences' (Hill, 1993: 20). Hill (1993: 228) suggests that the use of the Bible was a forced necessity in a society that regarded innovation as wrong. The experience of the 1640s and 1650s showed that biblical quotations could be used to support a wide range of conflicting points of view. This eventually had an outcome which in retrospect was totally predictable: if the Bible can prove anything, then paradoxically it can prove nothing. The result was that the use of the Bible as a source of knowledge declined sharply after about 1660 (Hill, 1993: chapter 19). From this same time, the Bible ceases to be the concern of the language historian.

In certain types of text, particularly literary texts, the authority of the ancients has actually been supplemented by the works of Shakespeare, and knowledge assumed to be held in common has continued to be used in creative writing, especially poetry. Writers today are still free to draw upon these sources without attribution, and display their learning by reference and allusion for the benefit of those who appreciate them. In order to interpret such texts, it remains the reader's task to trace the sources of information, and not the writer's task to make them explicit. For example, if a writer uses an expression such as *to be or not to be*, it is not seen as the writer's responsibility to make clear what the function of the expression is, and it is the reader who is expected to recognize it as a quotation from Shakepeare and to work out its relevance in the context. The same is true of some new text-types, including advertising and political propaganda. Of course readers who do not access information as intended by the writer may infer a different meaning. When we consider the meaning of texts of this kind, we therefore have to make a distinction between the writer's intention and the reader's interpretation.

There are still today certain restricted types of non-fictional text, such as popular and journalistic writing, and even dictionaries and grammar books, in which knowledge is treated as a common possession, so that ideas continue to be borrowed without attribution. But empirical knowledge is (at least superficially) discovered by individuals, and there are no biblical or classical precedents for it. This leads to the writing of texts in such a way that readers can in principle ascertain the truth of the text for themselves. A modern text is also likely to require specialized knowledge, but not of the classical kind.[5] In our modern culture, scholarship is generally regarded as a kind of intellectual property which belongs to individuals, and it is considered important to acknowledge the work of others, and make explicit the texts used as sources. Plagiarism, the unattributed use of somebody else's ideas, is tantamount to the theft of intellectual property. The term *plagiarism* originally referred to the kidnapping of a slave or child, and was first used in its modern sense in 1621. Much before that, it would probably have been a meaningless concept.

Finally, an archaic view of language of a rather different kind is illustrated by the following extract from George Fox (1660), *A battle-door for teachers and professors to learn singular and plural*:

> Do not they speak false English, false Latine, false Greek . . . that doth not speak *thou* to *one*, what ever he be, Father, Mother, King, or Judge, is he not . . . an Ideot, and a Fool, that speaks *You* to *one*, which is not to be spoken to a *singular*, but to *many*? O Vulgar Professors, and Teachers, that speaks Plural when they should Singular . . . Come you Priests and Professors, have you not learnt your Accidence (pp. 2–3).

On the surface, Fox is making a purely grammatical point. Leonard (1962: 10) takes his remarks in this passage at face value and cites him as an early prescriptive linguist. But we have to take into account the highly marked nature of Fox's usage. The use of the pronoun *thou* to address one person was already becoming archaic in normal conversation in the 1570s (see section 4.4 under *English grammar*). John Lewis was burnt at the stake in 1583 for heretical or subversive activities which included addressing everybody as *thou*. According to Thomas Fuller in 1655, 'Thou from superiors to inferiors is proper, as a sign of command; from equals to equals is passable, as a note of familiarity; but from inferiors to superiors, if proceeding from ignorance, hath a smack of clownishness; if from affectation, a tang of contempt' (Hill, 1975: 247).

It is significant that the people who according to Fox must be addressed as *thou* are all authority figures. Fox was a Quaker, and he was making a

---

5. To read a newspaper article on mad cow disease, for example, or on holes in the ozone layer, the reader needs detailed scientific information.

political point akin to that made in later revolutions by the use of *citizen* or *comrade*. He traces the use of the plural to the Roman emperors and blames the pope for what he regarded as the widespread misuse of the plural in European languages. Note that his argument is based on authority, not biblical authority but classical authority in the form of Latin grammar. He takes for granted that the rules of Latin also apply to English and other languages. He even addresses his opponents directly from within the text. In the early 1650s, the Quakers had been most successful in the north of England, where *thou* was still used more than in the south east: perhaps Fuller's 'clownishness' is an oblique reference to northerners. Shortly after this passage was written, the Quakers renounced the use of violence in pursuit of their political goals and became pacifists. Within a generation they retained only the familiar symbols of their revolutionary past: an old-fashioned style of dress, a refusal to doff the hat or swear oaths, and the continued use of *thou*.

The authoritarian views of the Latin master were never to be seriously challenged, and Fox was by no means alone in combining forward-looking social and political ideas with archaic and backward-looking views of language. When political parties emerged later in the century, they were to disagree on many things, but language was not one of them. This remains true: in the 1990s there is no reason to expect the Labour Party to be any more or any less enlightened on language matters than the Conservative Party.

8

The language of learned and polite persons

In 1660 the king was back, bishops were back, and so was the House of Lords. Censorship was already back. Latin and French were in use once again in courts of law. Over the next few years, parliament enacted the legislation now known as the Clarendon Code. Under the Corporation Act of 1661 support for the monarchy and the Church of England was a requirement for public office. The Act of Uniformity of 1662 required the clergy to assent to the new revised Prayer Book, and deprived those who refused of their livings; it also barred dissenters from Oxford and Cambridge, and – until the Toleration Act of 1689 – from teaching in schools. The legislation had the effect of distinguishing insider from outsider, the insiders being associated with the political and religious establishment. It is also from this time that we find insiders and outsiders in the use of the English language, and attempts by insiders to impose uniformity on the language.

8.1 *Language and science*

The situation after 1660 was far from a return to the status quo ante, and the old and the new were to co-exist in anomalous combinations. The new scientific outlook (see section 7.4), for example, resulted in the foundation of the Royal Society, which received its royal charter in 1662.

The science of language

In the new spirit of inquiry and observation, there were scholars who made astute observations about English. Richard Hodges, for example, observed spelling and pronunciation. In *The English primrose* (1644), he devised a method of annotating conventional spellings in order to convey pronunciation, and his method of placing numbers above vowel letters to indicate their pronuncation was continued until the development of modern phonetic alphabets. In *Most plain directions for true-writing* of 1653, he made a study of homophones. Most of these are individual words: for example, *I wrot the* lines *with my* loins *girded.* He indicates that the verbal ending spelt <eth> was actually pronounced [z], so that *courses, courseth* and *corpses* (with a silent <p>) were pronounced alike. He also gives homophonous phrases, cf. *Shee had* a sister, *which was an* assister, *who did greatly* assist her. This is interesting because since the eighteenth century the study of spoken language has rarely ventured beyond the single lexical item. In the spirit of the time, Hodges' avowed aim was not to study English phonetics, but to save time in reading the Scriptures.

Technical studies of speech are found from later in the decade, beginning with Jones's *Rationality of the art of speaking* (1659). Price's *The vocal organ* (1665) is designed to teach spelling and pronunciation 'by observing the instruments of Pronunciation' and includes a diagram of the organs of speech. William Holder's *Elements of speech* (1669) is a published version of a discourse presented to the Royal Society. It is an early account of phonetics, based on the 'natural production of letters', and contains an appendix on the deaf and dumb. This was followed in the next year by George Subscota's *The deaf and dumb man's discourse.*

There were other innovations in language study. Williams (1643) made the first attempt to study the native languages of America. Manwayring published a practical seaman's dictionary in 1644. Bishop Wilkins in 1668 described the creole origins of Bahasa Malaysia: 'the Malayan Tongue, the newest in the World . . . was invented . . . by a Concourse of Fishermen from Pegu, Siam, Bengala, and other nations at Malacca, where they . . . agreed upon a distinct Language made up of the easiest Words belonging to each Nation' (quoted by Leonard, 1962: 47). John Ray's *Collection of English words* (1691) contained 'two Alphabetical Catalogues, the one of such as are proper to the Northern, the other to the Southern Counties' and provided the entries with etymologies.

Interest developed in the possibility of a universal language (Salmon, 1979: 127–206). This was motivated partly by the practical need for an international language to replace Latin, and partly by frustration with natural languages that had caused so much religious and political division. Francis Lodowyck's *A common writing* of 1647 was followed in 1652 by *The ground-work of a new perfect language*; later in 1686 his 'Essay towards a universal alphabet' was published in the *Philosophical Transactions of the Royal Society.* Urquhart (1653) wrote an introduction to the universal language. But there is a change after the Restoration taking the study of language away from scientific inquiry. The new emphasis is on commerce and the beginnings of colonial expansion under the aegis of the monarchy. George Dalgarno's *Ars signorum* of 1661, another early attempt to design a universal language, included a recommendation from Charles II, which pointed out that it was 'of singula[r] use, for facilitating the matter of Communication and Intercourse between People of different Languages, and consequently a proper and effectual Means, for advancing all the parts of Real and Useful Knowledge, Civilizing barbarous Nations, Propagating the Gospel, and encreasing Traffique and Commerce'.

After the Restoration English manuals began to cater for the needs of business, and literacy ceases to be regarded as a privilege, and becomes the duty of the industrious student. Thomas Hunt's (1661) *Libellus orthographicus* was subtitled 'the diligent school boy's directory'. Thomas Lye's *The child's delight* of 1671, written in the earlier Old Testament style, contains a letter 'to the able and Industrious Instructors of youth in England'. Henry Preston's *Brief directions for true spelling* (1673) was designed for young people involved in trade. It included 'copies of letters, bills of parcels, bills of exchange, bills of debt, receipts'. Elisha Coles's *The compleat English schoolmaster* (1674) has the subtitle: 'or the Most Natural and Easie Method of Spelling English. ACCORDING to the present proper pronuntiation of the Language in OXFORD and LONDON'. Oxford was the ancient centre of medieval scholarship, and London was the newer mercantile centre. Coles claimed that his work was based on the principle that 'All words must be so spell'd, as they are afterwards to be pronounc'd'. He had obviously not read Smith or Mulcaster. Tobias Ellis, 'Minister of the gospel', produced a spelling book for children in 1680 with an engraving of Charles II in the frontispiece with the motto 'Fear God, and honour the King'. The vicar and schoolmaster Christopher Cooper produced his *Grammatica linguæ anglicanæ* in 1685, dealing with pronunciation, spelling and grammar for the benefit of foreigners and schoolchildren. Joseph Aicken's *The English grammar* of 1693 was intended for schools and designed to teach 'without the Assistance of Latin'.

In the generation following the Restoration such attempts as were made to apply scientific thinking to language had come to nothing. The dominant view, reinforced in schools, is in the old authoritarian tradition, and imposes on language the prevailing social and political views of the time.

The language of science

Renaissance rhetoric put a high value of the display of learning and virtuosity of form, and was well suited to texts composed for their own sake, whether as academic exercises, or for the delectation of courtiers. Rhetorical texts are works of art to be enjoyed at leisure, and can be appreciated by other scholars who share the conventions, and who can also admire the writer's wit and virtuosity. A text of this kind is a very different object from a text composed for purely utilitarian purposes, to inform or convince the reader. The rules of traditional rhetoric were at best irrelevant and at worst a hindrance for the radical preacher. John Wilkins (1646: 72) argued against rhetorical flourishes in preaching: 'Obscurity in the discourse is an argument of ignorance in the mind. The greatest learning is to be seen in the greatest plainnesse' (quoted by Jones, 1951: 78). Many preachers adopted a new Bible-based rhetoric, but by 1660 this was in turn outmoded. Ornamented styles of language had gone out of fashion.

Apart from fashion, scholars were facing a problem which was not fully recognized: they were having to develop new text-types for which the old styles were inappropriate. Hobbes, in 'Of Speech', chapter 4 of his *Leviathan* (1651), regards 'the use of Metaphors, Tropes, and other Rhetoricall figures' as 'causes of absurdity'. Hobbes's condemnation is general, but these things were not absurd in Shakespeare's plays. The point is that Shakespeare was not attempting to write political philosophy. After 1660, the scientific approach to language, which was influential in this respect alone, put a higher value on conveying meaning with precision.

The problems of scientific writing are discussed clearly and explicitly by Thomas Sprat in his *History of the Royal Society* (1667: 111–13). The Society had been 'most sollicitous' about 'the manner of their Discourse', and rejected 'specious Tropes and Figures', 'the easie vanitie of *fine speaking*', 'this vicious abundance of *Phrase*, this trick of *Metaphors*, this volubility of *Tongue*'. Sprat continues:

> They have therefore been most rigorous in putting in execution, the only Remedy, that can be found for this *extravagance*: and that has been, a constant Resolution, to reject all the amplifications, digressions, and swellings of style: to return back to the primitive purity, and shortness, when men deliver'd so many *things*, almost in an equal number of *words*. They have exacted from all their members, a close, naked, natural way of speaking; positive expressions; clear senses; a native easiness; bringing all things as near the Mathematical plainness, as they can: and preferring the language of Artizans, Countrymen, and Merchants, before that, of Wits, or Scholars.

This is the antithesis of the aristocratic style which was in favour at the court of Elizabeth. It also contrasted with the style of the revolutionary years. Sprat (1667: 42) argues that the English language generally improved until the Civil Wars when 'it receiv'd many fantastical terms, which were introduc'd by our *Religious Sects*; and many outlandish phrases'. He sees the possibility of solving the problem: 'set a mark on the ill Words; correct those, which are to be retain'd; admit, and establish the good; and make some emendations in the Accent, and Grammar'.

Sprat was making recommendations rather than describing general current practice, but he was successful in bringing about a new prose style, characterized by a lack of any fussiness of form. Although the need was specific, the effect was general, and for the next hundred years plainness of style was to be the outstanding feature not only of scientific writing but also of a wide range of text-types from published books to government decrees private papers. Even the private diary of the Lancaster ironmonger William Stout (Marshall, 1967) was composed with unadorned Quaker plainness.

This style has since been elevated to a myth. There is a long-standing belief that excellent prose was written in the century following the Restoration. The reign of Queen Anne is still sometimes called the Augustan Age, recalling the reign of Augustus (27 BC–AD 14), when the new men had been defeated in a power struggle, the aristocracy had reestablished its position, and writers had flourished. Dryden and Swift were on their own admission excellent writers, and this conviction underlies their attitudes to the English used by others. Prescriptive grammarians of the eighteenth century looked back on the work of Addison as a model of excellence (Wright, 1994). Samuel Johnson in *Lives of the poets* later suggested that 'Whoever wishes to attain an English style, familiar but not coarse, and elegant but not ostentatious, must give his days and nights to the volumes of Addison', although one should observe that this is not the style Johnson wished to attain for himself. Writing in 1966, I. A. Gordon argued that it is possible to read widely in the literature of this period 'without coming across a single page that deviates from the essentially colloquial norm of the time. It is difficult in this period to find *any* bad prose' (1966: 134). It is difficult to agree or disagree with such assertions, because they are not made with sufficient precision to be tested. The 'century of English prose' is also difficult to reconcile with the view frequently expressed during that century that everybody else was getting their language wrong.

8.2   *The improving language*

In a society that takes sanctions against people who do not conform in their religious and political views, it must seem reasonable to impose linguistic conformity too. One way of doing this is to set up an official body to oversee the language. Such ideas had already appeared in the 1570s (see section 6.2) but that had been in the very different climate of Elizabeth's reign, and they had come to nothing. Edmund Bolton proposed the establishment of a Royal Academy in 1617, to be devoted in part to literature, but nothing came of that either. Meanwhile on the continent, the Italians had established the Accademia della Crusca in 1582, and in 1612 the Accademia had published an Italian dictionary. It was followed in 1635 by Richelieu's Académie Française, which produced the *Grammaire de Port-Royal* in 1660, and a French dictionary in 1694. The aim of the Académie was to provide norms for the French language, and to secure supremacy for the French language. Faret argued: 'Notre langue . . . pourroit bien enfin succeder a la latine . . . si l'on prenoit plus de soin'. In the course of the seventeenth century a number of language societies grew up in Germany (Stoll, 1973), taking much the same attitude towards German as the Society of Antiquaries had towards English (see section 7.1).

A body which could have developed into an academy was the Royal

Society's committee for improving the English language which was set up in 1664. It had 22 members 'whose genius was very proper and inclined to improve the English tongue' and included John Dryden, the historian and later Bishop Thomas Sprat, and the diarist John Evelyn. The committee discussed a proposal from Evelyn for a grammar, spelling reform, a dictionary and models of elegance in style. The dictionary was to be a 'lexicon or collection of all the pure English words . . . so as no innovation might be us'd or favour'd, at least, 'till there should arise some necessity of providing a new edition'. In the event, there were several dictionaries published in the late seventeenth century, but they were produced by individuals, and the language was not subjected to official regulation and control.

The committee was not a linguistic body, but a political one. Several members, including Pepys and Sprat, had found it expedient to become monarchists in 1660. In 1659, John Dryden wrote a panegyric entitled *Heroique stanzas to the glorious memory of Cromwell.* In 1660 he wrote *A poem on the happy restoration and return of His Sacred Majesty Charles the Second*, and became Charles's propagandist and later Poet Laureate. The court party was well represented, but none of the committee members seems to have actually known anything about language, except perhaps Sprat, who made interesting remarks on prose style. The greatest language scholar of the time was not on the committee, and was attempting 'to justifie the wayes of God to men' in the writing of *Paradise lost.* The committee achieved nothing whatsoever in linguistic terms. On the other hand, it completely changed the political associations of the English language. The increasingly standardized written language was no longer the language of radicals or even of London and the court: it was now used by people who enjoyed privilege and power to attack people with whom they disagreed.

Dryden wanted the committee to function as an Academy, and in the dedication (to the earl of Orrery) of *Rival ladies* he writes with great approval of the French Academy. In the same essay he claimed that as a result of 'the practice of some few writers' (no doubt including himself) greater improvements had been made in the English language since 1660 than in all the years from the conquest to 1660. This is, of course, devoid of sense, but Dryden was not making serious remarks about the language, but rather asserting his own greatness as a writer.

Dryden commented at length on language in an essay entitled *Defence of the epilogue* appended to the second part of his play *The conquest of Granada* in 1672. He sets out to prove that 'the Language, Wit, and Conversation of our Age are improv'd and refin'd above the last'. This is all thanks to King Charles:

Now if any ask me, whence it is that our conversation is so much refin'd? I must freely, and without flattery, ascribe it to the Court: and, in it, particularly to the

King; whose example gives law to it. His own mis-fortunes and the Nations, afforded him an opportunity . . . of travelling. At his return, he found a Nation lost as much in Barbarism as in Rebellion. and as the excellency of his Nature forgave the one, so the excellency of his manners reform'd the other.

In order to argue for an improvement in the language, he attacks the past, not the immediate past, but the last generation but one: 'To begin with *Language*. That an Alteration is lately made in ours since the Writers of the last Age (in which I comprehend Shakespear, Fletcher and Jonson) is manifest.' He adduces examples 'enough to conclude that [Ben] *Johnson* writ not correctly'. He objects to the use of *his* in the line 'Though Heav'n should speak with all his wrath', presumably because he did not know that *his* was the old possessive form of *it*, which had relatively recently been replaced by the new form *its*. He objects to the double comparative of 'Contain your spirit in more stricter bounds' and to the final preposition in:

> The Waves, and Dens of beasts cou'd not receive
> The bodies that those Souls were frighted from.

Dryden comments: 'The Preposition at the end of the sentence; a common fault with him, and which I have but lately observ'd in my own writings.'

There are still people today who believe that sentences should not end with a preposition, and they are unlikely to be able to give a reason.[1] Final prepositions are a characteristic of the North Germanic languages, and at a guess the construction may originally have been borrowed into the dialects of the Danelaw. In other words it was probably in origin a regional feature, and what purports to be a judgement of syntax is almost certainly an expression of political views. The point that Dryden was trying to get across in this essay is that he was a greater dramatist than Jonson, Fletcher or Shakespeare.

He comments further on Shakespeare in the dedication (to the earl of Sunderland) of his play *Troilus and Cressida* in 1679: 'I have refin'd his Language which before was obsolete.' He compares English unfavourably with Latin:

I was often put to a stand, in considering whether what I write be the Idiom of the Tongue, or false Grammar . . . and have no other way to clear my doubts, but by translating my English into Latine, and thereby trying what sence the words will bear in a more stable language.

Such a view accords with those expressed 140 years before by opponents of Bible translations. He goes on to attack monosyllables: 'We are full of Monosyllables, and those clog'd with Consonants, and our pronunciation is

---

1. Latin sentences could not end with prepositions, but that is not relevant, because Latin is a different language. Even by Dryden's time grammarians had long been aware of structural differences between English and Latin.

effeminate.' At this point it becomes all but self-evident that he is not attempting a serious evaluation of language, but using language as a weapon in an ideological debate. Radicals before the revolution had used monosyllables as a weapon against the monarchy and the French: Dryden attacks monosyllables in defence of the monarchy. And the French connection? Charles II was at the time in the pay of the king of France (Hill, 1980a: 167–8).

In making these attacks Dryden is possibly the first person to select examples of the language usage of others and arbitrarily assert that they are intrinsically incorrect. To prove his points, Dryden attempted to find observable evidence in his opponents' texts. The problem was that he did not know enough about language to do this properly, and consequently from a linguistic point of view his remarks are ill founded. Nevertheless he did successfully establish the convention whereby people without any special knowledge of language feel entitled to assert that some other people have failed in the acquisition of their mother tongue.

8.3   *The uniform standard*

Although the language committee may have had no actual achievements, the basic ideas continued to be influential. In 1697 the dissenter Daniel Defoe called for an Academy in his extremely confused *Essay upon projects*. England was then at war against France, and, clearly motivated by rivalry with France, Defoe wanted an English Academy to rival the French one. He also took for granted that it makes sense to talk of purifying a language, and that this should be undertaken by an official body:

> The Work of this Society shou'd be to encourage Polite Learning, to polish and refine the *English* Tongue, and advance the so much neglected Faculty of Correct Language, to establish Purity and Propriety of Stile, and to purge it from all the Irregular Additions that Ignorance and Affectation have introduc'd.

The membership of the body is to exclude clergymen, physicians and lawyers, and to consist of twelve members of the nobility, twelve private gentlemen, and twelve chosen according to merit (which remains unexplained). Although this body is also to exclude 'Scholars . . . whose *English* has been far from Polite, full of Stiffness and Affectation, hard Words, and long unusual Coupling of *Syllables* and Sentences, which sound harsh and untuneable to the Ear', it is nevertheless expected to provide lectures on the English language.

When he attempts to explain what is actually wrong with the language, his argument quickly breaks down. What he was really worried about was the gentlemanly habit of of routinely swearing in conversation:

Jack, *God damn me* Jack, *How do'st do, thou little dear Son of a Whore? How hast thou done this long time, by God?* . . . Among the Sportsmen 'tis, *God damn the Hounds*, when they are at a Fault; or *God damn the Horse*, if he bau'ks a Leap: They call men *Sons of Bitches*, and *Dogs, Sons of Whores.*

He objects even more to women swearing:

The Grace of Swearing has not obtain'd to be a Mode yet among the Women; *God damn ye,* does not sit well upon a female Tongue; it seems to be a Masculine Vice, which the Women are not arriv'd to yet; and I woul'd only desire those Gentlemen who practice it themselves, to hear a Woman swear: It has no Musick at all there, I am sure. . . . Besides, as 'tis an inexcusable Impertinence, so 'tis a Breach upon Good Manners and Conversation . . . as if a man shou'd *Fart* before a Justice, or *talk Bawdy* before the Queen, or the like.

Fifty years before, swearing was associated with royalists – sometimes called 'Dammees', presumably from the expression *damn me!* – and with the Ranters, not with the sober and respectable middle classes (Hill, 1975: 210–13).

Towards the end of Queen Anne's reign, there were further calls, associated with Addison and Swift, for the official regulation of the language. From this period we encounter the view that the language has in some way deteriorated, and that change entails corruption. The arguments remain as irrational as those of Dryden and Defoe, and the same points are repeated again and again.

Joseph Addison launched an attack on monosyllables in the *Spectator* (135, 4 August 1711):

the English Language . . . abound[s] in monosyllables, which gives an Opportunity of delivering our Thoughts in few Sounds. This indeed takes off from the Elegance of our Tongue, but at the same time expresses our Ideas in the readiest manner.

He observes that some past-tense forms – e.g. *drown'd, walk'd, arriv'd* – in which the *-ed* had formerly been pronounced as a separate syllable (as we still do in the adjectives *blessed* and *aged*) had become monosyllables. A similar situation is found in the case of *drowns, walks, arrives*, 'which in the Pronunciation of our Forefathers were drowneth, walketh, arriveth'. He objects to the genitive *'s*, which he incorrectly assumes to be a reduction of *his* and *her*, and for which he in any case gives no examples. He asserts that the contractions *mayn't, can't, sha'n't, wo'n't* have 'much untuned our Language, and clogged it with Consonants'. He dismisses abbreviations such as *mob., rep., pos., incog.* as ridiculous, and complains about the use of short nicknames such as *Nick* and *Jack*. None of this, however, is the real reason for an Academy. An Academy was needed because people omitted relative pronouns, such as *who, which* and *that*. Such issues 'will never be decided till we have something like an Academy . . . that shall settle all Controversies between Grammar and Idiom.'

Perhaps the best-known call for an Academy was made by Jonathan
Swift in 1712, in *A proposal for correcting, improving and ascertaining the
English tongue* dedicated 'To the Most Honourable ROBERT Earl of
Oxford':

> I do here, in the Name of all the Learned and Polite Persons of the Nation,
> complain . . . that our Language is extremely imperfect; that its daily Improve-
> ments are by no means in proportion to its daily Corruptions . . . and, that in
> many Instances, it offends against every Part of Grammar (p. 8).

Swift is in part motivated by rivalry with continental languages – 'our
Language is less Refined than those of Italy, Spain or France' (p. 9) – but,
more importantly, he propounds a theory of the rise and decay of languages, and hopes that decay can be prevented:

> The *Roman* Language arrived at great Perfection before it began to decay: And
> the *French* for these last Fifty Years hath been polishing as much as it will bear,
> and appears to be declining by the natural Inconstancy of that people. . . . But the
> *English* Tongue is not arrived to such a degree of Perfection, as to make us
> apprehend any Thoughts of its Decay; and if it were once refined to a certain
> Standard, perhaps there may be Ways found out to fix it for ever; or at least till
> we are invaded and made a Conquest by some other State; and even then our best
> Writings might probably be preserved with Care, and grow into Esteem, and the
> Authors have a Chance for Immortality (pp. 14–15).

Swift was concerned for the long-term survival of his own writings, and
this is what the proposal is really all about. If one reads it with this in mind,
it is possible to understand why he argued as he did. He objects to change
on principle:

> But without . . . great Revolutions . . . (to which, we are, I think, less subject
> than Kingdoms upon the Continent) I see no absolute Necessity why any
> Language should be perpetually changing. . . . The *German*, *Spanish*, and *Ita-*
> *lian*, have admitted few or no Changes for some Ages past (pp. 15–17).

Many people have echoed this view since then. Swift looks back to a
golden age which ends a little later than Dryden's period of Shakespeare,
Fletcher and Jonson:

> The Period wherein the *English* Tongue received most Improvement, I take to
> commence with the beginning of Queen *Elizabeth*'s Reign, and to conclude with
> the Great Rebellion in Forty Two (p. 17).

Like Addison, he objects to monosyllables – *drudg'd, distrub'd, rebuk't,
fledg'd* – and blames poets:

> Poets . . . have contributed very much to the spoiling of the *English* Tongue . . .
> These Gentlemen, although they could not be insensible how much our Lan-
> guage was already overstocked with Monosyllables; introduced that barbarous
> Custom of abbreviating Words . . . so as to form such harsh unharmonious
> Sounds, that none but a *Northern* ear could endure (p. 21).

The 'Northern ears' are those of people of the north of Europe, where language is affected by the harsh climate:

> the same Defect of Heat which gives a Fierceness to out Natures, may contribute to that Roughness of our Language, which bears some Analogy to the harsh Fruit of colder Countries (p. 27).

Fortunately, female conversation offers some hope:

> if the Choice had been left to me, I would rather have trusted the Refinement of our Language, as far as it relates to Sound, to the Judgment of the Women, than of illiterate Court-Fops, half-witted Poets, and University-Boys. For, it is plain that Women in their manner of corrupting Words, do naturally discard the Consonants, as we do the Vowels. . . . Now, though I would by no means give Ladies the Trouble of advising us in the Reformation of our Language; yet I cannot help thinking, that since they have been left out of all Meetings, except Parties at Play, or where worse Designs are carried on, our Conversation hath very much degenerated (pp. 27–9).

We have to remember that Swift was the author of *Gulliver's travels*, in which he satirized the trivial arguments of politicians: the political parties of Liliput were divided on the correct way to open an egg. Nevertheless his proposal impressed Oxford, who might have set up a body as recommended by Swift; but before he did anything about it, Queen Anne died, and the Tory government fell.

John Oldmixon (1712) wrote a rejoinder to Swift's *Proposal*. Oldmixon shared the belief that the language needed to be fixed, but did not accept that Swift was the right person to do it (1712: 34). Part of the reason is that Swift was a Tory: ' 'tis impossible for a Tory to succeed in Eloquence' (p. 7). He objected to Swift's arrogance in claiming to speak in the name of learned and polite persons without first consulting them (p. 11), and in any case Swift's own English was not a good model because in *Tale of a tub* he used too many profane words and expressions (pp. 3–4). He ridicules Swift's claim that constant change would make the language incomprehensible within a hundred years (p. 22).

Calls for an official body to regulate the language continued until the end of the century. Lord Chesterfield in a letter to the World (28 November 1754) lamented that 'we had no lawful standard of our language set up, for those to repair to, who might chuse to speak and write it grammatically and correctly . . . The late ingenious doctor Swift proposed a plan of this nature . . . but without success.' In reality, it had already long been a dead issue.

A hundred years before, Francis Bacon had seen the same problem as Swift but, unlike Swift, Bacon made a rational analysis of the problem and found a rational solution. He protected his writings against change in English by translating them into Latin. Swift confused his problem with unconnected issues and irrelevant prejudice, and comes across as arrogant and absurd. If Defoe wanted to restrict swearing, an Academy was hardly an appropriate solution. Perhaps it is worth noting that he does not denounce the king of France as the Antichrist, as a Puritan of 50 years before might have done, and his objection to swearing is entirely secular, for he does not refer to the ten commandments. But public and popular discussion of language has never advanced beyond the stage reached by writers in the reign of Queen Anne.

8.4   *A controlled language*

The period from the Restoration of Charles II to the death of Anne marks an important transition in the standardization of English. Although a change in attitudes towards the language did not affect the language itself in the short term, the belief in correctness gave an impetus to conscious attempts to regulate the language. Swift's views were implemented in practice, and by the end of the eighteenth century the forms of standard written English had become more or less fixed in their modern form. Dryden's views are important because they became part of the new orthodoxy.

Since the fourteenth century, a combination of social forces and technology was ensuring that people all over the country were adopting the same written form. This is even true of handwriting, which is possibly the only area of the English language that has not been subjected to conscious regulation. Even in such a remote place as Denbigh in North Wales, the handwriting of parish clerks, lawyers' clerks and other individuals is subject to continuous change in the century after 1660 in the direction of new national norms. If standardization was happening anyway, it follows that the new authoritarian attitude which grew up after 1660 is not an essential part of the process, but something extraneous which was superimposed upon it. In view of the deep influence of this attitude on subsequent change in the language, it requires an explanation.

An important role was played by the Royal Society. In view of the scientific approach that was influential after 1660, one might expect language to be studied by induction from observed usage. The activities of a Royal Society which carried out scientific investigations under the patronage of the king and the nobility were inevitably limited to those things which did not challenge the social order. Scientists could study springs and gases, the recoil of guns and the growth of plants, but they could not tackle problems of a social and political nature. The scientific approach to language was restricted to areas of language which were socially uncontentious. There was, as a result, no serious challenge to the view that language was to be judged by deduction from assumptions laid down by authorities.

By default, the dominant approach to language remained traditional and authoritarian, and variation in language was interpreted like other aspects of social behaviour. In a society that believes that there is a correct way of doing things, whether dressing, bowing, holding a teacup or wearing a wig, it must appear self-evident that there is a correct way of using language. When scholars in this society take for granted the concept of language decay, the simplest explanation for social variation in language is that variants are corruptions that threaten the purity of the language. For people who start with assumptions of this kind, the views expressed on the English language by Jonathan Swift must have seemed straightforward common sense.

But the authorities had changed. In medieval culture, authority was vested in people who had been specially trained for the church, the law or medicine. Language issues were discussed by scholars professionally involved in language, by the Lollard translators, Arundel, Erasmus, Cheke and Gardiner. When the authority of the church crumbled in the time of Charles I, authority in matters of religion passed from professionals to anyone who asserted it. A simple man like Arise Evans would expound the meaning of the biblical text without having any real understanding of the issues involved, and his followers would accept what he said. In much the same way, authority in language was asserted by people such as Dryden, Defoe and Swift, who simply did not understand the issues. The need to know something about language before making judgements about language was simply not recognized in the late seventeenth century. This need hardly surprise us, as nothing has changed since.

Before 1660, attitudes to English would be shared by people from all social ranks and backgrounds, and opposed by another body of people from similar ranks and backgrounds. The divisions were thus vertical. Within a generation of 1660, the views of the royalist Dryden and the dissenter Defoe are marked more by their shared assumptions than by their differences. The same is true of Swift and Oldmixon. People who are willing to argue about the correct form of the language have already agreed that there is an intrinsically correct form to argue about.

It is also worth noticing that although language has always been a political issue, since the Restoration it has never properly been a party political issue. There may be a correlation between Tories and Anglicans (as opposed to Whigs and Dissenters) and authoritarian views on language, but there was a substantial measure of agreement between Whigs and Tories on the need to ascertain and fix a pure form of English. Then as now, the parties share beliefs about the English language which are part of a network of unquestioned assumptions about English society as a whole. The divisions in language have become horizontal, between those reckoned to be socially superior, and those regarded as inferior.

8.5   *A bourgeois language*

There is another interesting parallel between religion and language in that authority is linked to the social hierarchy. In a hierarchical society, it must seem obvious that those at the top are in possession of the correct forms, while everybody else labours with the problems of corruption. The logical conclusion is that the highest authority is associated with the monarchy. In Elizabeth's time, the usage of the court was asserted as a model for the language as a whole. After the Restoration, Dryden gave credit for the improvement of English to Charles II and his court. It must be said that this became less and less credible after 1688. William III was a Dutchman. Queen Anne was not credited with any special relationship with the language, and Addison and Swift were rather less than explicit in defining the learned and polite persons, other than themselves, who had in their possession the perfect standard of English. Anne's successor was the German-speaking elector of Hanover, who became George I. After 1714, even the most skilled propagandist would have found it difficult to credit the king with any authority with regard to a language he did not speak. Nevertheless, the monarchy was once again associated with correct English when the popular image of the monarchy improved in the time of Victoria.

After 1714 writers continued to appeal to the nobility for support and to act as patrons to their work on language. Some writers, such as Lord Chesterfield, were themselves of high social status. Robert Lowth became bishop of London. But ascertaining the standard language essentially became a middle-class activity. The social value of variation in language is that 'correct' forms can be used as social symbols, and distinguish middle-class people from those they regard as common and vulgar. The long-term effect of this is the development of a close connection in England between language and social class.

Where upper-class usage did not conform to the middle-class standard, it sometimes preserved forms which were later found to be remarkably similar to lower-class usage. The best-known example is *huntin', shootin' and fishin'*, but others include the h-less pronunciation of *humble*, and the pronunciation of *often* exactly like *orphan*, and *gone* to rhyme with *lawn*. The same form can be classed as refined or vulgar depending on whether it is used by the upper or the lower classes.

No mention has been made in this chapter of the language of ordinary people. The revolutionary government had begun to suppress democratic and anarchistic sects as soon as victory was won in the 1640s (Hill, 1975). Little is known about the language of ordinary people for some 200 years from the reimposition of censorship until the nineteenth century, when antiquarians began to study local dialects and mass education was introduced. By then it was apparent that ordinary people in the growing conurbations had not learned to use the middle-class norms of Standard English. To anybody observing working-class speech through the eyes of middle-class Victorian England it must have seemed perfectly obvious that the common people had failed to learn English properly.

9

The language of Great Britain

The familiar image of the eighteenth century is of an age of culture, taste and refinement before the values of old England were destroyed in the onslaught of the industrial revolution. It is an age of progress and prosperity, of economic expansion at home and overseas, the age of Jethro Tull and Turnip Townshend, when the majority of the population still lived in the countryside under the authority of the squire and the parson. This is a romantic image which reflects the outlook of the privileged few. Nevertheless it is of historical importance, because by the end of the century Standard English was more or less fixed in its modern form, having been shaped by the values of the eighteenth century.

9.1 *The codification of Standard English*

Language scholars of the eighteenth century are often dismissed as prescriptivists, but this is an overgeneralization. Great works of scholarship were produced, notably by Johnson and Lowth, but then as now, scholars proceeded from the common-sense views of the society in which they lived. When we look back on these works, it is the ill-informed and inappropriate prescriptive remarks that jump out of the page, and ironically these remarks have had a much greater influence on English culture than the scholarship itself.

Dictionaries

Early dictionaries (see section 6.3 under *Spelling reform*) were designed to explain hard words. Eighteenth-century dictionary writers began to compile an exhaustive list of the words of the language. In 1702, John Kersey produced a dictionary of about 28000 words, intended for 'Young Scholars, Tradesmen, Artificers, and the Female Sex, who would learn to spell truely'. This implies that there was at this time a concept of a normal or correct spelling for words, which everybody was expected to use.

The major lexicographer of the eighteenth century was of course Samuel Johnson, whose *A dictionary of the English language* appeared in 1755. Some of Johnson's definitions have become famous:

PIE: Any crust baked with something in it.

NETWORK: Any thing reticulated or decussated, at equal distances, with interstices between the intersections.

OATS: A grain, which in England is generally given to horses, but in Scotland supports the people.

TORY: One who adheres to the antient constitution of the state, and the apostolical hierarchy of the Church of England, opposed to a whig.

WHIG: 1. Whey
2. The name of a faction.

These are all special in some way, for example, in being particularly witty or pompous, or reflecting Johnson's own political views. Many of Johnson's definitions and much of his methodology, including his use of illustrative quotations, were copied by his successors.

If instead of concentrating on what Johnson actually did, we look at what he said about it, a different picture emerges. In his *Plan* for the intended dictionary (1747), he echoes Swift in the desire to improve the language, and 'preserve the purity and ascertain the meaning of our English idiom' for the benefit of posterity (pp. 2–4), and asserts baldly (p. 10) that 'all change is of itself an evil'. In the preface to the dictionary in 1755, by contrast, having done the work and understood the problems, he adopts an ambivalent tone:

When I took the first survey of my undertaking, I found our speech copious without order, and energetick without rules; wherever I turned my view, there was perplexity to be disentangled, and confusion to be regulated; choice was to be made out of boundless variety, without any established principle of selection; adulterations were to be detected, without a settled test of purity; and modes of expression to be rejected or received, without the suffrages of any writers of classical reputation or acknowledged authority.

This can be read in two different ways, either 'the language must be sorted out', or 'there are no suitable criteria'. He is clearly inconsistent in asserting both that 'it is the duty of the lexicographer to correct or proscribe' 'improprieties and absurdities' and that his aim is not to 'form, but register the language', not to 'teach men how they should think, but relate how they have hitherto expressed their thoughts'. He pours scorn on the idea of fixing the language:

the lexicographer [may] be derided, who being able to produce no example of a nation that has preserved their words and phrases from mutability, shall imagine that his dictionary can embalm his language, and secure it from corruption and decay.

Note that he retains the idea of language corruption: 'every language has a time of rudeness antecedent to perfection, as well as of false refinement and declension.' He looks back to a golden age which has crept forward again, starting in the 1580s but now extending to 1660:

> So far have I been from any care to grace my pages with modern decorations, that I have studiously endeavoured to collect examples and authorities from the writers before the Restoration, whose works I regard as *the wells of English undefiled*, as the pure sources of poetic diction. . . . I have fixed Sidney's work for the boundary, beyond which I make few excursions.

In basing his definitions on real examples, he takes for granted that these should be taken from literary works of the past. Only certain kinds of English are worth recording, and the 'fugitive cant' 'of the laborious and mercantile part of the people' 'must be suffered to perish with other things unworthy of preservation'.

Johnson's dictionary has been highly influential, and in different ways. His scholarship has been developed by later generations of lexicographers. The spelling of the vast majority of English words was fixed in 1755; apart from the simplification of the final <ck> in *musick,* and the American innovations, there have been no systematic changes in spelling. Linguists may think of modern spellings as the ones which happened to have widespread currency in the middle of the eighteenth century, but people who do not know the origin of standard spellings probably assume that in some way they are intrinsically 'correct'. Judging by the way dictionaries are used in word-games such as Scrabble, or in popular quizzes on radio and television, the general assumption in modern culture is that the dictionary is the appropriate authority to determine the correct form and meaning of words.

Grammars

While most literate people know what a dictionary is for, or at least think they do, the same is not true of a grammar. What a grammar does is to provide an outline of the forms of a language, usually for someone who does not already know them. This information is useful for someone learning a foreign language, and early grammars were designed to teach Latin and other languages. By the eighteenth century there was already a tradition of English grammars designed to teach standard written English to native speakers of English. This is a very different activity because it involves making people consciously aware of linguistic information they intuitively possess anyway. Teaching standard grammar is a different activity again, and involves making people consciously aware of the differences between their own language and the standard.

These subtle distinctions were not made by eighteenth-century grammarians. By this time grammars were divided into conventional sections. *Orthography*, for example, is concerned with the way letters of the alphabet are used to spell different words. Words which are used in similar ways are grouped into classes or *parts of speech*. Related words such as *boy/boys* or *sing/sings/sang/sung* are treated in what we now call *morphology*, but what in older grammar books is often called *accidence* or *etymology*. The study of grammar was also conventionally confused with the development of literacy skills. Writing requires literacy skills which people do not pick up intuitively, and rather different skills are required for different types of text, such as a shopping list, a love-letter, and an inspector's report. Composing a text and monitoring the spelling and morphology are, of course, very different activities. However, grammarians did not make a distinction between learning the forms of a language and developing literacy skills, and so to them it must have superficially seemed sensible to use a grammar to teach people to write.

One of the most influential grammars was Robert Lowth's *A short introduction to English grammar* of 1762. As an account of the structure of English, as it was understood at the time, this is a work of outstanding scholarship. The main text gives a concise account of the forms of English, and contains many objective and descriptive statements, for example, that adjectives come before nouns (p. 121). When discussing final prepositions (p. 127) he wittily remarks that 'This is an Idiom which our language is strongly inclined to'. In the preface, on the other hand, he gives vent to extreme reactionary views which he takes straight out of Swift's *Proposal*, asserting that 'the English Language as it is spoken by the politest part of the nation' 'oftentimes offends against every part of grammar' (p. iii). He goes on to argue that 'It is not the Language, but the practice, that is in fault' (p. vi), and that the grammarian's task is 'besides shewing what is right' to explain 'by pointing out what is wrong' (p. x). Now this is perfectly reasonable with regard to a foreign-language grammar. Learners made mistakes in writing Latin, and it was the schoolmaster's job to correct them. It is very different with regard to native speakers. It does not make sense to tell native speakers of English who have learnt the form *I have fell* that they have not in fact learnt that at all, or that what they have learnt is not English. It may be the case that *I have fell* is not now Standard English, but that is a separate matter.

Lowth was later bishop of London. Like Samuel Johnson, he was a Tory and an Anglican. At the same time, Joseph Priestley was teaching at the Dissenting Academy at Warrington. In his *Course of lectures on the theory of language* (1762), he hinted at the political implications of prescriptive grammar:

In modern and living languages, it is absurd to pretend to set up the compositions of any person or persons whatsoever as the standard of writing, or their conversation as the invariable rule of speaking. With respect to custom, laws and every thing that is changeable, the body of a people, who, in this respect, cannot but be free, will certainly assert their liberty, in making what innovations they judge to be expedient and useful. The general prevailing custom, whatever it happen to be, can be the only standard for the time that it prevails.

Priestley was an eminent scientist, and is best known for his discovery of oxygen. His enlightened views on language are not so celebrated. The dominant view, and the one that affected the teaching of grammar in schools, was that expressed in Lowth's preface. Popular discussions of Standard English (e.g. Marenbon, 1987) still confuse grammatical knowledge and writing skills.

English usage

Despite the prescriptive presentation, Johnson and Lowth produced major works of scholarship. Most of the claims they made about the forms of English would be accepted by linguists today, and one has to recognize that it is intellectually difficult to assemble and sort grammatical and lexical information, and present it in a coherent way. It is much easier to compile a list of alleged errors in the use of English. Books devoted to other people's incorrect language tend to jumble up points of grammar and vocabulary with pronunciation, spelling and punctuation, and even points of style. This linguistic jumble is commonly known as *usage*.

One of the most remarkable books on usage was Robert Baker's *Reflections on the English language* of 1770. He proposes the setting-up of an Academy (pp. i–iii), presumably not having heard of Swift's proposal. He had not seen Johnson's *Dictionary*, and he was apparently unaware that anybody had ever written an English grammar. Baker had had a classical education, but expressed his views on the language without any knowledge of the relevant scholarship. He made 127 remarks illustrating alleged errors in other people's English. He objects to *went* as a past participle (remark VIII); *different to* (IX) and *different than* (XCIX); misuse of the apostrophe (XXV); the confusion of *fly* and *flee* (XXIX), *set* and *sit* (XXXII) and *lie* and *lay* (XXXIII); alleged misuse of *whom* (XXXIX) and *him, her, me* and *them* (XL); *mutual* meaning 'common' (XLIII), and *less* meaning 'fewer' (XLVII); and *the reason is because* (LXXX). What is remarkable is how many of these have been echoed by later writers, and how many of the condemned forms were eventually banished from the standard language.

Lists of this kind have been passed on in the education system, with the result that it has become an observable fact that educated users of English really do write in accordance with prescribed usage. Educated writers do

not in general use the double comparatives or routine double negatives –
e.g. *worser* or *I didn't say nothing* – which were originally condemned as
corruptions of the language. They use conventional spelling and punctuation as a matter of course. Educated speakers monitor their word-stress
patterns, and modify their pronunciation of words to conform to what they
perceive as the norm. This has led to the concept of 'correct' English which
conforms to the arbitrary rules, and which is regularly confused with the
effective use of English. 'Correctness' has been cultivated at least as much
in Scotland, Ireland and in independent America as in England. Priestley
(1761) argued that usage 'will never be effected by the arbitrary rules of
any man, or body of men whatever'. He was enlightened, but he was
wrong.

The use of a common standard language has in itself a number of
practical advantages, and in social terms is at best cohesive and at worst
neutral. The confusion of 'standard' with 'correct' created a new kind of
standard, a standard of acceptability which most people would in one way
or another fail to achieve. This is in its nature socially divisive. English
usage has assumed an important role in Anglo-Saxon culture and society
which transcends the use of 'correct' forms. People's literacy skills, their
command of English, their social class and even their intelligence have
come to be routinely measured according to the degree to which they
conform to the arbitrary conventions of usage.

9.2 *London and the provinces*

By the eighteenth century, London English had a long-established and
dominant role in the development of the language. In the case of the written
language, it is scarcely necessary to make a distinction between London
English and the standard. The situation is more complicated with respect to
speech. During the medieval period, the prestigious form of speech in
England was not English at all but French, and this prestige lingered on
for another two centuries after the phasing-out of French. At first, London
English would not appear to have had any special status. Indeed, the
southward movement of northern and east midland forms into London
points to a prestigious centre further north, presumably York. But as
spoken English became prestigious, London English began to affect speech
in the rest of the country.

The English of the capital

Comments on spoken English by sixteenth-century scholars such as Hart
and Puttenham (see sections 6.2–6.3) reflect the new situation in which the

speech of the capital had attained prestige. But they were referring to the language of the court, and this was already markedly different from the language of ordinary Londoners. Perhaps the first record of ordinary speech is found in the diaries of Henry Machin, who was a Merchant Taylor (Wyld, 1920: 141–7). Some of Machin's spellings, dating from the 1550s, suggest characteristics of nineteenth-century Cockney, such as the interchange of <v> and <w> as in <woyce> ('voice') but <voman> ('woman'), a feature immortalized by Dickens in his portrayal of the speech of Sam Weller. Other spellings which deviate markedly from what has become the standard reflect the kind of variation in speech which was characteristic of all classes at the period. But some of the most interesting spellings suggest pronunciations which became generally current only very much later, for example, the vowel shortening of *sweat* <swett>, the vowel lengthening of *guard* <gaard>, and the pronunciation of <wa> as [wo] as in *wash* <wosse>. The unrounding of the vowel in *morrow* <marow> is now associated particularly with American English.

A society that interprets variation in speech in terms of 'correctness' will understandably give a social evaluation to the variants themselves. Innovations are classed as vulgar or polite, and archaic forms as vulgar or quaint, according to the prestige of the people who use them. This social evaluation is important for two reasons. First, descriptions of London English, unless they specifically deal with Cockney, deal with the polite forms. Second, it is the polite forms that spread from London to middle-class speech in the towns.

Provincial English

Before the eighteenth century, the vast majority of English speakers had spoken the local country dialects that had developed out of the dialects of the early Anglo-Saxon settlers. But now the towns were beginning to grow rapidly, and attracting people from the surrounding countryside. The newcomers would originally speak a wide variety of dialects, but the differences would gradually be lost and the town would eventually develop its own relatively homogeneous dialect, related to that of the countryside. For example, such evidence as remains of the old town dialect of Liverpool indicates that it was similar to the dialects of south-west Lancashire (Knowles, 1975). Town dialects were prestigious and influenced the speech of the surrounding rural areas. The speech of Johnson and Garrick was influenced by the town dialect of Lichfield. Even in the late nineteenth century, the speech of Gladstone was marked by the old dialect of Liverpool.

Social and technological change made it inevitable that the speech of many (but not all) English speakers would be modified in the direction of London English. Improved methods of transport by the new turnpike roads, by sea, by inland waterways and canals created for the towns a network of communication centred on London. This enabled new fashionable forms of speech to spread from London to the rest of the country. The degree of influence reflects the quality of communications: for example, Yorkshire was more heavily influenced than Lancashire, in view of its better road system, and the speech of ports such as Lancaster and Liverpool was in turn more influenced than that of the cotton towns further inland. To give a specific example, the new [r]-less pronunciation of words such as *learn* and *arm* penetrated Yorkshire much earlier than Lancashire, and Lancashire ports before the cotton towns. The rhotic forms now survive in the towns of east Lancashire, but are rare elsewhere in that part of the north of England.

Within any town, London forms were adopted more readily by the middle classes than the working classes. This has brought about the social stratification of speech in towns, creating a close connection between social class and the way people speak. Traditional working-class speech typically retains some features of the surrounding rural dialects, and some features no longer in fashion in middle-class speech. It also contains local innovations which on account of their lack of prestige have not been widely adopted. Because middle-class speech in different towns began to share London features in common, middle-class speech became more homogeneous than working-class speech. It is still much easier to tell where working-class people come from than middle-class people.

In view of the extent of London influence, speech in England has become worthy of comment only to the extent that it differs from London usage. Sometimes regional speech retains the old forms. For example, northern English generally retains the old vowels in *muck* and *brass*, which rhyme with the London vowels of *book* and *gas* respectively. In other cases, innovations arose in regional varieties: for example, postvocalic [l] was lost in words such as *call* and *old* in many parts of the north of England and the south of Scotland. In this case, the change has subsequently been reversed by London influence, and the [l] has been restored except in occasional forms such as *owd*. Today, [l]-dropping is probably regarded as a Cockney innovation.

Superimposed on this normal process of change was the conscious attempt to regulate the way people speak, and given the prevailing ideas of the eighteenth century, it was perhaps inevitable that regional dialects would be interpreted as corruptions of the pure English of London. This attitude is expressed by Jones (1724: 11):

> For want of better Knowledge, and more Care, almost every Country in *England* has gotten a distinct Dialect, or several peculiar Words, and odious Tones, perfectly ridiculous to Persons unaccustomed to hear such Jargon: thus as the Speech of a *Yorkshire* and *Somersetshire* downright *Countryman* would be almost unintelligible to each other; so would it be good Diversion to a polite *Londoner* to hear a Dialogue between them.

This intolerance is of fundamental importance in the subsequent history of English pronunciation. People modify their speech anyway according to fashion much as they modify the way they dress or decorate their houses. But the currency of the belief that non-fashionable forms are actually corruptions adds a further dimension to the problem. Anybody with any social standing, whether or not they accept the values on which the intolerance is based, has little choice but to conform in the way they speak.

9.3   *English beyond England*

By the time English began to spread beyond England, the written language was already well on the way to its modern standard form. The printing industry was in a position to impose standard forms, and the people who had access to publishing would be unlikely to question the superiority of such standard forms as existed. There has consequently never been any serious question of a rival written standard. There have always been geographical differences in the use of the standard, but the formal differences that remain are matters of detail, such as minor spelling differences, or the survival of *gotten* in American English corresponding to *got* in British English.

In the case of spoken language, the technology required to impose uniformity did not yet exist, and communications were such that London influence was limited to the polite classes even in England. As a result many other prestigious varieties of spoken English have developed out of the kind of English spoken by the original settlers in former colonies. Differing patterns of change have given rise to claims which are as bizarre as they are familiar: that American English is archaic, that the purest English is to be heard at Inverness, or that the people of Ulster still speak like Elizabeth I.

English in Scotland

The history of English in Scotland parallels in some interesting ways its history in England, but with significant differences in timing. Medieval Scotland used Latin as the language of record, and French was highly influential not through conquest but through the Auld Alliance of 1295. French borrowings were of the same kind as in England, but different actual forms were borrowed, e.g. *tassie* ('cup') and *hogmanay*. The English of Scotland – also known as *Inglis* and later as *Scots* – began to be used as a written language in the later fourteenth century (Murison, 1979: 6–8), at about the same time as in England (see section 4.3). It was used as a literary language by the 'Scottish Chaucerians'.

By the sixteenth century Scots was developing as a written language parallel to English. The Spanish ambassador to the court of James IV compared the differences to those between Castilian and Aragonese (Murison, 1979: 8–9). The same need was perceived to enlarge the vocabulary (cf. section 5.4). William Harrison in his *Of the languages spoken in this iland* of 1587 comments:

> The Scottish english hath beene much broader and lesse pleasant in vtterance than ours, because that nation hath not till of late indeuored to bring the same to any perfect order . . . Howbeit in our time the Scottish language endeuoreth to come neere, if not altogither to match our toong in finenesse of phrase, and copie of words.

The problem for Scots is that printing did not provide the same boost as in England. Caxton in Westminster had clearly perceived the need to choose his language according to the needs of the market (see section 4.5 under *Incunabula*), and in this respect Scots was unable to compete with London English. After the Reformation of 1560, there was the same need as in England for a vernacular translation of the Bible, but it was the Geneva Bible that was introduced, and it was written in London English. As in England, the Bible was a major influence in the spread of literacy, and literate Scots would be familiar with London English. The Psalter too was in London English (Murison, 1979: 9).

When James VI moved to London in 1603 to become James I of England, the prestige of his court was transferred from Edinburgh to London. From about this time the prestige of Scots declined. One of James's courtiers, Sir William Alexander, actually apologized for using Scottish forms in his written English (Aitken, 1979: 89). In the course of the century, not only the writing but also the speech of the Scottish gentry was anglicized, partly by intermarriage (Aitken, 1979: 90–2). By the time of the Act of Union of 1707, it was thus inevitable that London English should be used as the official language of Great Britain.

Eighteenth-century comments on Scottish English, particularly after 1760, typically involve alleged errors in the speech and writing of Scots. J. Johnson's *Dictionary* of 1762, for example, lists Scottish solecisms in the writings of Hume (quoted by Leonard, 1962: 178). According to a writer in the *Oxford Magazine* in 1768, 'The Article – THE – before Superlatives, is frequently omitted by the SCOTS (who have not contributed a little to corrupt our Language by the Multiplicity of their Works)' (quoted by Leonard, 1962: 90). While such comments may be regarded as somewhat condescending, it is also the case that a large number of Scots were glad to be instructed how to improve their linguistic ways (Romaine, 1982: 62). Scots who did not stand out became linguistically invisible. Unless one happens to know where writers come from it is easy to assume by default that they come from London. Hume complained in 1757: 'Is it not strange that, at a time when we . . . in our Accent and Pronunciation, speak a very Corrupt

Dialect of the Tongue which we make use of . . . shou'd really be the People most distinguish'd for Literature in Europe' (Frank, 1994: 55). The paradox is that English linguistic attitudes were shared by many Scots themselves.

A long-term view, especially one that concentrates on texts intended to be used outside Scotland, can give the misleading impression of a unidirectional change towards London English. In fact, texts written for local Scottish purposes had a significantly higher proportion of Scots forms than those intended for international distribution.[1] Educated speakers in Scotland reflect to differing degrees the normalizing pressures general in England, but this has not extended to the adoption of Received Pronunciation (RP) in Scotland (see section 10.5 under *The King's English*). Strong RP influence is a feature of the genteel accents of Kelvinside in Glasgow and Morningside in Edinburgh, but these are not typical of Scottish speech.

English in Ireland

English involvement in Ireland can be traced to the twelfth century, when Anglo-Norman settlers took over the old Norse settlements in the area round Dublin (Geipel, 1971: 56). This is the area that came to be known as the Pale. As in England, Latin and French became the languages of English administration until the middle of the fourteenth century. The Statutes of Kilkenny of 1366 (Kallen, 1994: 150–2) were intended to protect the position of English, but in this case against the use of Irish as the vernacular. The use of English gradually declined, although remnants of the old dialects can be traced into the nineteenth century (Barry, 1982).

The English used in Ireland today does not derive from the medieval language of the Pale, but was introduced by settlers from England and Scotland in the sixteenth and seventeenth centuries. The settlers were encouraged to migrate by the English government as part of a policy to control the Irish. Whereas in England the use of English was associated with nationalism, for the native Irish it became associated with the domination of a foreign power. Irish was associated with opposition to English involvement in Ireland, and since the settlers were typically Protestants, Catholicism was also associated with Irishness. In this way, from the very beginning, the political associations of the English language were completely different in Ireland from what they were in England.

Written Irish English was always virtually indistinguishable from the English of England. On the other hand, settlers brought with them different spoken varieties which are still characteristic of different parts of Ireland. Although they came from many different parts of Britain, they were subject to the same social pressures in Ireland. Forms would spread or die out

---

1. A. Meurman-Solin, personal communication.

according to what was locally prestigious, and eventually relatively homogeneous dialects emerged from the original variety. This process must have been very similar to the development of Old English dialects (see section 2.3). Nevertheless Ulster Scots, spoken in the northern part of Ulster, still clearly reflects the speech of settlers from Scotland. Further south, it is still possible to detect the influence of the English north west. For example, a characteristic of Belfast speech is the identical pronunciation of *fir* and *fair*, and this is also found in the region of the river Mersey. Other features of Ulster English are reminiscent of Elizabethan English (Braidwood, 1964).

Ireland was formally incorporated into the United Kingdom by the Act of Union of 1800, and during the next century, the use of Irish declined dramatically, being seen as a stumbling block to progress even by Irish nationalists (Barry: 1982: 92). (The present association of the Irish language and Irish nationalism is a twentieth-century phenomenon.) When the Irish republic gained its independence, English had long since become the dominant language. The republic has developed its own norms for spoken English based on educated Dublin speech (Barry, 1982: 90), which differ from the kind of RP which at the same time was becoming established in England. Meanwhile the six northern counties followed a similar path to Scotland. Belfast even has its *Malone Road* accent to match those of Kelvinside and Morningside.

English in the American colonies

English was first taken across the Atlantic to Newfoundland by John Cabot in 1497 in the search for the north-west passage to China (Bailey, 1982: 137). The early colonists were in general people who were forced to emigrate by economic necessity (Cassidy, 1982: 178), and therefore not in general the people with the power to set the fashion in England. In these circumstances one can expect innovations to be condemned by English prescriptivists. Perhaps the first recorded innovation in American English dates from 1663 and is the use of the word *ordinary* in the sense of 'tavern' rather than 'boarding house' as in England, and the first Americanism to be condemned was the use of *bluff* in the sense of 'headland', first recorded in 1735 (Cassidy 1982: 186).

The first colonists in New England came from many parts of Britain, but predominantly from the east midlands (Cassidy, 1982: 178), and the resulting dialect mixture produced a relatively homogeneous variety. This has remained a characteristic of American speech, which has had little dialect variation, geographical or social. Using the same kind of thinking as was prevalent in England, this could be construed as evidence that American English was a good kind of English. The first claim for the 'purity' of American English dates from 1724 (Cassidy, 1982: 187), and soon after independence Americans were claiming that their English was superior to that of England. Thus Noah Webster:

> the people of America, in particular the English descendants, speak the most *pure English* now known in the world . . . The people of distant counties in England can hardly understand one another, so various are their dialects; but in the extent of twelve hundred miles in America, there are very few . . . words . . . which are not universally intelligible (1789: 288–9).

Webster also saw the political significance of linguistic independence:

> Our political harmony is concerned in a uniformity of language. As an independent nation, our honor requires us to have a system of our own, in language as in government.

The irony is that American radical thinkers, while challenging British authority, nevertheless took for granted British attitudes on issues of language correctness. In the event, the clearest sign of linguistic independence in the short term was in a minor spelling reform. Words such as *honour* and *colour* lost the <u>, *waggon* lost a <g>, and *plough* was spelt <plow>. It is also difficult to distinguish American prescriptive attitudes from British ones. As late as the 1920s, S. A. Leonard could complain on the one hand about the damage done by 'schoolmastered language' (1962: 246), and then go on to refer to 'grossly illiterate forms against which there is genuine and strong consensus of feeling among reasonably cultivated persons in this country' and take comfort in the fact that 'the very conservative larger dictionaries may be trusted to delay acceptance of an expression long enough' (1962: 247).

9.4   *English pronunciation*

Increased social contact in the eighteenth century was drawing attention to differences in speech, and the fixing of the written form set the precedent for the standardization of spoken English. Jonathan Swift had the habit of listening for pronunciation errors in the sermons of visiting preachers, and remonstrating with them afterwards (Lounsbury, 1904: 62). In the course of the century, attention was increasingly paid to the spoken language, or at least to the pronunciation of words, and speech also became subjected to conscious regulation and attempts were made to impose conformity and bring about a national standard. Johnson's dictionary was an important factor in creating the new attitude. In his *Plan*, he talks of 'an English dictionary . . . by which the pronunciation of our language may be fixed' (1747: 32), and discusses the need to fix the accentuation of polysyllables and the sounds of monosyllables. In the latter case, *wound* and *wind* 'will not rhyme to *sound*, and *mind*' (1747: 11–13).

Johnson's thinking looks back to Swift, but already in the 1740s the issue was becoming international, as attempts were made to establish the London forms in Scotland and Ireland. Elocutionists began to attack the Scottish accent from about 1748 (Aitken, 1979: 96). In 1761, Thomas Sheridan, an Irishman, lectured in Edinburgh on 'those points with regard to which Scotsmen are most ignorant, and the dialect of this country most imperfect'. As a result, a society was established in Edinburgh to promote [London] English in Scotland, and 'Scotch' was banned from the classroom (Romaine, 1982: 61).

Sheridan had no doubts about the need to standardize pronunciation:

> it can not be denied that an uniformity of pronunciation throughout Scotland, Wales and Ireland, as well as through the several counties of England, would be a point much to be wished (1762: 206).

Sheridan was confident that he himself knew what the correct pronunciation was. This was because his father had learnt it at the time of Queen Anne, when English was spoken with the greatest uniformity and with the utmost elegance. He had also learnt it from the best authority, namely Jonathan Swift (Lounsbury, 1904: 59–66). Swift was of course another Irishman. Very similar views were put forward by the Scot James Buchanan (1764), who saw 'the establishing an uniform pronunciation' as 'doing an honour to our country', by which he meant the United Kingdom. Buchanan was a little vaguer about the source of the standard, but made it clear that Scots had to modify their pronunciation.

It must also be said that Sheridan in the course of his scholarly work achieved a genuine insight into the nature of spoken language, but in this case the insights were not developed by later scholars. He comments (1762: 29): 'Pronunciation . . . which had such a comprehensive meaning among the ancients, as to take in the whole compass of delivery, with its concomitants of look and gesture; is confined with us to very narrow bounds, and refers only to the manner of sounding our words.' The study of the spoken language was in practice to be confined to the pronunciation of individual words, and that remains true today. The study of prosody was taken up by Steele (1775), but this has never been given the same emphasis as the sounds of words. Sheridan also saw the complexity of the relationship between speech and writing (1762: 95): 'I am aware it will be said, that written language is only a copy of that which is spoken, and has a constant reference to articulation; the characters upon paper, being only symbols of articulate sounds.' The view that he warns against here embodies a naïve view of literacy which has nevertheless dominated the thinking of linguists and phoneticians until relatively recently.

As in the case of Johnson and Lowth, it is Sheridan's simple-minded remarks that have proved influential and had a permanent effect on the history of the language. William Kenrick asserted in the preface to his

Dictionary (1773): 'There seems indeed a most ridiculous absurdity in the pretensions of a native of Aberdeen or Tipperary to teach the natives of London to speak and read.' He claimed to give the pronunciation of words 'according to the present practice of polished speakers in the metropolis'. John Walker (1791) provided 'Rules for the natives of Ireland in order to obtain a just Pronunciation of English', followed by a parallel set of rules for the natives of Scotland. He asserted that London English was superior to provincial English, 'being more generally received', but nevertheless made a list of the faults of Londoners.

The kind of issue raised in these and other works was restricted to the 'manner of sounding words'. Should *balcony* and *academy* be stressed on the first syllable or the second, and *European* on the second syllable or the third? Should *Rome* sound like *roam* or *room*, and should *gold* rhyme with *cold* or *cooled*? Should the first vowel of *quality* be as in *wax* or *was*? Some disputed words had popular pronunciations based on fanciful etymologies, for example *cucumber* was pronounced 'cowcumber', and *asparagus* 'sparrow-grass'. People still argue today whether *controversy* should be stressed on the first syllable or the second, and whether *vase* should rhyme with *face*, *shahs* or *cause*.

Pronouncing dictionaries, particularly Walker's dictionary, proved increasingly influential in the nineteenth century (Ellis, 1875). This created the belief that there was a standard pronunciation, although the details remained phonetically vague, and that it was spoken by some ill-defined group of people connected in some way with London. These vague ideas were given a more definite form by Henry Sweet (see section 10.4 under *Received Pronunciation*).

9.5   *Change in Standard English*

The fixing of the language can give the superficial impression that the history of English came to an end some time towards the end of the eighteenth century. It is true that there has been little subsequent change in the forms of the standard language, at least in the written standard language. There have been substantial changes in non-standard spoken English. In any case what were actually fixed were the forms of Standard English. The way these forms have been used in different social situations has continued to change.

New words and expressions have continued to be introduced, and old ones have changed their meaning. Archaic forms continue to become obsolete, although they may be sustained beyond their natural span by prescriptive rules. For example, many people must have a vague feeling that they ought to use the old subjunctive in the phrase *if I were you*, when what comes naturally is *if I was you*. Similarly some old dual forms still linger on, including *the bigger of two* or *between two* in contrast to the plurals *the biggest of three* or *among three*. In such cases there is a clash between the normal forces of change and conscious attempts to regulate the language.

The way people used the language – in writing prose and verse, letters and wills – continued to change. Here also we can trace the influence of the prevailing irrational views of the time, particularly with regard to what is conventionally and vaguely referred to as prose style. At a time when the national prosperity depended on such things as commerce, the navy and colonial expansion, the study of mathematics and other useful subjects was considered below the dignity of a gentleman (Lawson and Silver, 1973). A classical education, now that Latin had ceased to have any practical value, was considered more suitable.

The typical prose style of the period following the Restoration of the monarchy (see section 8.1) was essentially unadorned. This plainness of style was a reaction to the taste of the preceding period. Early in the eighteenth century taste began to change again, and there are suggestions that ordinary language is not really sufficient for high literature. Addison in the *Spectator* (no. 285) argues: 'many an elegant phrase becomes improper for a poet or an orator, when it has been debased by common use.' By the middle of the century, Lord Chesterfield argues for a style raised from the ordinary; in a letter to his son he writes: 'Style is the dress of thoughts, and let them be ever so just, if your style is homely, coarse, and vulgar, they will appear to as much disadvantage, and be as ill-received as your person, though ever so well proportioned, would, if dressed in rags, dirt and tatters.' At this time, Johnson's dictionary appeared, followed by Lowth's grammar and Sheridan's lectures on elocution. By the 1760s, at the beginning of the reign of George III, the elevated style was back in fashion.

The new style is associated among others with Samuel Johnson. Johnson echoes Addison and Chesterfield: 'Language is the dress of thought . . . and the most splendid ideas drop their magnificence, if they are conveyed by words used commonly upon low and trivial occasions, debased by vulgar mouths, and contaminated by inelegant applications' (Wimsatt, 1941: 105). This gives rise to the belief that the language of important texts must be elevated above normal language use. Whereas in the medieval period Latin was used as the language of record, in the late eighteenth century Latinate English was used for much the same purpose.

Boswell in his *Life of Johnson* reports Johnson's comment on *The rehearsal* that 'it has not wit enough to keep it sweet', which he later revised to 'it hath not vitality enough to preserve itself from putrefaction'. Another comment taken from a letter – 'When we were taken upstairs a dirty fellow bounced out of the bed in which one of us was to lie' – was later written up for publication as 'Out of one of the beds, on which we were to repose, started up, at our entrance, a man black as a *Cyclops* from the forge' (Wimsatt, 1941: 78). This kind of artificial prose survived into the nineteenth century, and was used in some newspapers and literary reviews.[2]

2. Verse was also conventionally written in an artificial (but actually very different) style. Here the reaction came earlier, from William Wordsworth in *Lyrical ballads*.

10

The language of empire

By the nineteenth century, English had become the language of a world-wide empire, and it was beginning to be influenced by its worldwide context. For the purpose of a general history of the language, however, England and London can still be treated as the natural focus of events. In the short term, in view of developments in England, the linguistic processes of half a millennium must have appeared to culminate in Victorian English.

10.1   *The international spread of English*

The means by which English spread over the new empire that grew up after the loss of the American colonies differed from one colony to another, but there are three discernible main patterns. In the first case, English was transplanted by native speakers; in the second it was introduced as an official language alongside existing national languages; and in the third case, it interacted in complex ways with native languages.

The spread of English by native-speaker settlers to places such as Australia and New Zealand is remarkably parallel to the development of Old English (see section 2.3) and American English. The settlers paid little attention to the languages of the original inhabitants, and conventional accounts (e.g. Turner, 1966) describe the new kinds of English as though the colonies grew up in empty lands. If there was contact with other languages, it was with other colonial languages, including French in Canada, or Dutch in South Africa.

The penal settlement at Botany Bay was begun in 1788 (Turner, 1966: 4), shortly after American independence meant that former outlets for convicted criminals were no longer available. Many of the early enforced immigrants were from the economically depressed towns of the south of England, and from Ireland. English was first spoken in New Zealand by whalers, and in 1792 a gang of sealers were left on the South Island. Missionaries arrived in 1814 (Turner, 1966: 5), and many of the early settlers were Scots. The language of such people was not the kind held in high esteem by the polite English society of the time. The speech of transported Londoners in particular contained innovations which in the thinking of the time would have been classed as evidence of the corruption of the language.

English was introduced as a second language in places such as India, China and other countries of the east. Here the early English traders encountered ancient civilizations which they recognized as at least as advanced as their own. In India, for example, the interest taken in Sanskrit by Sir William Jones in the 1780s led to intense research in Europe into the historical relationships among languages, and eventually to the reconstruction of Indo-European. By the end of the century, however, the belief in the superiority of English was leading to a decline in respect for other languages. By 1813 the official education policy in India was to impart 'to the Native population knowledge of English literature and science through the medium of the English language'. According to Bentinck, the English language was the 'key to all improvements'. English was also used as an official language in Singapore and Hong Kong, Malaya and the East Indies, and in East Africa.

Whether as a transplanted native language or as an official language, the language used in the colonies was essentially the same as that used in England. A very different situation developed in West Africa. Here special trade languages, or *pidgins*, had long been in use for communication with Portuguese traders, and they used elements from Portuguese and African languages. When the British arrived, they also began to incorporate elements from English. Mixed groups of Africans transported to the Caribbean by slave traders would not have a language in common, and pidgins would form the most effective means of communication. Eventually they would be adopted as a native language, called a *creole*. From a linguistic point of view the development of a creole means the emergence of a completely new language; but that is not how Caribbean creoles would have been seen by typical eighteenth-century Englishmen.

In these very different ways, imperial expansion encouraged the belief in the superiority of English, by which was understood Standard English. The use of 'broken' English, including pidgins and creoles, encouraged the view that there were some human beings who did not have a proper language at all. Such a view has political implications which go far beyond language, and was to prove influential in England itself.

10.2   *The illustrious past*

Language scholars provided Standard English with an illustrious past by their interpretation of the history of the language, the publication of our ancient linguistic heritage, and most of all by the historical codification of the language in the form of *The Oxford English dictionary.*

The Oxford English dictionary

The Oxford dictionary was an outstanding work of historical scholarship, but it was not the first historical dictionary. This was Charles Richardson's *A new dictionary of the English language*, which appeared in 1836–7, and which attempted to trace the historical development of the meanings of words using historical quotations rather than definitions. The original intention of the Philological Society in 1857 was simply to produce a supplement to the dictionaries of Johnson and Richardson, but it was soon clear that a completely new work was required. The new project was begun in 1858 with Herbert Coleridge as editor, with the aim of completing the work in two years. In 1861, on the death of Coleridge, F. J. Furnivall was appointed editor, and he was followed in 1879 by James Murray, who was appointed full-time editor. Murray's aim was a complete history of all English words 'known to have been in use since the middle of the twelfth century', and he built a special scriptorium in his garden to store the millions of slips of paper on which the illustrative quotations were written by the readers. The first instalment of the new dictionary – originally called *The new English dictionary on historical principles* – appeared on 1 February 1884. Publication was not completed until 19 April 1928. Murray was not to see the project finished, for he died in 1915.

The preparation of the dictionary was accompanied by an increased interest in the study of words, notably by Archbishop Trench (1878). Grammars at this period routinely added a historical section, usually with a list of words. Trainee teachers were faced with lists of etymological roots, as in Daniel (1883). Whatever the editors of the dictionary might have intended, and despite the haphazard changes in the meanings of words that they recorded, the picture given in textbooks and popular works of the time is that the English vocabulary had evolved from humble origins to its culmination in Victorian English.

Ancient records

One of the problems facing the dictionary compilers was that they lacked sufficient information to trace words back into the medieval period. Manuscripts were simply not available in an easily usable form. In order to provide texts, Furnivall founded the Early English Text Society in 1864, followed by the Chaucer Society in 1868. The work of these societies led to the publication of a large number of scholarly editions of ancient texts.

There was, however, from the beginning an ambivalent attitude towards dialects in the presentation of ancient texts to non-specialists. Henry Sweet restricted the first edition of his highly influential *Anglo-Saxon reader* (first published 1876) and the associated *Primer* (1882) to West Saxon. The texts were presented in a modernized format, with full stops and capital letters and other modern punctuation. Verse was divided into lines, instead of continuous text. This inevitably gives the impression that West Saxon was a kind of standard Old English[1] parallel to standard Modern English. Sweet simultaneously insisted on the importance of other dialects, and added Anglian and Kentish texts at the end of his later editions of the *Reader*. But in the ninth edition, revised by C. T. Onions, the texts were divided into three sections, 'Verse', 'Prose' and 'Examples of Non-West-Saxon dialects'; this surely suggests that dialects are an oddity. After the conquest, there was no English dialect that could be taken as a national norm, and consequently Middle English is presented in its natural dialectal variety.

History of the language

In the course of the second half of the nineteenth century, the story of English gradually emerged in its modern form (Crowley, 1989). The study of words was fitted into a familiar account of English history identifying the different events that had led to the enlargement of the vocabulary: the coming of the Saxons, and the Danish and Norman invasions. Caxton could be seen as the harbinger of the new age that dawned at the end of the Middle Ages. A particular interest was taken in the sixteenth century, the growth of the vocabulary at this time being interpreted as an expression of the Renaissance. From an Anglican point of view, the Reformation was a major advance which led to Elizabethan English.

The belief in progress can give the impression that the language has marched onward and upward, while suffering setbacks on the way. Thus West Germanic leads on to late West Saxon, which in turn leads to Elizabethan English, and eventually modern Standard English. The emphasis on literary texts led to an interpretation of major literary figures as creators of the language, with the result that the Beowulf poet, Chaucer, Shakespeare and Milton were taken to illustrate the rise of the language (see, for example, Bradley, 1904: 215–40).

As the understanding of language broadened at the end of the nineteenth century, the 'internal' history branched out to cover the attributes of words, including spelling and pronunciation, semantic change and (to a limited extent) their changing grammatical behaviour. This 'internal' history has preserved some older beliefs about language change, including the ambiva-

---

1. It is not necessary to treat one dialect as the norm in this way. Early German is studied as a group of related dialects. But the study of early German pre-dates the formation of the unified German state.

lence towards dialects. Although the relationship between dialects and Standard English has long been perfectly well understood, and this is made clear in explicit descriptions, conventional accounts of change in English pronunciation, grammar and vocabulary have never quite fitted the known 'external' history. Changes are given precise dates, as though they took place everywhere at about the same time in a standard language. In fact, there are changes usually ascribed to the Anglo-Saxon period which have still not taken place in the rural dialects of Cumbria. This approach to change is consistent with an older story, according to which (standard) Saxon collapsed after the Norman conquest, not to be reestablished until the end of the Middle Ages. Some scholars, such as Chambers (1932) and Gordon (1966), have even sought to establish a historical link between the old and new kinds of Standard English.

10.3 *Working-class English*

The kind of English which was provided with a historical background in the nineteenth century was also the kind that resulted from the normalizing forces of the previous century. Standard English now apparently had a rigorous scientific underpinning. Scholarly study also gave an impression of what constituted a typical sample of English. A paragraph from Dickens – standard, written, literary, Victorian English – would appear to be typical in a way that, say, the transcript of a conversation between working-class youths in Bradford would not. The reality was that scholars had not yet even begun to describe the normal language activity of the vast majority of English speakers.

Rural dialects

The idea that rural dialects, particularly in the west and the north, preserved features that had become archaic elsewhere had been known for centuries. The dialect origin of Standard English itself is explicitly brought out in Murray's preface to the Oxford dictionary:

> Down to the Fifteenth Century the language existed only in dialects, all of which had a literary standing: during this period, therefore, words and forms of all dialects are admitted on an equal footing into the Dictionary.

Even so the use of *only* here indicates that recognition of dialects is something of a concession. The second half of the century saw the compilation by vicars, schoolteachers and gentlemen in different parts of the country of lists of local dialect words.

More scholarly interest in dialects increased after about 1870, when linguists began to look for regularity in sound change. It was soon found that standard languages did not exhibit regularity. With hindsight, this is not surprising in the case of English, in view of the dialect mixture which gave rise to the standard language. Search for regularity in rural dialects led to dialect surveys (e.g. by Ellis, 1875) and the preparation of dialect dictionaries (e.g. Wright, 1961). A particular urgency was added by the belief that the process of standardization was destroying local dialects. The same belief many years later led to the survey of English dialects (Orton and Dieth, 1962).

Although dialectologists were trying to understand the nature of sound change, they took no interest whatsoever in the rapid changes taking place around them in the formation of urban dialects. However, even the study of the dialects of small communities showed that their speech was not regular or uniform, and that it was necessary to take account of social variation in speech. It was not until the late 1960s that sociolinguists began to study the speech of the English urban masses (Trudgill, 1974; Knowles, 1975).

Urban dialects

In the course of the nineteenth century, a number of industrial towns grew into enormous conurbations with massive working-class populations. The population of Liverpool, for example, passed 5000 in about 1700, 50 000 in the 1780s, and the Merseyside conurbation as a whole had passed 500 000 by the time of the 1841 census. From the 1840s on, the conurbation continued to grow as a result of large-scale immigration, particularly from Ireland, with the result that, according to the 1861 census, one Liverpudlian in four had actually been born in Ireland. The evidence suggests that, until 1830 or later, Liverpool had a dialect similar to that of local areas of Lancashire, but that a new urban dialect must have developed from about the 1840s (Knowles, 1975: 14–24).

Urban dialects are not confined to large towns, but grow with the conurbation, spreading to neighbouring small towns and then along local communication networks over the the surrounding countryside. The great conurbations of Manchester–Salford and Leeds–Bradford were built up from conglomerations of small towns and villages. Merseyside, on the other hand, developed by continuous expansion from a central hub at the waterfront (Smith, 1953: 2). By the 1880s, the new Scouse dialect had spread across the river to Birkenhead (Ellis, 1875–89: v. 408). Since then it has spread west across the Wirral into North Wales, and east across south Lancashire, where it is limited by the influence of Manchester. Popular London speech (of which Cockney is the prototypical example) has influenced the speech of ordinary people all over the Home Counties and the south east. As a result of the growth of these and other conurbations, the speech of most people in towns and their urban fields – and that means most people in the country – has been influenced by the local urban accent.

At the same time, especially after the building of railways, an increasing number of people were in direct or indirect contact with 'polite' London English. The resulting competition between national and local norms has led to the social stratification of urban speech. Middle-class speech typically shows the modification of the traditional town dialect by national norms, while working-class speech is more influenced by local norms. A study of Liverpool speech in the 1960s (Knowles, 1975) indicated that in middle-class speech national norms were superimposed on the north western features of the original town dialect. (As elsewhere, women's speech tended to show more national influence than that of men.) The Scouse accent, on the other hand, has incorporated features of the speech of immigrants, and developed pronunciations of certain vowels and consonants, and some prosodic patterns, which are markedly different from national norms. Repeated across the country, the linguistic outcome of the growth of conurbations was a *de facto* challenge to the national supremacy of 'polite' London English.

Universal education

The prevailing perception of working-class urban speech has undoubtedly been determined not by scholarly dialect surveys but by the experience of compulsory mass education. For a long time the non-conformist churches had been active in educating the poor, and the Church of England had also begun Sunday schools. For most of the nineteenth century, the National Society, established in 1811 to promote the claim of the Church of England to control education, was balanced by the British Society set up to promote the the rival claim of the non-conformists. The increasing need for an educated workforce was balanced by fear of social unrest (Levine,1986: 82–3), and the cost to the public purse. The result was slow progress, following in the wake of social reform. The Reform Act of 1832 was followed in 1833 by the first parliamentary grant for education, the sum of £20000 to be distributed by the National and British Societies (Lawson and Silver, 1973: 268). The Reform Act of 1867 was followed by the Education Act of 1870.

Even before 1870, state funding was linked to the testing of children's performance in the three Rs. According to the revised code of 1862, schools received a payment of eight shillings per child, but lost a third of this for a child's failure in any of the tests (Lawson and Silver, 1973: 290). These tests were no doubt based on the belief that they provided a useful measure of literacy, but the concept of literacy was itself impoverished. A literate person is able to carry out socially useful tasks involving the written language, and while this includes the ability to recognize words and spell them, it also includes the ability to apply these skills in practice (cf. Barton, 1994).[2] The effect of payment by results, as people such as T. H. Huxley and Matthew Arnold complained at the time (Lawson and Silver, 1973: 290–1), is that it distorted the whole educational provision of the school. It also introduced the concept of failure into the evaluation of language. An illiterate serf of the 1460s was someone who had not learned to read; an illiterate child of the 1860s had failed to learn to read. This failure was something that had apparently been objectively measured in an official examination.

Language deficit

From the later nineteenth century there is a growing association between allegedly bad or incorrect English and educational failure. At this time scholars knew a lot about the etymological roots of English words and nothing about the sociology of language. For the teacher in the classroom faced with the clash of cultures, the obvious inference to be made was that working-class usage was incorrect. There must also have been a high correlation between this usage and failure on educational tests, and in the absence of an understanding of statistics, the inference to be made is that working-class usage is the cause of educational failure.

By the 1920s it was being alleged that the working classes were suffering from a serious language deficit. The view was put forward not in the form of an overt attack, but as an expression of concern, and of the need to propagate civilized values. The Newbolt Report (Newbolt, 1921), for example, asserted that 'the first and chief duty of the Elementary School is to give its pupils speech – to make them articulate and civilised human beings'. In so far as the report recognized that children need to develop language skills, it made a significant advance in the teaching of English. The problem was that the compilers of the report did not have any clear idea what these skills were and how they might be taught. By default the skilled use of language was equated with the use of standard forms in speech and writing, and standard speech was in turn equated with the forms of middle-class speech usage. The paradoxical result was that the report, having set out to make an enlightened review of English teaching, gave official sanction to the crudest and most reactionary views of working-class speech which were current at the time.

The same paradox is found in George Sampson's *English for the English*

2. A rough comparison can be made with the problems of computer literacy in the 1990s. It would not make sense to administer a test on understanding a computer manual or writing a command for a concordance program to someone who had no idea what they could actually do with a computer.

of 1921. Sampson argued strongly that education for the working classes should be a training for life not for factory work, and that the teaching of English should be spread across the curriculum. He saw a clear difference between the teaching of grammar and the teaching of writing, and supported an education in English as opposed to the traditional Latin education. In this context his views on language are quite startling:

> Much of the failure in elementary and even in secondary education is due to the fact that the children do not possess language, and are treated as if they did. . . . Boys from bad homes come to school with their speech in a state of disease, and we must be unwearied in the task of purification (pp. xvi–xvii).

He accepted contemporary views of Standard English, and of its imperial role:

> This country is torn with dialects, some of which are, in the main, degradations. . . . The language of all English schools should be Standard English speech. . . . There is no need to define Standard English speech. We know what it is, and there's an end on't. We know Standard English when we hear it just as we know a dog when we see it, without the aid of definitions. . . . it is the kind of English spoken by a simple unaffected Englishman like the Prince of Wales (pp. 47–8).

> English is now incontestably the language of the world. Where should the standard of spoken English be found if not in England? But there is no standard here. Each county, almost each town, is a law to itself and claims the right purity for itself. This is not independence, it is mere provincialism; and it is not the duty of the schools to encourage provincialism, but to set the standard of speech for the Empire (p. 51).

The message is quite clear: people who depart from the standard are not to be regarded as proper English speakers, and working-class people are suffering from a language deficit. The concept of deficit reappears later in the work of Basil Bernstein (1973), who made this inference from the observation that working people are less successful on language-based measures of intelligence than on non-verbal ones. Bernstein distinguished an 'elaborated' code from a 'restricted' code, the former being possessed only by the middle class and not the working class. The idea that some people have access to areas of language denied to others is a key to the understanding of the problem of language skills. On the other hand, a simple dichotomy of codes cannot be sustained in the light of more recent studies of pragmatics and discourse, and investigations of different registers. The problem is aggravated by the implication in Bernstein's early work that language differences can be traced to actual cognitive differences between classes, and although his later work is ambivalent on this point, it is still open to the interpretation that working-class people suffer from some kind of cognitive defect. Such a conclusion would push the evidence too far.[3] In the USA, the concept of language deficit was even used in an attempt to explain Black English (Labov, 1969).

10.4   *The standard of English pronunciation*

The development of a standard pronunciation is the latest stage in the movement to fix the language which starts with Swift for the language as a whole and with Sheridan for pronunciation in particular. Throughout the nineteenth century, and into the twentieth (e.g. Lounsbury, 1904), books appeared discussing the pronunciation of contested words. But there were now three important new factors. First, as a result of interest in local dialects, much more was now known about variation in English speech. Second, the growth of conurbations had led to the emergence of new urban accents. These were essentially used by the working classes, and were subjected to the same criticisms as working-class language in general. Third, the study of phonetics had advanced to the stage where speech could be studied in much more detail than before. It was now possible to go beyond discussing which syllable should be stressed in *balcony*, or which vowel should be used in *vase*, and specify minute details of pronunciation. The new standard of pronunciation draws on the resources of phonetic science and defines correct pronunciation in such a way that the masses cannot possibly attain it.

Received Pronunciation

In the second half of the nineteenth century, Alexander Ellis (later president of the Philological Society) made a monumental and detailed study of English pronunciation, including both the history of sound changes, and variation in contemporary dialects. He must have known more than anybody else about English pronunciation and its variation. He raised the question of a standard, and commented (1875: 1089): 'I have not even a notion of how to determine a standard pronunciation.'

The concept of a standard pronunciation as it later developed elaborated the ideas of Sheridan and Walker, and involved the usage of a restricted élite rather than the speech of the population as a whole. This usage could to some extent be defined negatively as the avoidance of 'varieties in which no speaker can indulge without being condemned as ignorant' (Ellis, 1878: 183). The obvious examples of condemned pronunciations are dropped and

---

3. I am not denying the possibility of significant correlations between language skills and social class. My point here is that this is a complex problem which is not to be solved by simple-minded models of language and social class.

inserted [h], and intrusive [r] in phrases like *law and order*. Ellis was here reporting the prevailing views, rather than taking personal responsibility for them, and the point that comes across is that in English society at large, there was at this time a growing judgemental attitude towards variation in speech (see also Crowley, 1989: 129–63).

It is much more difficult to describe standard pronunciation in positive terms. However, we can make inferences from the kind of influence that spread from London to other conurbations. Judging by later variation, we can infer with some confidence that it involved the distribution of sounds: for example, in standard pronunciation *class* rhymes with *farce* rather than *gas*, and *singer* does not rhyme with *finger*. It is even possible to reconstruct some important socio-linguistic variables. For example, Liverpool speech derives from Lancashire dialects which used a postvocalic [r] in *burn* or *square*, and it was heavily influenced by Irish English, which also retains postvocalic [r]. The Liverpudlian Mr Gladstone's use of this [r] raised comment at the time. There is no trace of it in the modern dialect, even in the speech of people born before 1914. From this we can infer that the r-less forms were perceived as standard in late-nineteenth-century Liverpool and eventually replaced the local rhotic forms.

By the end of the nineteenth century, phoneticians took for granted that a well-defined standard existed, and that they were able to describe it in detail. It was their own kind of English. Henry Sweet described his own speech, and described it as a *class dialect* (1910: 7). The important distinction was between middle-class urban speech on the one hand and working-class and country speech on the other: 'Standard English . . . is still liable to be influenced by . . . a rustic dialect or the vulgar cockney of London.' The difficulty is that, leaving aside obvious shibboleths such as [h]-dropping, the main class variation in London speech involves not the distribution of sounds, but the details of their pronunciation, for example, the vowel of *bad* or *house*, the [l] of *bell* or the [k] of *baker*.

Sweet used his knowledge of phonetic science to define the standard in positive terms and in much finer detail than had been possible before, going beyond the distribution of sounds and into minute phonetic detail. This shift is socially important because it restricts membership of the class of standard speakers. It is relatively easy to recognize differences of distribution, and modify one's pronunciation accordingly. But by the time people are old enough to identify shades of sound, their articulatory habits have long since become established, and it is virtually impossible to change them.

Sweet's views were reinforced by other phoneticians, including Jones, Ripman and Lloyd James, and the language historian H. C. Wyld (on Jones and Wyld, see Crowley, 1989: 164–206). During the First World War, claims began to be made that a standard or 'received' pronunciation ('RP') had in fact developed in the second half of the nineteenth century in English public schools. It is difficult to find any evidence to support this claimed origin of RP, and if it were true it would be surprising that Alexander Ellis knew nothing about it. Jones describes RP in the preface to his *English pronouncing dictionary* of 1917 as:

> the pronunciation . . . most usually heard in everyday speech in the families of Southern English persons whose men-folk have been educated at the great public boarding-schools. This pronunciation is also used by a considerable proportion of those who do not come from the South of England but who have been educated at these schools. The pronunciation may also be heard, to an extent which is considerable though difficult to specify, from persons of education in the South of England who have not been educated at these schools.

Note that Jones took for granted that the speech of a privileged group within the population of England – public schoolboys – could be equated with the *English* of his dictionary's title. Jones (1918) described RP in considerable detail in his *Outline of English phonetics*, and the position he adopted then has not been seriously challenged since.

While the actual descriptions of language phenomena made by early twentieth-century phoneticians were as objective and scientific as possible, their social assumptions about speech belonged to an intellectual tradition going back to Sheridan and Swift. George Sampson was clearly reflecting his training in phonetics when he wrote:

> a teacher of speech untrained in phonetics is as useless as a doctor untrained in anatomy. . . . the untrained ear cannot isolate the real cause of the trouble – often, in London speech, for instance, a defect of one element in an unrecognized diphthong (1921: 49).

H. C. Wyld's *A history of modern colloquial English* of 1920 gives an extremely detailed account of changes in pronunciation over the previous 500 years. Again, the first impression is of objective scholarship. However, the changes seem to lead inevitably and inexorably to the standard pronunciation of the early twentieth century. Wyld selects his material carefully, and ignores the rich evidence of changes in other kinds of English, and thereby gives the contentious impression that RP has really been in existence for centuries.

RP was soon being credited with other desirable attributes. It was said to be more generally intelligible and more beautiful than other varieties; Wyld (1934) even attempted to argue on linguistic and phonetic grounds that it was inherently superior. At about the same time, Ripman (1931: 6–9) was arguing that people should learn RP in order not to be disadvantaged by non-standard accents. This view, while superficially reasonable, leaves unchallenged the contentious basis on which RP was established in the first place. By the early 1930s, British phoneticians had added pronunciation to the standardized part of the language.

10.5 *Good English*

Books on English usage continue the tradition of the eighteenth century, often with the same examples. After about 1860, there is an increasing association of incorrect English with the language of the working class. Educated usage is equated with middle-class usage, and is asserted to be the natural standard for the nation, and even promoted to the rank of royalty. In the twentieth century, attention is increasingly drawn to matters of pronunciation.

There is also a positive side to this tradition, for there is an increasing awareness that people need to know how to use the language effectively. In a parallel tradition, elocutionists attempt to investigate the effective delivery of speech. The problem is that the effective use of language continues to be confused with grammar on the one hand, and conformity to arbitrary rules of usage on the other. Saxon English and simplicity of style are even brought back as the examples to follow. It is only relatively recently that language scholars have come to recognize the effective use of language as a subject worthy of serious investigation.

The Queen's English

Henry Alford, whose *The Queen's English* first appeared in 1864, saw the language as a highway of progress:

> the Queen's English . . . is, so to speak, this land's great highway of thought and speech . . . There was a day when it was as rough as the primitive inhabitants. Centuries have laboured at levelling, hardening, widening it (1870: 2–3).

Its progress has been hampered by its enemies, including grammarians:

> most of the grammars, and rules, and applications of rules, now so commonly made for our language, are in reality not contributions towards its purity, but main instruments of its deterioration (1870: vii)

and it is threatened by the use of Latin words:

> The language . . . is undergoing a sad and rapid process of deterioration. Its fine manly Saxon is getting diluted into long Latin words not carrying half the meaning. . . . The greatest offenders . . . are the country journals (p. 177).

and by the sort of semi-literate who, incapable of understanding the apostrophe, could paint RAILWAY STATION'S on the side of an omnibus (p. 12), or mis-spell words in provincial newspapers (p. 24), or remain ignorant of the use of /h/, like the commercial gentleman in the refreshment-room at Reading station who complained that 'his *ed* used to *hake* ready to burst' (p. 31). Those who applied themselves to their linguistic problems could succeed:

I have known cases of men who have risen from the ranks, – whose provincial or vulgar utterances I could myself remember, – who yet before middle age have entirely cast off every trace of these adverse circumstances, and speak as accurately as their high-born and carefully trained compeers (p. 30).

Alford was a Greek scholar, but his work on English is a mixture of second-hand scholarship and crude prejudice. A later book by the educationist W. B. Hodgson (1882) is superficially similar but subtly different. Hodgson's list of alleged *Errors in the use of English* was the result of 30 years of systematically noting down usages of which he disapproved. His aim, which echoes Lowth, was 'to set forth the merits of correctness in English by furnishing examples of the demerits of incorrectness', but he gave no criteria whatsoever for his judgements.

Some of his examples have become famous: for example, *A piano for sale by a lady about to cross the Channel in an oak case with carved legs.* While this sentence is not ungrammatical, it is difficult to deny that it lacks elegance. When we encounter such examples in real life we may note the clumsiness of the potential ambiguity, and pedants may pretend to misunderstand them. But we are able to interpret them, and we can be confident that we know what the writer meant. At the same time, Hodgson is intuitively tackling something new, namely the effective use of language.

The King's English

The study of the effective use of language is a matter of rhetoric rather than grammar, and it developed within the tradition of prescriptive usage. *The King's English* (1919) was written by the Fowler brothers during the First World War. Unlike the work of Alford and Hodgson, it is organized, and an attempt is made to base judgements on general principles. These include a preference for the familiar word to the far-fetched, the concrete word to the abstract, the single word to the circumlocution, the short word to the long, and the Saxon word to the Romance (Fowler and Fowler 1919: 1). Old nostrums are repeated: for example, *as* and *than* 'take the same case after them as before' (pp. 62–3), and this is defended on the grounds that *I love you more than him* differs in meaning from *I love you more than he.* (Another view, of course, is that the *than him* version is actually ambiguous and that the ambiguity is accepted by normal users of English.) *Shall* and *will* are given extensive treatment (pp. 133–54), combining description and prescription. Among the later works in this tradition are Fowler's *Modern English Usage*, which is still in widespread use.

In 1948, Sir Ernest Gowers was appointed to find ways of improving the standard of writing in the Civil Service, and his work culminated in the publication of *The complete plain words* in 1954. Superficially his discussions of the misuse of words and the rules for the use of punctuation marks are very similar to the ideas found in many books of usage. However, the starting point is fundamentally different, because he saw the aim of the writer 'to get an idea as exactly as possible out of one mind into another'. He saw clearly the need to recognize change in the language, and differences of style (i.e. variation according to register). He attacked the prolixity of bureaucratic communications, and advocated a simpler mode of expression,[4] and this was not because it was incorrect but because it was not effective. He also saw the problem 'not that official English is specially bad', as that it is specially important for it to be good.

4. Echoes of this approach are found in present-day attempts at 'user-friendly' literature from the inland revenue and other public bodies. The result is a mixture of distance and intimacy which Fairclough (1992: 114–17) calls *interdiscursivity*.

11

Conclusion

Among the events of the twentieth century which have already had a profound effect on the course of the English language are the collapse of British power after the Second World War and the growth of communications technology on a global scale. In the course of the twentieth century, the power to affect change in the English language has begun to shift away from prestigious groups in Britain to transnational commercial organizations. English now has to be considered not in a British context but in a world context, and in this new context most people who use English are not native speakers of the language.

11.1   *The aftermath of empire*

After more than 500 years, the dominant position of London with respect to the English language – and the cultural values which it embodied – must have seemed permanent. Nevertheless, the situation changed dramatically after 1945, as British military forces withdrew from colonies and bases around the world. English was the language of one of the new superpowers, namely the United States. In addition, communications technology had created the need for an international language, a role English had already developed in the context of the empire. Factors of this kind maintained and enhanced the position of English as the international language.

New kinds of English

In some countries where English was established as a native language, the prestige of the local variety has increased at the expense of British English. Australia has become an influential centre, one result of which is that New Zealanders sound to many people like Australians. English in Canada and other former colonies in America is similarly influenced by the English of the United States. Where English was formerly used as an official language, there is a clash between its role as the old colonial language, and its new role as the language of international communication. In some countries, including Egypt and Mesopotamia, which had never been fully part of the empire, English was replaced by the native language. In Malaysia and East Africa, English has been replaced in its internal roles by Bahasa Malaysia and Swahili respectively, although English is still used for international purposes. In the case of India, English has the ironic advantage of being neutral with respect to competing native languages, and has been retained for many internal purposes as well as for international communication.

A different situation again has been created in West Africa and the Caribbean, where English has been adopted with varying degrees of creolization, forming a pattern known as a *creole continuum*. Standard English has been introduced through the education system.

The ownership of English

Two thousand years ago, a major consequence of the decline of Roman power was that Rome lost its automatic authority with respect to the language. The written language passed into the control of the church (see section 2.3 under *The beginnings of written English*), while the spoken language was largely dominated by kingdoms set up by Germanic-speaking Goths and Franks. Similarly, the inevitable consequence of the loss of British power is that London, England and even Britain no longer have control over written and spoken English.

The international spread of standard written language means that many groups of people now have equal rights to it. Even in the nineteenth century, James Joyce and Mark Twain had as much right to determine how to write English as Charles Dickens. The same is now true of Zimbabweans and Australians. The spoken language is more obviously variable, but Sidney and New York have the same right (and, more importantly, the economic power) to determine its form as London. For that matter, English is not the exclusive property of people who regard themselves as native speakers. At some point Irish and English scholars assumed the right to say how Latin should be used, and now businessmen in Delhi or Hong Kong have exactly the same right with respect to English.

An area where the spread of English promises to have interesting consequences is Europe. In the Germanic countries especially, English is becoming not so much a foreign language as a second language. This is true not only of the small languages such as Dutch and Danish, but even of German. Germans tend to speak English at international events even when they are held in Germany. The European Union has a language policy which seeks to protect small languages, but in practice English is likely to have an increasingly dominant role.

The one place which has been little affected by such developments is Britain itself, where the old assumptions about Standard English and Received Pronunciation (RP) remain unchallenged. In British schools and universities, the study of 'English' deals by default with the written standard, and the study of the spoken language rarely goes beyond the sounds of RP. In fact, the continued use of English worldwide has given a temporary boost to British English and RP in the field of English-language teaching. This has been attacked as language imperialism (Phillipson, 1992). In the longer term, as the United Kingdom becomes one of the states of Europe, it is going to be less and less able to lay claim to the ownership of the language.

11.2   *English in the media*

Something we take for granted in the twentieth century is that we hear how people speak outside our own social circle, and even how they spoke in former times. This was made possible by the invention of the phonograph, which meant that for the first time speech could be stored and distributed. The phonograph has been followed by the gramophone record, talking films, radio broadcasting, television, the tape recording and the video recording. This means that the range of spoken varieties that any individual comes into contact with has increased many times. A decreasing proportion of the speech we hear is in the traditional face-to-face setting.

Broadcast English

Broadcasting in England was introduced in the 1920s, at the time when Daniel Jones was promoting RP as a standard. Lord Reith, ironically a Scot, implemented RP as the spoken norm for British broadcasting. In this way the new technology gave credibility to RP, which became *de facto* the most widely recognized form of British English, and the accent generally taken to be typically British.

There are special occasions, such as the coronation of a monarch, for which the broadcast report has come to constitute the spoken equivalent of a language of record. Lloyd James, one-time linguistic adviser to the BBC and professor of phonetics at London, saw this as an essential occasion for RP: 'We also know [*sic*] that for serious purposes, solemn occasions, or indeed for such ordinary occasions as reading the news bulletin, all purely local standards i.e. "dialects," are considered unsuitable by the vast majority of listeners' (1938: 170).

Lloyd James regarded provincial speech as a social handicap, and argued (1938: 172): 'The eradication of those details of the local standard that are recognized as not educated is always to be encouraged.' Such a view seemed to be vindicated during the Second World War when Wilfrid Pickles read the news in a Yorkshire accent, and listeners complained. It was noted with some surprise that the complaints came not from the Home Counties, but from Yorkshire. It was of course precisely in Yorkshire that middle-class people felt threatened by working-class Yorkshire accents. There must have been many more people in Yorkshire who responded positively, but did not have the confidence to write to the BBC about it.

Speech styles

Lloyd James confused the phonetic forms of the RP accent with speaking skills.[1] It is easy to talk about accents, and more difficult to identify the new speech skills and speaking styles that broadcasters have had to develop. Early broadcasters predominantly made use of two styles, namely public speaking and reading aloud, but the microphone rendered the traditional styles obsolete. Public speakers had to find a way of addressing a mass audience as though they were talking to an individual. Readers operated within new constraints, so that, for example, the newsreader had to convey headlines as in a newspaper, and weather forecasters had to keep to a fixed time slot. Sports commentators have learnt to react in speech to rapid events, and keep in touch with the listener even when there is nothing to say. Journalists speak their reports as well as writing them down. The teleprompter has created a new kind of speech, intermediate between spontaneous speech and reading aloud.

The employment of RP speakers by the BBC could give the impression that these new skills were a property of the accent itself, so that in order to read the news well, it was necessary to use RP. However, broadcasting was from the first international, and in Scotland and Ireland, in the United States and all over the English-speaking world, broadcasters were being equally successful using other accents of English. The obvious conclusion is that the speaking skills of the broadcaster are totally independent of the accent which happens to be used. In England, other accents began to be used for certain specialized purposes, such as gardening programmes and cricket commentaries, and in the 1960s for local broadcasting and some relatively unprestigious channels, such as those broadcasting pop music. However, Lloyd James's confusion lives on. In the mid 1990s, although any world variety of English can be used for serious broadcasting in England, it is still relatively unusual to hear in a programme which could

---

1. This is analogous to the widespread confusion of the use of standard grammatical forms with writing skills.

be regarded as an important record an accent which both belongs to England and differs markedly from RP.

Estuary English

An important effect of broadcasting is that almost the whole population has been brought into immediate contact with different kinds of speech. In the short term this must have led to the increased influence of RP, but ordinary people have gradually obtained greater access to the medium in the form of such events as telephone discussions, street interviews and quiz programmes. This means that other accents can spread rapidly too.

In the early part of the century it made sense for Daniel Jones to define the standard according to the speech of English public schoolboys. The situation has changed since 1945, and particularly since the 1960s, when there has been a marked decline in deference in English society. The new models for young people are more likely to be footballers or pop stars than public schoolboys. By the 1980s there was increasing evidence that speech was being subjected to new kinds of influence. The fact that people regularly hear a wide range of different kinds of English means that they have a wide choice of forms to imitate. They do not always choose the RP form. For example, a marked change in pronunciation in England is the use of a glottal stop for a [t] in words such as *water* and *better*. This change has taken place very rapidly in different parts of the country. For example, it was virtually unknown in Liverpool in the 1960s, but extremely common a generation later. This change clearly did not spread along traditional lines, and can only be a response to the mass media.

In the south east, a new kind of pronunciation has been recognized and is commonly called *Estuary English* (Rosewarne, 1994). The main characteristics of this accent are taken from the popular speech of London. Examples include the use of a glottal stop for [t] in a word such as *water*, pronouncing postvocalic [l] as [w] in *bell* [bew], and dropping the [j] in *news*, making it 'nooz' rather than 'nyooz'. Essentially this continues the process whereby an urban dialect spreads over its urban field. What is new is that successful people retain the accent instead of moving towards RP.

Estuary English is particularly associated with young upwardly mobile people known as *yuppies*, the sort of enterprising self-made people who benefited considerably from government policies of the time. The social change was rapidly followed by a change in the social structure of the language. But Estuary English is spoken by many different kinds of people ranging from politicians to academics and trade union leaders, and by no stretch of the imagination can these be described as a coherent group. It is difficult to see how this accent could have come about so quickly without the influence of the mass media.

Global convergence in a multimedia environment

The storage and distribution of spoken materials in the form of gramophone records and films led to the worldwide domination of American English followed by British English. The increasing familiarity of American English in Britain led to American influence on British speech, with the result that the varieties began to converge. This has arrested the normal process of divergence which had been taking place since English was first taken to America.

More recently, spoken materials have been developed in other parts of the world. Since the 1980s the successful marketing of Australian soap operas in Britain has led to Australian influence in English speech. One apparent example is the use of a rising pitch at the end of a turn, as though the speaker is asking 'Are you with me?' On the surface Australian English might not be considered prestigious, but it clearly has covert prestige for the people who adopt Australian patterns of speech. What is interesting is that linguistic influence follows commercial success. The prestige of the traditional English class system has suddenly become totally irrelevant. Nor does it matter whether the producers are native speakers of English: a film made in Bombay could be as influential as one made in Hollywood.

Since speech and writing are fused with image in a multimedia environment, it is no longer possible to make a simple distinction between spoken and written language. Many people's language has been deeply influenced in the last ten years or so by the computer industry, but the effects belong to speech and writing together. Some words such as *analog* or *program* can be identified as American on account of their spelling, but the people who did the research and development might well have come from Bangalore or Belfast. Worldwide English embraces speech and writing, and nobody owns it.

11.3   *Speech and language technology*

Throughout history the study of the English language has been guided by the prevailing beliefs about language in the society of the time, and in the long run studies of the language have affected the way people actually use the language. In relatively recent years, new computer-based technology has made it possible to study large amounts of natural language data. A large body of language texts is known as a *corpus*.[2] The idea of corpora is not new — Johnson used one for his dictionary in 1755 — but what is new is

---

2. The traditional plural is *corpora*, although *corpuses* is also used.

the ability to store a corpus on disk and recover information quickly and easily.

The first modern corpus was the Brown Corpus of American English, which consists of a million words of texts published in 1961. The LOB (Lancaster–Oslo–Bergen) corpus (Johansson *et al.*, 1978) contains a parallel million words of British English. More recent corpora reflect the new speakers of English. The Kolhapur corpus (1986), for example, consists of a million words of Indian English. More recently, the International Corpus of English (ICE) (1996) has collected large samples of English from around the world, including non-native varieties, such as East African English. The importance of this work is that for the first time claims made about the English language are being based not on subjective opinion, but on careful research on a large body of natural data. Interesting results are beginning to appear for people who are not expert linguists, for example in the Cobuild dictionary and grammar (Sinclair, 1987).

It was already possible in the 1980s to program machines to produce and recognize speech (Holmes, 1988). Most of the work was based on American English, and work on British speech concentrated on RP. While speech scientists in the short term followed conventional views about speech standards, in the long term the technology is likely to affect the perceived standard. From a commercial point of view, a speech-recognition device has to work for the variety of accents that people actually speak. There is little point is designing a machine to recognize RP, if it spoken by only 3 per cent of the population. If any accent is going to be imposed, so that people have to modify their accents to work the machine, then commercial reality dictates that it will be some kind of General American. Speech-recognition devices could thus have indirect influence on the way people actually speak. In this new situation the old social values are meaningless and irrelevant.

11.4   *The information superhighway*

Within a generation of the invention of the computer, the computer industry was established on a global scale, using English as its language. As the computer culture has expanded into large-scale databases, electronic mail (e-mail) and so on, the expansion of English has followed, and the technology is so designed that the user needs to interact in English. Individual programs can of course use other languages, but the program itself will almost certainly use English-based commands. Whereas in previous technological revolutions the technology has had to be adapted for different languages, in this case languages other than English have to be interfaced with the resident language of the technology.

English is the dominant language of the Internet or the so-called 'information superhighway', which links together networked computers all over the world. Although still in its infancy, the Internet has led to the development of new types of text which require new skills. Conventional skills, such as the ability to write prose, are largely irrelevant, and this is to the advantage of the many users whose native language is not English.

For private communication, e-mail has recently created a situation in which writers have to produce a completely new kind of document without quite knowing what the rules are. A conventional letter begins with an address, the date and perhaps the address of the addressee. But if the system itself inserts these things, is there any point in the writer putting them in too? Conventional written texts are non-interactional, but with e-mail it is possible to include parts of the original in the reply. An e-mail letter can consequently be written quickly, so is it necessary to include a greeting and a farewell? Is it rude to leave them out? By using the extended alphabet the writer can emulate other aspects of spoken language: for example, to *emphasize* a word, or the use of smileys such as :-) or :-(to indicate the writer's attitude. In this way e-mail texts depart from the norm for written texts. Not all users of e-mail are concerned with the conventional niceties of written texts, such as standard spellings, and complete and standard syntax.

Public documents on the Internet typically consist of short, interlinked pages of information. A conventional document is organized on rhetorical principles (see section 6.2) and linearly ordered with a beginning, a middle and an end. Using a *hypertext* format, the writer can organize information in many different ways, and readers are free to navigate their own route through the information. Leaving aside crude attempts to link the text to the spoken word by the use of accompanying tapes or cassettes, a conventional text is also silent. A network exploiting the resources of a multimedia environment can link pictures or sound recordings to an exact point in the text.

In writing this book, incidentally, I feel much as a copyist must have done in a scriptorium at the end of the 1470s (see section 4.5). The technology which is already here is undoubtedly going to change completely the way documents are constructed in the future, but where these changes will lead we cannot even begin to guess. In the meantime, there is still a need for conventional documents because that is what readers expect. Much of the effort of writing this book has gone into forcing the information into a linear order, and patching up with cross-references when this proves impossible. It would have been easier to write, and more logically organized, in hypertext format.

11.5   *English in the future*

It is impossible to foretell the future, and probably foolish to attempt to do so. Nevertheless it is possible to identify some of the major changes which have already taken place and which will undoubtedly affect the course of future events.

English has changed in the course of the present century from being the language of the British empire to the international language of communication. Beliefs which seemed perfectly sensible in the old context are already looking quaint and dated. The idea that the monarch has some special authority in matters of language – or for that matter the upper classes or even the middle classes – has more in common with a world in which the monarch's touch cures disease than with the world of the Internet. In the 1990s the idea that correct English pronunciation was discovered by Victorian public schoolboys carries much the same conviction as the idea that Adam and Eve spoke German in the Garden of Eden (see sections 1.4 and 6.1 under *Saxon and classical*). In the new world as it now is, England is adopting much the same relationship to English as Italy did towards Latin in the medieval period.

We can be reasonably sure that the present power vacuum will not last for ever. Two thousand years ago, after the collapse of Roman power, control over the language shifted north to the Franks, the Irish and even the Anglo-Saxons. The Roman soldiers guarding the east coast of Britain in the fifth century could not have foreseen that the language of the Saxon pirates would eventually be used all over the world not only by people but also by inanimate machines. With this precedent, we can predict that some organization will assume the power to control the English language. In the late 1990s the most likely contenders are native speakers not of English but of the languages of East Asia. As commercial logic determines that more and more skilled computer work will be done in India, so the balance of power will shift to the east. As the tiger economies continue to grow, using English to communicate with Germans, Finns and Russians, so the balance will shift further east again. The typical English user of the future is unlikely to have read the Authorized Version of the Bible, and may never even have heard of William Shakespeare.

Appendix: Further suggestions

In this appendix I shall outline some of the main issues that arose in the writing of the main text. I refer to published work where appropriate, or indicate topics that require further investigation.

Among the most valuable historical sources is the collection of over 360 titles reprinted in facsimile by the Scolar Press in the series English Linguistics 1500–1800. At the time of writing, the five-volume *Cambridge history of the English language* is in the process of publication.

Chapter 1

This opening chapter deals with the social context within which language change takes place. The study of languages in contact goes back to German dialect studies in the 1920s, and an important early work is Weinreich (1953). The notion of diglossia goes back to the work of Ferguson (1959). The concept of standard language has been studied extensively by socio-linguists. See, for example, Joseph (1987), or for a more recent discussion Stein (1994) and Milroy (1994).

Chapter 2

The account I give here keeps to the received view that apart from some topographical terms, river names and a handful of lexical items, Celtic had virtually no influence on early English (see, for example, Jackson, 1953: 246–61). However, it must be said that the story defies credibility, especially as the grammar and pronunciation of Old English are traced in a purely Germanic context. The sound changes described for English (Campbell, 1959) have so many similarities with those described for Celtic

(Jackson, 1953) that it is difficult to believe that they arose independently by chance. This area merits further investigation.

Chapter 3

For a detailed survey of the survival and continued influence of Norse in Britain, see O. Jespersen (1905) and J. Geipel (1971) *The Viking legacy*. Judging by the evidence of the dialect maps in McIntosh *et al.* (1986), I suspect I have underestimated the linguistic importance of York in the later Middle Ages.

There has been much discussion over whether the result of Anglo-Danish and later Anglo-French contact was that Middle English was a creole. The evidence is reviewed by Goerlach (1986), who decides against classifying it as a creole. The evidence in this chapter and in chapter 4 is of obvious relevance for anyone interested in pidgins, creoles and language contact. However, I have avoided this issue in the main text because it makes no difference to the main thesis of the book.

Chapter 4

Historians of English understandably foreground the English texts that survive from the medieval period. It is important to interpret the English data in the light of medieval literacy practices. M. T. Clanchy (1979) gives an invaluable account of literacy in the early medieval period in *From memory to written record.*

The study of French influence in English, going back to Jespersen (1905), has tended to treat English as a homogeneous variety. The work assessed by Dekeyser (1986) is essentially based on the dictionary. Using corpus-based techniques it would be possible to go further, and investigate the distribution of French forms in different kinds of text.

In the past, historians have emphasized the role of creative writers in forming the standard language: for example, McKnight (1928: 17) claims it as the personal achievement of Chaucer. It is more realistic, if more prosaic, to interpret it as the outcome of capitalist enterprise and bureaucracy. Important sources here are Samuels (1963) and Fisher (1977). Blake (1969) gives a good introduction to the work of Caxton.

Chapter 5

The linguistic aspects of the Renaissance and Reformation are conventionally treated as products of the new world ushered in after the ending of the Middle Ages on the field of Bosworth. I have here treated the events of the 1530s and early 1540s as the ending of a story which began long before with John of Gaunt and Wyclif. A classic work on the events of the fourteenth century, seen from an Anglican point of view, is G. M. Trevelyan (1899) *England in the age of Wycliffe*, recently reissued with a new introduction by J. A. Tuck. For the language of the Lollards see Hudson (1985), and the biography of Reginald Pecock by V. H. H. Green (1945).

There is a problem with regard to Lollard English which I have not been able to resolve. On the one hand it is associated with opposition to church and state, and on the other it is regarded as one of the strands that contributed to Standard English. It is difficult to construct a social context in which this could in reality have taken place.

Chapter 6

R. F. Jones (1953) *The triumph of the English language* makes a detailed and valuable study of comments on the language by sixteenth- and seventeenth-century writers. However, Jones tends to take remarks at face value, and does not investigate the issues that lead writers to adopt particular views on language.

Chapter 7

An interesting aspect of the linguistic history of the revolution is that it was entirely ignored in conventional histories of the language: see, for example, Bradley (1904), McKnight (1928) and Baugh (1959). Nothing of any linguistic interest, it would appear, happened between the death of Shakespeare and the Restoration of the monarchy. McKnight mentions Puritans in passing, but presents a grotesque caricature, dismissing them as pedants in 'need of the sobering influence of classical taste' (1928: 262). The changes of this period were not of the kind traditional historians looked for, and in any case clash with the evolutionary model of language history.

For the history of the English revolution, see the many books by Christopher Hill; the book that is most directly relevant to language is *The English Bible and the seventeenth century revolution*, published by

Penguin in 1994. Useful examples of revolutionary writing are to be found in the facsimile editions of fast sermons in the 34 volumes of *The English revolution I: fast sermons to parliament 1640–53* edited by a team headed by Robin Jeffs and published in 1970–1.

The use of biblical references is an example of what Norman Fairclough (1992: chapter 4) calls *intertextuality*. Most references, metaphors and precedents illustrate *manifest intertextuality* (pp. 117–18), but their use in non-religious texts illustrates *interdiscursivity* (pp. 124–30). Note, however, that whereas in a modern context the latter involves the 'colonization' of one discourse type by another, in the seventeenth century writers developed a new political discourse type within religious discourse. This area merits more detailed study than it has been possible to give it in this book.

I have hinted that there were several developments in the early part of the century that led to plainness of style after the Restoration. The connections between these developments need further clarification.

Chapter 8

The language attitudes of the eighteenth century have been studied and analysed many times. See, for example, Leonard (1961).

Chapter 9

Aitken and McArthur (1979) *Languages of Scotland* give a historical and contemporary account of Gaelic and English in Scotland. For a good overview of the international spread of English, see Leith (1996).

Chapter 10

There is a widespread view that at the end of the nineteenth century linguists were taking a more descriptive view of language. The mass of evidence actually points the other way (see Crowley, 1989). In the preparation of this chapter, I examined a collection of over 70 books written between 1860 and 1960 on 'correct English', and traced the beginnings of the concepts of the effective use of language on the one hand, and 'language deficit' on the other. The concept of language deficit reappeared, in a suitably revised post-war form, in Basil Bernstein's concept of 'restricted code' (Bernstein, 1973). Labov (1969) attacks similar assumptions about Black English. The deficit hypothesis is found in an even milder form in the works of John Honey (1989). The prescriptive approach was revived in the 1980s by right-wing thinkers such as Marenbon (1987).

Bibliography

For some of the older works it has not been possible to give a full bibliographical reference. For works which have been reprinted in the Scolar Press series English Linguistics 1500–1800, I have given the Scolar reprint number.

Adams, G. B. (ed.) 1964: *Ulster dialects*. Belfast: Ulster Folk Museum.
Aicken, J. 1693: *The English grammar*.
Aitken, A. J. 1979: Scottish speech: a historical view, with special reference to the Standard English of Scotland. In A. J. Aitken and T. McArthur (eds.) *Languages of Scotland*. Edinburgh: Chambers, 85–118.
Aitken, A. J. and T. McArthur (eds.) 1979: *Languages of Scotland*. Edinburgh: Chambers.
Alford, H. 1864: *The Queen's English*. London: George Bell and Sons.
Anon. 1550: *A very necessary boke*. Menston: Scolar Reprint 43.
Anon. 1575: *A plaine pathway to the French tongue*. Menston: Scolar Reprint 70.
Anon. 1680: *A treatise of stops*. Menston: Scolar Reprint 65.
Aston, M. 1977: Lollardy and literacy. *History* 62: 347–71.
Bailey, R. W. 1982: The English language in Canada. In R. W. Bailey and M. Goerlach (eds.) *English as a World Language*. Cambridge: Cambridge University Press, 134–76.
Bailey, R. W. 1991: *Images of English: a cultural history of the English language*. Cambridge: Cambridge University Press.
Bailey, R. W. and M. Goerlach (eds.) 1982: *English as a world language*. Cambridge: Cambridge University Press.
Baker, R. 1770: *Reflections on the English language*. Menston: Scolar Reprint 87.
Bammesberger, A. 1992: The place of English in Germanic and Indo-European. In R. M. Hogg (ed.) *The Cambridge history of the English language*. Cambridge: Cambridge University Press, 26–66.
Baret, J. 1573: *An alvearie or triple dictionarie, in Englishe, Latin and French*.
Barry, M. V. 1982: The English language in Ireland. In R. W. Bailey and M. Goerlach (eds.) *English as a world language*. Cambridge: Cambridge University Press, 84–133.
Barton, D. 1994: *Literacy: an introduction to the ecology of written language*. Oxford: Blackwell.
Bates, D. and A. Curry (eds.) 1994: *England and Normandy in the Middle Ages*. London: Hambledon Press.
Baugh, A. C. 1959: *A history of the English language*. London: Routledge.
Bellot, J. 1580: *Le maistre d'escole Anglois or the Englishe scholemaister*. Menston: Scolar Reprint 51.

Bernstein, B. 1973: *Class, codes and control*. St Albans: Paladin.

Blake, N. F. 1969: *Caxton and his world*. London: André Deutsch.

Bradley, H. 1904: *The making of English*. London: Macmillan.

Braidwood, J. 1964: Ulster and Elizabethan English. In G. B. Adams (eds.) *Ulster dialects*. Belfast: Ulster Folk Museum, 5–109.

Brinsley, J. 1612a: *The grammar schoole*. Menston: Scolar Reprint 62.

Brinsley, J. 1612b: *The posing of the past*. Menston: Scolar Reprint 35.

Brown, R. and A. Gilman 1960: The pronouns of power and solidarity. In T. Sebeok (ed.) *Style in language*. Cambridge, MA: MIT Press.

Buchanan, J. 1764: *An essay towards establishing a standard for an elegant and uniform pronunciation of the English language*.

Bullockar, J. 1616: *An English expositor.* Menston: Scolar Reprint 11.

Bullockar, W. 1580: *Booke at large*.

Burchfield, R. (ed.) 1994: *English in Britain and overseas*. Cambridge: Cambridge University Press.

Butler, C. 1634: *The English grammar*. Oxford: William Turner.

Camden, W. 1595: *Institutio Graecae grammatices*. Menston: Scolar Reprint 202.

Camden, W. 1605: *Remaines concerning Britain*.

Campbell, A. 1959: *Old English grammar*. Oxford: Clarendon.

Casaubon, M. 1650: *De quatuor linguis*.

Cassidy, F. G. 1982: Geographical variation of English in the United States. In R. W. Bailey and M. Goerlach (eds.) *English as a world language*. Cambridge: Cambridge University Press, 177–209.

Cawdrey, R. 1604: *A table alphabeticall . . . of hard vsuall English wordes*.

Chambers, R. W. 1932: The continuity of English prose from Alfred to More and his school. In E. V. Hitchcock (ed.) *Harpsfield's life of More*. London: Early English Text Society, pp. xlv–clxxiv.

Chambers, R. W. and M. Daunt (eds.) 1931: *A Book of London English 1384–1425*. Oxford: Clarendon.

Chapman, H. W. 1961: *The last Tudor king: a study of Edward VI*. London: Arrow Books.

Cheke, J. 1555: *De pronuntiatione graecae linguae*. Menston: Scolar Reprint 81.

Clanchy, M. T. 1979: *From memory to written record: England, 1066–1307*. Cambridge, MA: Harvard University Press.

Clement, F. 1587: *The petie schole*. Menston: Scolar Reprint 2.

Cocker, E. 1696: *Accomplish'd school-master*. Menston: Scolar Reprint 33.

Cockeram, H. 1623: *The English dictionarie*. Menston: Scolar Reprint 124.

Coles, E. 1674: *The compleat English schoolmaster*. Menston: Scolar Reprint 26.

Cooper, C. 1685: *Grammatica linguæ anglicanæ*. Menston: Scolar Reprint 86.

Coote, E. 1596: *The English schoole-maister*. Menston: Scolar Reprint 98.

Cope, J. I. and H. W. Jones (eds.) 1959: *History of the Royal Society by Thomas Sprat*. London: Routledge.

Corro, A. del 1590: *The Spanish grammer*. Menston: Scolar Reprint 36.

Cottle, B. 1969: *The triumph of English, 1350–1400*. London: Blandford.

Crouch, D. 1994: Normans and Anglo-Normans: a divided aristocracy? In D. Bates and A. Curry (eds.) *England and Normandy in the Middle Ages*. London: Hambledon Press.

Crowley, T. 1989: *The politics of discourse*. London: Macmillan.

Crowley, T. 1991: *Proper English? Readings in language, history and cultural identity*. London: Routledge.

Daines, S. 1640: *Orthoepia anglicana*. Menston: Scolar Reprint 31.

Dalgarno, G. 1661: *Ars signorum*. Menston: Scolar Reprint 116.

Danes, J. 1637: *A light to Lilie*. Menston: Scolar Reprint 58.

Daniel, E. 1883: *The history and derivation of the English language.* London: National Society.

Davies, J. 1621: *Antiquae linguae britannicae rudimenta.* Menston: Scolar Reprint 70.

Dekeyser, X. 1986: Romance loans in Middle English: a re-assessment. In D. Kastovsky and A. Szwedek (eds.) *Linguistics across historical and geographical boundaries.* Berlin: Mouton de Gruyter, 253–65.

Dickens, C. 1858: Saxon-English. *Household words* **18**.

Dolman, J. 1561: translation of Cicero's *Those fyue questions.*

Duncan, A. 1595: *Latinæ grammaticæ pars prior.* Menston: Scolar Reprint 121.

Duncan, A. A. M. 1984: The kingdom of the Scots. In L. M. Smith (ed.) *The making of Britain: the dark ages.* London: Macmillan.

Edmundson, H. 1655: *Lingua linguarum.* Menston: Scolar Reprint 259.

Ellis, A. 1875–89: *On early English pronunciation, with special reference to Shakspere and Chaucer* (5 vols.). London: Philological Society.

Ellis, A. 1877: *Pronunciation for singers.* London: Curwen.

Ellis, T. 1680: *The English school.* Menston: Scolar Reprint 184.

Elyot, T. 1531: *The boke named the gouernour.*

Elyot, T. 1541: *Castel of helth.*

Erasmus, Desiderius 1528: *Dialogus de recta latini graecique sermonis pronuntiatione.*

Evans, J. 1621: *The palace of profitable pleasure.* Menston: Scolar Reprint 32.

Fairclough, N. 1989: *Language and power.* London: Longman.

Fairclough, N. 1992: *Discourse and social change.* Cambridge: Polity Press.

Fairclough, N. 1995: *Critical discourse analysis: the critical study of language.* London: Longman.

Farnaby, T. 1641: *Systema grammaticum.* Menston: Scolar Reprint 160.

Ferguson, C. A. 1959: Diglossia. *Word* **15**: 325–40.

Fisher, J. H. 1977: Chancery and the emergence of standard written English in the fifteenth century. *Speculum* **52**: 870–99.

Fisiak, J. 1994: The place-name evidence for the distribution of Early Modern English dialect features: the voicing of initial /f-/. In D. Kastovsky (ed.) *Studies in Early Modern English.* Berlin: Mouton de Gruyter, 97–110.

Fowler, H. W. and F. G. Fowler 1919: *The King's English.* Oxford: Clarendon.

Fox, G. *et al.* 1660: *A battle-door for teachers and professors to learn singular and plural.* Menston: Scolar Reprint 115.

Frank, T. 1994: Language standardization in eighteenth-century Scotland. In D. Stein and I. Tieken-Boon van Ostade (eds.) *Towards a Standard English 1600–1800.* Berlin: Mouton de Gruyter, 51–62.

Frantzen, A. J. 1986: *King Alfred.* Boston: Twayne.

Free, J. 1749: *An essay towards an history of the English tongue.* Menston: Scolar Reprint 125.

Freeborn, D. 1992: *From Old English to Standard English.* London: Macmillan.

Frings, T. 1950: *Grundlegung einer Geschichte der deutschen Sprache.* Halle: Niemeyer.

Geipel, J. 1971: *The Viking legacy: the Scandinavian influence on the English and Gaelic languages.* Newton Abbot: David and Charles.

Gil, A. 1621: *Logonomia anglica.* Menston: Scolar Reprint 61.

Goerlach, M. 1986: Middle English – a creole? In D. Kastovsky and A. Szwedek (eds.) *Linguistics across historical and geographical boundaries.* Berlin: Mouton de Gruyter.

Goeurot, J. 1544: *Regiment of lyfe, whereunto is added a treatise of the pestilence.*

Gordon, I. A. 1966: *The movement of English prose.* London: Longman.

Gowers, E. 1954: *The complete plain words.* London: HMSO.

Grantham, H. 1575: *An Italian grammar*. Menston: Scolar Reprint 69.

Green, V. H. H. 1945: *Bishop Reginald Pecock: a study in ecclesiastical history and thought*. Cambridge: Cambridge University Press.

Greenbaum, S. (ed.) 1996: *Comparing English worldwide*. Oxford: Clarendon.

Hare, J. 1647: *St Edwards ghost*.

Harrison, W. 1587: *Of the languages spoken in this iland*.

Hart, J. 1551: *The opening of the unreasonable writing of our Inglish tongue*. MS.

Hart, J. 1569: *An orthographie*.

Hart, J. 1570: *A methode or comfortable beginning for all vnlearned, whereby they may bee taught to read English, in a very short time, with pleasure*.

Hewes, J. 1624: *A perfect survey of the English tongue*. Menston: Scolar Reprint 336.

Hewes, J. 1633: *Florilogium phrasicon*. Menston: Scolar Reprint 264.

Higham, N. 1986: *The northern counties to AD 1000*. London: Longman.

Hill, C. 1968: *Puritanism and revolution*. London: Panther.

Hill, C. 1972: *The intellectual origins of the English revolution*. London: Panther.

Hill, C. 1975: *The world turned upside down*. London: Penguin.

Hill, C. 1980a: *The century of revolution 1603–1714*. London: Routledge.

Hill, C. 1980b: *Some intellectual consequences of the English revolution*. London: Weidenfeld and Nicolson.

Hill, C. 1994: *The English Bible and the seventeenth century revolution*. London: Penguin.

Hitchcock, E. V. (ed.) 1932: *Harpsfield's life of More*. London: Early English Text Society.

Hodges, R. 1644: *The English primrose*. Menston: Scolar Reprint 183.

Hodges, R. 1653: *Most plain directions for true-writing*. Menston: Scolar Reprint 118.

Hodges, R. 1984: The Anglo-Saxon migrations. In L. M. Smith (ed.) *The making of Britain: the dark ages*, 35–47.

Hodgson, W. B. 1882: *Errors in the use of English*. Edinburgh: David Douglas.

Hogg, R. M. (ed.) 1992: *The Cambridge history of the English language*, vol. 1: *The beginnings to 1066*. Cambridge: Cambridge University Press.

Holder, W. 1669: *Elements of speech*. Menston: Scolar Reprint 49.

Holmes, J. N. 1988: *Speech synthesis and recognition*. London: Chapman and Hall.

Honey, J. 1989: *Does accent matter: the Pygmalion factor*. London: Faber.

Hope, J. 1993: Second person singular pronouns in records of Early Modern 'spoken' English. *Neuphilologische Mitteilungen* 1 **XCIV**: 83–100.

Hudson, A. 1985: *Lollards and their books*. London: Hambledon.

Hudson, A. 1986: Wyclif and the English language. In A. Kenny (ed.) *Wyclif and his Times*. Oxford: Clarendon, 85–103.

Hunt, T. 1661: *Libellus orthographicus*. Menston: Scolar Reprint 94.

Jackson, K. 1953: *Language and history in early Britain*. Edinburgh: Edinburgh University Press.

Jeffs, R. (ed.) 1970: *The English revolution I: fast sermons to parliament 1640–53* (34 vols.) London: Cornmarket Press.

Jespersen, O. 1905: *Growth and structure of the English language*. Oxford: Blackwell.

Jewel, J. 1567: *A defence of the apologie of the Churche of Englande*.

Johansson, S., G. N. Leech *et al.* 1978: Manual of information to accompany the Lancaster-Oslo/Bergen corpus of British English. University of Oslo: Department of English.

Johnson, S. 1747: *The plan of a dictionary*. Menston: Scolar Reprint 223.

Johnson, S. 1755: *A dictionary of the English Language*.

Jones, B. 1659: *Herm'aelogium: or an essay at the rationality of the art of speaking*. Menston: Scolar Reprint 238.

Jones, D. 1909: *The pronunciation of English*. Cambridge: Cambridge University Press.

Jones, D. 1917: *An English pronouncing dictionary*. London: Dent.

Jones, D. 1918: *An outline of English phonetics*. Cambridge: Heffer.

Jones, H. 1724: *An accidence to the English tongue*. London.

Jones, R. F. 1951: *The seventeenth century: studies in the history of English thought and literature from Bacon to Pope*. Stanford: Stanford University Press.

Jones, R. F. 1953: *The triumph of the English language*. Stanford: Stanford University Press.

Jonson, B. 1640: *The English grammar*. Menston: Scolar Reprint 349.

Joseph, J. E. 1987: *Eloquence and power: the rise of language standards and standard languages*. London: Frances Pinter.

Kallen, J. L. 1994: English in Ireland. In R. Burchfield (ed.) *English in Britain and overseas*. Cambridge: Cambridge University Press.

Kastovsky, D. (ed.) 1994: *Studies in Early Modern English*. Berlin: Mouton de Gruyter.

Kastovsky, D. and A. Szwedek 1986: *Linguistics across historical and geographical boundaries*. Berlin: Mouton de Gruyter.

Kenny, A. (ed.) 1986: *Wyclif and his times*. Oxford: Clarendon.

Kenrick, 1773: *A new dictionary of the English language*. London.

Kersey, J. 1702: *A new English dictionary*. Menston: Scolar Reprint 140.

Klein, L. 1994: 'Politeness' as linguistic ideology in late seventeenth- and eighteenth-century England. In D. Stein and I. Tieken-Boon van Ostade (eds.) *Towards a Standard English 1600–1800*. Berlin: Mouton de Gruyter, 31–50.

Knowles, G. 1975: Scouse: the urban dialect of Liverpool. Unpublished Ph.D. thesis, University of Leeds.

Knowles, G. 1987: *Patterns of spoken English*. London: Longman.

Kortlandt, F. 1986: The origin of Old English dialects. In D. Kastovsky and A. Szwedek (eds.) *Linguistics across historical and geographical boundaries*. Berlin: Mouton de Gruyter, 437–42.

Kyngston, R. 1403: Letter to Henry IV. *Royal and historical letters during the reign of Henry IV*, 1, pp. 155–9. Rolls Series.

Labov, W. 1969: The logic of non-standard English. *Georgetown monographs on language and linguistics* **22**: 1–31.

Lass, R. 1994: Proliferation and option-cutting: the strong verb in the fifteenth to eighteenth centuries. In D. Stein and I. Tieken-Boon van Ostade (eds.) *Towards a Standard English 1600–1800*. Berlin: Mouton de Gruyter, 81–113.

Lawson, J. and H. Silver 1973: *A social history of education in England*. London: Methuen.

Leith, D. 1983: *A social history of English*. London: Routledge and Kegan Paul.

Leith, D. 1996: English – colonial to postcolonial. In D. Graddol, D. Leith and J. Swann (eds.) *English: history, diversity and change*. London: Routledge.

Leonard, S. A. 1962: *The doctrine of correctness in English usage 1700–1800*. New York: Russell and Russell.

Lever, R. 1573: *The arte of reason*. Menston: Scolar Reprint 323.

Levine, K. 1986: *The social context of literacy*. London: Routledge.

Lily, W. and J. Colet 1549: *A short introduction of grammar*. Menston: Scolar Reprint 262.

Linacre, T. 1523: *Rudimenta grammatices*. Menston: Scolar Reprint 312.

Linacre, T. 1524: *De emendata structura latini sermonis*. Menston: Scolar Reprint 83.

Lloyd James, A. 1938: *Our spoken language*. London: Nelson.

Lodge, R. A. 1993: *French: from dialect to standard*. London: Routledge.

Lodowyck, F. 1647: *A common writing*. Menston: Scolar Reprint 147.

Lodowyck, F. 1652: *The ground-work of a new perfect language*. Menston: Scolar Reprint 103.

Lodowyck, F. 1686: Essay towards a universal alphabet. *Philosophical Transactions of the Royal Society*.

Lounsbury, T. R. 1904: *The standard of pronunciation in English*. New York: Harper.

Lowth, R. 1762: *A short introduction to English grammar*. Menston: Scolar Reprint 18.

Lupset, T. 1533: *A treatise of charitie*.

Lye, T. 1671: *The child's delight*. Menston: Scolar Reprint 91.

Manwayring, H. 1644: *The seaman's dictionary*. Menston: Scolar Reprint 328.

Marenbon, J. 1987: *English our English: the new orthodoxy examined*. London: Centre for Policy Studies.

Marshall, J. D. (ed.) 1967: *The autobiography of William Stout of Lancaster 1665–1752*. Manchester: Manchester University Press.

McFarlane, K. B. 1972: *Lancastrian kings and Lollard knights*. Oxford: Clarendon.

McIntosh, A. *et al.* 1986: *A linguistic atlas of late mediaeval English*. Aberdeen: Aberdeen University Press.

McIntosh, C. 1994: Prestige norms in stage plays, 1600–1800. In D. Stein and I. Tieken-Boon van Ostade (eds.) *Towards a Standard English 1600–1800*. Berlin: Mouton de Gruyter, 63–80.

McKisack, M. 1959: *The fourteenth century 1307–1399*. London: Oxford University Press.

McKnight, G. 1928: *Modern English in the making*. Toronto: General Publishing Co.

Milroy, J. 1994: The notion of 'standard language' and its applicability to the study of Early Modern English pronunciation. In D. Stein and I. Tieken-Boon van Ostade (eds.) *Towards a Standard English 1600–1800*. Berlin: Mouton de Gruyter, 19–29.

Mittins, W. H., M. Salu *et al.* 1970: *Attitudes to English usage*. London: Oxford University Press.

Morrish, J. 1986: King Alfred's letter as a source of learning in England. In P. E. Szarmach (ed.) *Studies in earlier Old English prose*. Albany: State University of New York Press, 87–107.

Mulcaster, R. 1582: *The first part of the elementarie*. Menston: Scolar Reprint 219.

Murison, D. 1979: The historical background. In A. J. Aitken and T. McArthur (eds.) *Languages of Scotland*. Edinburgh: Chambers, 2–13.

Murphy, J. 1972: *The Education Act 1870*. Newton Abbot: David and Charles.

Murray, K. M. E. 1977: *Caught in the web of words: James A. H. Murray and the Oxford English dictionary*. New Haven: Yale University Press.

Mustanoja, T. F. 1960: *A Middle English syntax*. Helsinki: Société Néophilologique.

Newbolt, H. 1921: *The teaching of English in England*. London: HMSO.

Oldmixon, J. 1712: *Reflections on Dr Swift's Letter to the Earl of Oxford*. Menston: Scolar Reprint 254.

Orton, H. and E. Dieth 1962: *Survey of English dialects*. Leeds: E. J. Arnold.

Parson, J. 1767: *Remains of Japhet*. Menston: Scolar Reprint 64.

Partridge, A. C. 1973: *English Bible translation*. London: Deutsch.

Phillips, E. 1658: *The new world of English words*. Menston: Scolar Reprint 162.

Phillipson, R. 1992: *Linguistic imperialism*. London: Oxford University Press.

Pichonnaye, G. de la 1575: *A playne treatise to learn in a short space the Frenche tongue*. Menston: Scolar Reprint 66.

Poole, J. 1646: *The English accidence*. Menston: Scolar Reprint 5.
Poussa, P. (1995): Ellis's 'Land of Wee': a historico-structural revaluation. *Neuphilologische Mitteilungen* 1 xcvl: 295–307.
Powell, T. G. E. 1980: *The Celts*. London: Thames and Hudson.
Preston, H. 1673: *Brief directions for true spelling*. Menston: Scolar Reprint 85.
Price, G. 1984: *The languages of Britain*. London: Edward Arnold.
Price, O. 1665: *The vocal organ*. Menston: Scolar Reprint 227.
Priestley, J. 1761: *The rudiments of English grammar*. Menston: Scolar Reprint 210.
Priestley, J. 1762: *A course of lectures on the theory of language*. Menston: Scolar Reprint 235.
Prins, A. A. 1952: *French influence in English phrasing*. Leiden: Leiden University Press.
Puttenham, G. 1589: *The arte of English poesie*. Menston: Scolar Reprint 110.
Ramée, P. de la 1585: *Latin grammar*. Menston: Scolar Reprint 305.
Randsborg, K. 1984: The Viking nation. In L. M. Smith (ed.) *The making of Britain: the dark ages*. London: Macmillan.
Ray, J. 1691: *A collection of English words*. Menston: Scolar Reprint 145.
Richards, M. P. 1986: The manuscript contexts of the Old English laws: tradition and innovation. In P. E. Szarmach (ed.) *Studies in earlier Old English prose*. Albany: State University of New York Press, 171–92.
Richardson, M. 1980: Henry V, the English Chancery, and Chancery English. *Speculum* **55**: 726–50.
Ripman, W. 1931: *English phonetics*. London: Dent.
Rissanen, M., M. Kytö et al. (eds.) 1993: *Early English in the computer age: explorations through the Helsinki corpus*. Berlin: Mouton de Gruyter.
Robinson, O. W. 1992: *Old English and its closest relatives*. London: Routledge.
Romaine, S. 1982: The English language in Scotland. In R. W. Bailey and M. Goerlach (eds.) *English as a world language*. Cambridge: Cambridge University Press, 56–83.
Rosewarne, D. 1994: Estuary English: tomorrow's RP? *English Today* **37** (10.1): 3–8.
Salmon, V. 1979: *The study of language in seventeenth century England*. Amsterdam: Benjamins.
Sampson, G. 1921: *English for the English*. Cambridge: Cambridge University Press.
Samuels, M. L. 1963: Some applications of Middle English dialectology. *English Studies* **44**: 81–94.
Sebeok, T. (ed.) 1960: *Style in language*. Cambridge, MA: MIT Press.
Shastri, S. V., C. T. Patilkulkarn and Geeta S. Shastri 1986: Manual of information to accompany the Kolhapur corpus of Indian English. Department of English, University of Kolhapur.
Sheridan, T. 1762: *Course of lectures on elocution*. Menston: Scolar Reprint 129.
Shirley, J. 1651: *Grammatica anglo-latina*. Menston: Scolar Reprint 193.
Sinclair, J. 1987: *Looking up: an account of the Cobuild project*. London: Collins.
Smith, L. M. (ed.) 1984: *The making of Britain: the dark ages*. London: Macmillan.
Smith, T. 1568: *De recta & emendata linguæ anglicæ scriptione, dialogus*. Menston: Scolar Reprint 109.
Smith, W. (ed.) 1953: *A scientific study of Merseyside*. Liverpool: Liverpool University Press.
Sprat, T. 1667: *History of the Royal Society*. London: J. Martyn and J. Allestry.
Stafford, P. 1984: One English nation. In L. M. Smith (ed.) *The making of Britain: the dark ages*. London: Macmillan.
Stanbridge, J. 1496: *Accidence*. Menston: Scolar Reprint 134.

Starnes, de Witt Talmage and G. E. Noyes 1946: *The English dictionary from Cawdrey to Johnson: 1604–1755*. North Carolina University Press.

Steele, J. 1775: *The melody and measure of speech*. Menston: Scolar Reprint 172.

Stein, D. 1994: Sorting out the variants: standardization and social factors in the English language 1600–1800. In D. Stein and I. Tieken-Boon van Stade (eds.) *Towards a Standard English 1600–1800*. Berlin: Mouton de Gruyter, 1–17.

Stein, D. and I. Tieken-Boon van Ostade (eds.) 1994: *Towards a Standard English 1600–1800*. Berlin: Mouton de Gruyter.

Stoll, C. 1973: *Sprachgesellschaften in Deutschland des 17. Jahrhunderts*. Munich: List Verlag.

Stone, L. 1969: Literacy and education in England, 1640–1900. *Past and Present* **42**: 69–139.

Strype, J. 1705: *The life of the learned Sir John Cheke*.

Subscota, G. 1670: *The deaf and dumb man's discourse*. Menston: Scolar Reprint 8.

Sutherland, J. (ed.) 1953: *The Oxford book of English talk*. Oxford: Clarendon.

Sweet, H. 1882: *Anglo-Saxon primer*. Oxford: Clarendon.

Sweet, H. 1887: *Second Anglo-Saxon reader*. Oxford: Oxford University Press.

Sweet, H. 1892: *A short historical English grammar*. Oxford: Clarendon Press.

Sweet, H. 1910: *The sounds of English*. Oxford: Clarendon Press.

Sweet, H. 1978: *A second Anglo-Saxon reader: archaic and dialectal*. Oxford: Oxford University Press.

Swift, J. 1712: *A proposal for correcting, improving and ascertaining the English tongue*. London.

Szarmach, P. E. (ed.) 1986: *Studies in earlier Old English prose*. Albany: State University of New York Press.

Tawney, R. H. 1926: *Religion and the rise of capitalism*. London: Penguin [1938].

Thomas, A. 1994: English in Wales. In R. Burchfield (ed.) *English in Britain and overseas*. Cambridge: Cambridge University Press.

Thomas, W. 1550: *Principal rules of the Italian grammer*. Menston: Scolar Reprint 78.

Toon, T. E. 1983: *The politics of early Old English sound change*. New York: Academic Press.

Trench, R. C. 1878: *On the study of words*. London: Macmillan.

Trevelyan, G. M. 1899: *England in the age of Wycliffe*. London: Longman.

Trudgill, P. 1974: *The social differentiation of English in Norwich*. Cambridge: Cambridge University Press.

Turner, G. W. 1966: *The English language in Australia and New Zealand*. London Longman.

Tyndale 1528: *The obedience of a Christen man*.

Urquhart, T. 1653: *Logopandecteison, or An introduction to the vniversal language*. Menston: Scolar Reprint 239.

Valence, P. 1528: *Introductions in frensshe or Introdvctions en francois*. Menston: Scolar Reprint 38.

Verstegan, R. 1605: *A restitution of decayed intelligence*.

Viereck, W. 1993: The medieval common market and its impact on Middle English. *Neophilologische Mitteilungen* **1 XCIV**: 69–78.

Walker, J. 1791: *A critical pronouncing dictionary of the English language*. Menston: Scolar Reprint 117.

Wallis, J. 1653: *Grammatica linguæ anglicanæ*. Menston: Scolar Reprint 142.

Warner, A. 1961: *A short guide to English style*. London: Oxford University Press.

Wartburg, W. von 1946: *Evolution et structure de la langue française*. Bern, Francke.

Webbe, J. 1622: *An appeale to truth*. Menston: Scolar Reprint 42.

Webbe, J. 1627: *Pueriles confabuliunculae*. Menston: Scolar Reprint 74.

Webster, N. 1789: *Dissertations on the English language*. Menston: Scolar Reprint 54.

Weinreich, U. 1953: *Languages in contact*. The Hague: Mouton.

Whitelock, D. 1952: *The beginnings of English society*. London: Penguin.

Wilkins, J. 1646: *Ecclesiastes, or a discourse concerning the gift of preaching*.

Wilkins, J. 1668: *Essay towards a real character, and a philosophical language*. London: The Royal Society.

Williams, D. 1950: *A history of Modern Wales*. London: John Murray.

Williams, R. 1643: *A key into the language of America*. Menston: Scolar Reprint 299.

Wilson, T. 1553: *The art of rhetorique*.

Wimsatt, W. K. 1941: *The prose style of Samuel Johnson*. New Haven: Yale University Press.

Wright, J. 1961: *The English dialect dictionary*. London: Oxford University Press.

Wright, L. 1994: Early Modern London business English. In D. Kastovsky (ed.) *Studies in Early Modern English*. Berlin: Mouton de Gruyter, 449–65.

Wright, S. 1994: The critic and the grammarians: Joseph Addison and the prescriptivists. In D. Stein and I. Tieken-Boon van Ostade (eds.) *Towards a Standard English 1600–1800*. Berlin: Mouton de Gruyter, 243–84.

Wyld, H. C. 1920: *A history of modern colloquial English*. Oxford: Blackwell.

Wyld, H. C. 1934: The Best English: a claim for the superiority of Received Standard English. *Proceedings of the Society for Pure English* **4**.

Index